Visual Studio 2019 In Depth

Discover and make use of the powerful features of the Visual Studio 2019 IDE to develop better and faster mobile, web, and desktop applications

by

Ockert J. Du Preez

FIRST EDITION 2019

Copyright © BPB Publications, India

ISBN: 978-93-89328-325

Distributors:

BPB PUBLICATIONS
20, Ansari Road, Darya Ganj
New Delhi-110002
Ph: 23254990 / 23254991

DECCAN AGENCIES
4-3-329, Bank Street,
Hyderabad-500195
Ph: 24756967 / 24756400

MICRO MEDIA
Shop No. 5, Mahendra Chambers,
150 DN Rd. Next to Capital Cinema,
V.T. (C.S.T.) Station, MUMBAI-400 001
Ph: 22078296 / 22078297

BPB BOOK CENTRE
376 Old Lajpat Rai Market,
Delhi-110006
Ph: 23861747

Published by Manish Jain for BPB Publications, 20 Ansari Road, Darya Ganj, New Delhi-110002 and Printed by him at Repro India Ltd, Mumbai

Dedicated to

My Wife and Daughter
Elmarie Du Preez and Michaela Du Preez

About the Author

Ockert J. Du Preez has always had a love for computers, but never thought he would end up working as a systems developer, never mind writing a book.

His real interest in programming started in 1998 when he encountered Visual C++ 6 and Visual Basic 6.

After his wife, .NET is his greatest love.

He has been writing online articles for platforms such as CodeGuru, DevX, Developer.com, and Database Journal for several years. He was a .NET Microsoft MVP from 2009 to 2017.

About the Reviewer

Sunny Sharma is a Tech Lead, Microsoft Certified Trainer, Microsoft Certified Solutions Expert, and Microsoft Azure MVP with 8+ years of application development on .NET platform. He is a speaker, one of the organizers of geek97 tech community, and has conducted various technical sessions related to the .NET platform, Microsoft Azure Cloud technologies. He writes blogs and articles in his spare time at devsdaily.com

Acknowledgement

First and foremost, I would like to thank God for giving me the courage to write this book. I would like to thank everyone at BPB Publications for giving me this opportunity to write and publish this book.

Thank you to my wife and my daughter for always believing in me.

Thanks, Richard Newcombe, for your inspiration.

Thanks, NCC Vereeniging for educating me.

I would like to thank Bradley Jones and Susan Moore for giving me the opportunity to write my articles for CodeGuru.

Lastly, I would like to thank my critics. Without their criticism, I would never be able to write this book.

– Ockert J. Du Preez

Preface

This book peeks into every corner of the Visual Studio IDE and help you get started with the latest 2019 version. Right from installation, you'll discover new areas within the tool, and also the optimal way to use the features you may already know. You'll learn, for example, how to extend Visual Studio with your own customizations, so that you can make it perform the way you want. You will then explore everything about NuGet package, testing applications using Live Unit Testing and how to make code templates with the T4 Code generation tool. You'll get to grips with the richer JavaScript IntelliSense, which will help you focus more on coding. Moving on, you'll learn to work with the dedicated workloads for Data Storage and Data Science. You will also review the more advanced architecture tools concealed within the IDE and finally create cloud-first applications powered by Microsoft Azure with the built-in suite of Azure tools. This book is divided into 15 chapters and it provides a detailed description of the core concepts of Visual Studio 2019.

Chapter 1 focuses on Installing Visual Studio 2019. It covers all the options and Add-ons to install and explore the new Visual Studio 2019 features.

Chapter 2 inspects the Visual Studio 2019 IDE and examine its features and updates from previous versions of Visual Studio.

Chapter 3 explores the new JavaScript Intellisense and its AI capabilities to cater for a better coding experience.

Chapter 4 covers the new features in the C# language.

Chapter 5 details the new features in .NET Core 3.

Chapter 6 discusses all the built-in tools in Visual Studio 2019. It will describe their purpose as well as explain how to use them.

Chapter 7 teaches us about the awesome debugging tools Visual Studio 2019 has as well as their innerworkings.

Chapter 8 explores the use of various Testing tools.

Chapter 9 digs into tools dedicated to the ASP.NET environment.

Chapter 10 explains the need for simulators, emulators and tools that help with creating beautiful responsive mobile apps for any market.

Chapter 11 explores Azure tools and more.

Chapter 12 details the most common and most popular extensions that can be added to Visual Studio 2019.

Chapter 13 details all the powerful extensions specific for your ASP.NET applications.

Chapter 14 focusses on IDE Extensions especially for Mobile app development purposes. You will delve into each.

Chapter 15 explores Azure tools and more.

Errata

We take immense pride in our work at BPB Publications and follow best practices to ensure the accuracy of our content to provide with an indulging reading experience to our subscribers. Our readers are our mirrors, and we use their inputs to reflect and improve upon human errors if any, occurred during the publishing processes involved. To let us maintain the quality and help us reach out to any readers who might be having difficulties due to any unforeseen errors, please write to us at :

errata@bpbonline.com

Your support, suggestions and feedbacks are highly appreciated by the BPB Publications' Family.

Table of Contents

SECTION I: Getting Started

1. **Getting Started with Visual Studio 2019**.. 3

    Structure 3

    Objective 4

    Why Visual Studio 2019? 4

    The Solution Explorer 4

    The Properties window 5

    The Data Sources window 6

    The Server Explorer window 7

    Toolbox 9

    New features of Visual Studio 2019... 10

    Visual Studio 2019 Updates 12

    Requirements and prerequisites 13

    Supported Operating Systems 13

    Hardware... 13

    Additional requirements 13

    Supported languages... 14

    Visual Studio 2019 Editions 14

    Visual Studio 2019 Preview.. 15

    Visual Studio 2019 Preview 1.. 15

    Visual Studio 2019 Preview 2.. 17

    Visual Studio 2019 Preview 3.. 18

    Visual Studio 2019 Community 19

    Visual Studio 2019 Professional 19

    Visual Studio 2019 Enterprise.. 19

    Integrated Development Environment (IDE) Comparison 20

    Installation options 21

    Windows 21

    Web and cloud... 22

    Mobile and gaming 23

Other toolsets 23

Choose what to install 23

Launching Visual Studio 2019 28

Conclusion 30

2. **Digging into the Visual Studio 2019 IDE** 31

Structure 31

The standard IDE Windows 31

Menus 32

Toolbars 32

Design window 32

Data Sources 32

Toolbox 38

Team Explorer 39

Notifications 40

Cloud Explorer 40

Resource view 41

JSON outline 41

Project properties window 42

Reference window 42

Code window 43

Debugging window 44

Output window 44

Quick watch 44

Locals 45

Tasks List 46

Comparing desktop, mobile and web IDEs 46

Windows Forms 46

ASP.NET 47

Xamarin.Forms (mobile) 48

.NET Core IDE 48

Visual Studio Code IDE 48

Desktop IDE 48

Mobile IDE 50

Web IDE 54

Visual Studio 2019 Extensions...57
   Finding and installing extensions 57
   Image optimizer...58
   Creating a very basic extension 59
IDE Productivity Power Tools...62
Conclusion 62

3. **Visual Studio 2019 IntelliSense** **63**
Structure 63
IntelliSense 63
Template IntelliSense Improvements in C++...........................66
   Peek window UI and live edits...66
   Nested template support 66
   Default argument watermarks..66
Artificial Intelligence (AI)..66
IntelliCode Extension for Visual Studio 2019 67
Advantages of using IntelliCode 67
   Assisted IntelliSense 67
   Recommendations for your types based on your code (C#)......67
   Inferring code style and formatting conventions.....................68
      EditorConfig...68
      Add an EditorConfig file to a solution or project..............73
   Find issues faster...74
   Focused code reviews...74
   Installing the IntelliCode extension 74
Conclusion 78

4. **Latest Features and Changes in C# 8.0** **79**
Structure 79
Objective...80
The C# language 80
Variables and constants...80
   Data types 81
   Creating or declaring variables 82
   Naming conventions 83

Arrays and collections 83

    Arrays 83

    Collections 84

        Queues 85

        Stack 85

        Hashtable 86

Enums 87

Selection statements 88

    The if statement 88

    Switch 90

Iteration statements 91

    The for loop 91

    The foreach loop 92

    The do…while loop 92

    The while loop 93

New features in C# 8.0 93

    Pattern matching 93

    Switch expressions 94

    Property patterns 94

    Tuple patterns 95

    Using declarations 95

    Static local functions 96

    Disposable ref structs 97

    Nullable reference types 98

    Nullable contexts 98

    Asynchronous streams 99

    Ranges and indices 99

Conclusion 101

5. **What's New in .Net Core 3.0** **103**

Structure 103

Objective 104

.NET Core 3.0 104

Installing .NET Core 3.0 104

The .NET framework 4.8 106

The .NET platform dependent intrinsics 107

    Platform dependent intrinsics guidelines 107

Local .NET tools 108

    Build Windows applications with .NET Core 3.0 110

XAML Islands 110

    NuGet packages 111

    Windows community toolkit 111

    Creating an app using XAML Islands 112

Cryptographic key import/export 113

MSIX deployment for desktop apps 114

    Prerequisites for MSIX 114

Open-source WPF, Windows Forms, and WinUI 115

Conclusion 115

SECTION II: Tools

6. **Built-in Tools** **119**

Structure 119

Visual Studio Live Share 120

Profiling tools.. 121

    CPU usage 121

    Memory usage.. 123

    GPU usage 125

        Using the GPU profiler tool... 126

    Application Timeline 126

    PerfTips 127

    IntelliTrace 128

    Network usage... 128

    HTML UI responsiveness 128

    JavaScript memory 128

Solution Explorer 128

    Solution filtering 129

    Showing and hiding unloaded projects 131

    Solution filter files 132

Conclusion 133

7.   Debugging Tools... **135**

Structure 135

Objective 136

Code Cleanup 136

Apply implicit/explicit type preferences............................... 138

Apply 'this.' qualification preferences 139

Apply language/framework type preferences 139

Add/remove braces for single-line control statements 140

Add accessibility modifiers.. 140

Sort accessibility modifiers 141

Make private fields read-only when possible........................ 141

Remove unnecessary casts 141

Apply expression/block body preferences 141

Apply inline 'out' variables preferences 142

Remove unused variables 142

Apply object/collection initialization preferences 142

Search bar on debugging windows.. 142

Search and highlighting 143

Search navigation.. 143

Search Depth 144

Debugging applications 144

Breakpoints.. 144

Navigating code during the debug mode 145

Debug multiple processes 147

Visual Studio 2019 remote debugging tools................................. 147

Download the remote debugging tools.................................. 148

Install and run the remote configuration wizard.............. 148

Code generation tools.. 150

Quick actions 151

Code snippets 151

Design time T4 templates 152

Runtime T4 text templates... 153

Conclusion 155

8. **Testing Tools** 157

    Structure 157

    Objective 158

    Unit testing in Visual Studio 2019 158

        Creating unit test projects and test methods 158

        Create a unit test project and unit test stubs 158

        Writing a small test 160

        Test Explorer 161

    Coded UI tests 162

        Creating a Coded UI test 162

    Selenium 164

        Selenium IDE 164

        Selenium RC 168

            Installing the Selenium RC server 168

            Running the server 168

            Getting the client libraries to work 168

        Selenium WebDriver 169

            Installing WebDriver 169

        Selenium Grid 169

    Appium 169

    Apache JMeter 171

    Blazemeter 172

    Akamai CloudTest 174

    Conclusion 175

SECTION III: Advanced Tools

9. **ASP.NET Tools** 179

    Structure 179

    Objective 179

    Web frameworks 180

        ASP.NET MVC framework 180

        DotNetNuke (DNN platform) 182

            Using DotNetNuke 182

        MonoRail 183

        Vue.js 183

Getting started with Vue.js and Visual Studio 2019 184

React.js 187

.NET Core 3 189

Blazor 189

Getting started with Blazor and Visual Studio 2019 189

Setting up Blazor 190

ASP.NET Core Identity Provider for Amazon 196

Cognito 196

User pools 196

Identity pools 197

Setting up and getting started with Amazon Cognito 197

Web API 198

Creating a new Web API application 199

Visual Studio Kubernetes Tools 201

Installing Kubernetes 202

Conclusion 205

10. **Mobile Tools** **207**

Structure 208

Objective 208

JSON 208

JSON structure 208

JSON schemas 210

Combining multiple subschemas 211

Complex schemas 213

Xamarin 216

Installing Xamarin 216

Xamarin.Forms 217

Creating a Xamarin.Forms app 217

DevExtreme 222

Installing DeveExtreme 222

Emulators and Simulators 223

Differences between Simulators or Emulators to test apps 223

Visual Studio 2019 Android Emulator 223

Setting up a new device 224

Conclusion 225

11. Azure Tools 227

Structure 227

Objective 227

Internet of Things (IoTs) 228

SAP on Azure 229

Artificial intelligence (AI) 231

Microsoft AI platform 231

Azure AI 232

Knowledge mining 232

Machine learning 232

API apps and agents 233

Azure DevOps 241

Practicing a DevOps model 242

Azure Blockchain Service 242

Conclusion 244

SECTION IV: Extensions

12. IDE Extensions 247

Structure 247

Objective 247

Visual Studio 2019 Extensions 248

Preview label for Visual Studio Extensions 248

Creating a very basic Extension 249

Add a preview label to an Extension 252

GitHub 253

Creating a new repository 253

Forking a repository 254

GitHub for desktop 257

Pull Requests for Visual Studio 257

Using the Pull Requests for Visual Studio Extension 258

Connect to an Azure Repo 258

Microsoft Visual Studio Live Share 259

Using Microsoft Visual Studio Live Share 259

Arduino IDE for Visual Studio 260

Installing Arduino IDE for Visual Studio 260

Redgate SQL Change Automation Core 263

Installing Redgate SQL Change Automation Core in
Visual Studio 2019 263

Conclusion 263

13. **ASP.NET Extensions** 265

Structure 265

Objective 265

Markup language 266

Markdown 266

Markdown Editor 267

Working with the Markdown Editor 268

Web Compiler 269

Less 269

Less variables 270

Less mixins 270

Less nesting 271

Scss (Sass) 271

Stylus 272

JSX (React) 273

Using the Web Compiler extension 273

Web Accessibility Checker 275

Web accessibility 275

Working with the Web Accessibility Checker Visual Studio extension. 276

ASP.NET core vs Code Extension Pack 280

Open VS Code 281

Conclusion 281

14. **Mobile Extensions** 283

Structure 283

Objective 283

SQLite 283

SQL features not implemented in SQLite.. 284

Installing and using SQLite for Visual Studio 2019............................ 285

Coding the logic for the database operations.. 287

NuGet Package Manager 292

Creating and publishing a NuGet package using
Visual Studio 2019... 292

Creating the Class Library to be used as a NuGet package 293

Publishing the NuGet package.. 297

JSON Viewer 299

Installing and using JSON Viewer... 299

Conclusion 300

15. Azure DevOps Extensions 301

Structure 301

Objective 301

Azure DevOps 302

Practicing a DevOps model 302

Azure Artifacts 302

Getting started with Azure Artifacts... 303

AWS Tools for Microsoft Visual Studio Team Services 306

Getting and installing AWS Tools for
Microsoft Visual Studio Team Services.. 308

Code Search 309

Installing and using the Code Search extension 309

Other noteworthy Azure DevOps extensions.................................... 310

Test Case Explorer 310

IIS Web App Deployment Using WinRM.. 310

Conclusion 311

Index.. 313

Section I

Getting Started

Introduction

In the *Getting Started* section, we will discover all the installation options as well as learn how to install Visual Studio 2019 to suit our needs. We will take a look at the **Integrated Development Environment (IDE)** and all its associated windows. Next, in *Chapter 3: Visual Studio 2019 IntelliSense,* we will take a look at IntelliSense and see how it can save hundreds of keystrokes while writing a big program. Finally, we will explore the language changes in C# 8.0 and .NET Core 3.0.

This section will have the following chapters:

1. Installation
2. Visual Studio IDE
3. Intellisense
4. Language and Coding Changes in C# 8
5. .NET Core 3.0

CHAPTER 1
Getting Started with Visual Studio 2019

The first version of Visual Studio was released in 1997, and it was the first time all Microsoft's programming tools were integrated into one common IDE. Now, more than 20 years later, the technology landscape has changed tremendously, and Visual Studio has adapted continuously with it. Therefore, Visual Studio 2019 includes the best and newest tools to work with modern-day problems and technologies properly.

In this chapter, we will focus on installing Visual Studio 2019. We will cover all the options and add-ons to install and explore the new Visual Studio 2019 features, including DevOps, IntelliCode, new Debugging windows updates, new Open Windows, and many more!

Structure

- Why Visual Studio 2019?
- Requirements and prerequisites
- Visual Studio 2019 Editions
- Installation options
- Choose what to install
- Launching Visual Studio 2019

Objective

In this chapter we will cover Visual Studio 2019 in general. It will cover the requirements to install it, how to install it, and how to start using Visual Studio 2019. Most importantly, it will answer the question: why Visual Studio 2019?

Why Visual Studio 2019?

The answer is simple: productivity. Visual Studio 2019 allows us to create, debug, and deploy desktop, web, and mobile applications with great ease. Visual Studio 2019 boasts a powerful debugger and vast amount of debugging windows, which aid in exception handling and debugging. Developer productivity in Visual Studio 2019 is increased immensely with the widening of the Code Editor, Code Health, and Document Indicator tools and quick project creation. Working in a team is also easier and better with the addition of DevOps. Visual Studio 2019 also has an inviting IDE with windows such as the `Solution Explorer, Server Explorer, Team Explorer, Data Sources, Properties` window and the `Toolbox` window.

Visual Studio 2019 also has many new features, which we will go into as well. First, let us understand some of the well-known Windows for the newbies reading this book.

The Solution Explorer

The `Solution Explorer` window shows all the files in our projects, including classes, references, forms, or pictures. It serves as a quick way to switch between windows as well as do project or solution-oriented tasks, which are as follows:

- Renaming of files
- Adding references quickly
- Removing project items
- Adding project items

The following screenshot displays the **Solution Explorer** window:

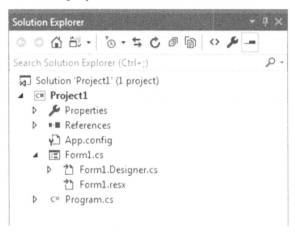

Figure 1.1: *Solution Explorer*

The Properties window

The Properties window hosts all the **Properties** of an object such asforms, any controls on the form, web pages, the project or solution itself. Properties are characteristics of objects; for example, its name, size, location, color, or file name. Properties describe objects. The following screenshot displays the **Properties** window:

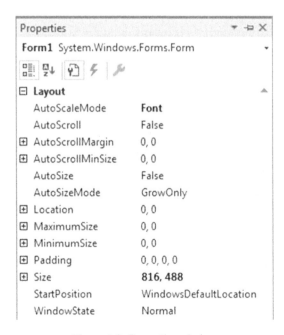

Figure 1.2: *Properties window*

In the **Properties** window, we can also add the event handlers for the controls on the form, web page, or mobile screen; it looks similar to the following screenshot:

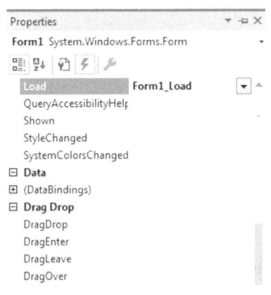

Figure 1.3: Properties window events

Each object has different events, and our job as developers would be to program these events to suit our purpose. In the preceding screenshot, we will notice that **Load** has an event. This event is named **Form1_Load**.

The naming convention of an event is **Objectsname_eventname**. The specific event's name is added to the object's name. This makes it easy for us to identify and search for certain events when the need arises.

The Data Sources window

The **Data Sources Configuration Wizard** window allows us to add data sources to our project. A data source is explained as a place or object from which we obtain data. This can be a database such as Microsoft SQL Server, Microsoft Access, Oracle, and so on. The following screenshot displays the **Data Source Configuration Wizard** window:

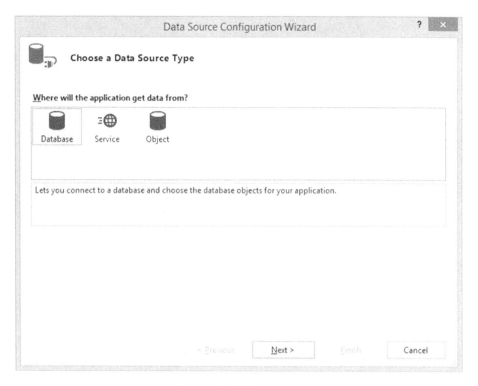

Figure 1.4: *Add Data Source*

Specify the location of the obtained data, then the table name, stored procedure name, or query name, which will fetch the data or contains the data. After a data source is added, we can use it throughout our Windows form, web page, or mobile screen.

The Server Explorer window

The **Server Explorer** window shows the details of all the servers that we are connected to. These include **Cloud Services, SQLDatabases**, and **Virtual Machines**, as shown in the following screenshot:

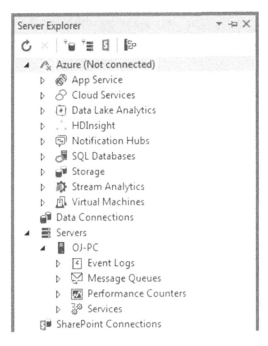

Figure 1.5: Server Explorer

It is divided into four parts and each of them is explained, which are as follows:

- **Azure**
  - o **App Services:** Azure App Service is a managed **PaaS (Platform as a ServiceS)** that integrates Mobile Services, Microsoft Azure Websites, and BizTalk Services into one single service. This adds new capabilities that enable integration with on-premises or cloud systems.
  - o **Cloud Services:** Azure Cloud Services, also a PaaS, is designed to support applications that are scalable, reliable, and most importantly, inexpensive to operate. Azure Cloud Services are hosted on VMs and you can install your own software on them, and you can access them remotely.
  - o **Data Lake Analytics:** Azure Data Lake Analytics is an analytics job service that simplifies big data. You do not need to deploy or configure hardware; you simply write queries to transform your data and extract insights.
  - o **SQL Databases:** SQL Azure is Microsoft's cloud database service. With SQL Azure, organizations can store relational data in the cloud and scale the size of their databases, depending on the business needs.
  - o **Storage:** Azure Storage is a service providing cloud storage that is highly available, secure, durable, and scalable. It includes Azure Blobs, Azure Data Lake Storage Gen2, Azure Files, Azure Queues, and Azure Tables.

  o **Virtual Machines:** Azure Windows Virtual Machines provides secure, high-scale, on-demand, virtualized infrastructure using Windows Server.

- **Data Connections:** As explained in the *Data Source window* section, data connections can also be added here. After a connection has been made, a data source is created and added in the **Server Explorer** window as well as the **Data Sources Configuration Wizard** window.

- **Servers:** The servers in the services window are the actual servers you are connected to. The items such as the Event Log and Services help testing services you create and deploy to these servers. It saves a lot of time. Message queue allows us to trace various application messages that are sent to the servers. Performance counters show how the applications perform and it is easy to see where a problem might be. This parts includes following options:

  o **Event Logs**

  o **Services**

  o **Performance Counters**

  o **Message Queues**

- **SharePoint Connections:** SharePoint is a web-based collaborative platform. In Server Explorer, we can navigate through all the components of a SharePoint site on our system.

Toolbox

The Toolbox contains all the controls, or tools, that we can add to our form, web page, or mobile screen. Windows Forms controls differ from ASP.NET Web Forms Controls and that differ from Mobile or Cloud Controls.

For example, a windows textbox behaves differently on a web application and a mobile application. On a mobile platform, a windows textbox is known as an entry field. In all the three platforms, similar controls are used differently and programmed differently.

ASP.NET includes controls such as DropDown List, Hidden Fields, and Ad Rotators, whereas a Windows Forms project includes a ComboBox (which is similar to the ASP.NET's Dropdown List) and Panel. A mobile application includes different controls specific to the mobile platform, which will not work on a Windows Forms application.

In the following screenshot, we will see the Windows Forms Toolbox as well as an ASP.NET Web Form Toolbox:

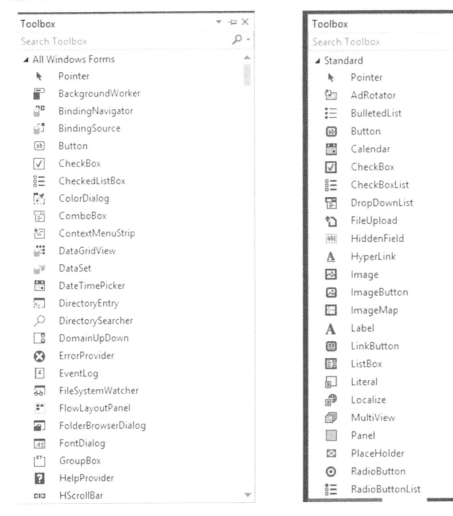

Figure 1.6   Figure 1.7

Examples of the different Toolboxes

New features of Visual Studio 2019

Visual Studio 2019 has a lot of new and exciting features and changes, including the following:

- **New project dialog box:** The New project dialog box features an improved search experience and filters to create projects faster. It looks similar to the following screenshot:

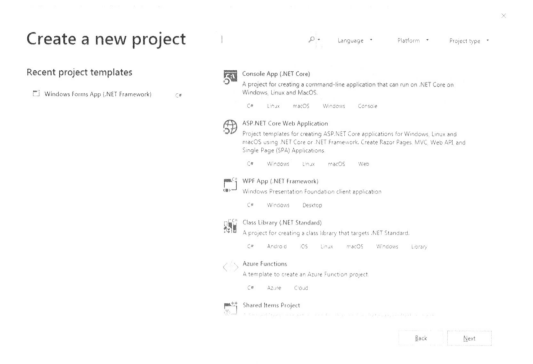

Figure 1.8: New project dialog box

- **Document health indicator:** Document indicator enables us to check and maintain our code's issues. The Document Health Indicator enables us to check and maintain our code's issues. It works because of its Code Cleanup command. With Code Cleanup we can identify and fix warnings and suggestions with one simple click of a button.

  Code Cleanup formats the code and applies any and all code fixes as suggested by its current settings and `.editorconfig` files. EditorConfig files, as discussed in depth in *Chapter 3: Visual Studio 2019 IntelliSense* helps us to maintain a consistent coding style while working with multiple developers on the same project with different editors and IDEs. An EditorConfig project consists of a file format that defines coding styles, and plugins that enable editors to read the file format and adhere to defined styles.

  The Health Inspector can be accessed at the bottom of the Code Window, indicated by a little brush icon *Chapter 7: Debugging Tools,* explains this tool even more with practical examples. It looks similar to the following screenshot:

Figure 1.9: Document health indicator

Solution filter: Solution filter files enable us to choose which projects should be loaded when a solution is opened. Solution filtering enables us to open a large solution but only load a selective few projects. It is common for large teams to have large solutions with many projects. Developers in this team do not always work on all the projects; they may work on a subset of projects whereas others will work on a different subset of projects. By filtering the solution large solutions can be opened more quickly, as not all the projects have to be loaded. In *Chapter 6: Built-in Tools*, we will delve into the solution filter more, and create filters practically.

- **Debug windows search keywords:** Search keywords inside the `Watch,` `Autos,` and `Locals` windows while busy debugging. It looks similar to the following screenshot:

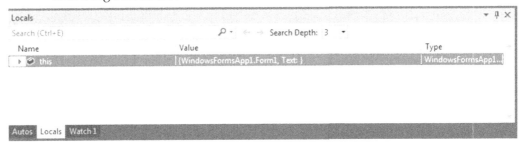

Figure 1.10: Search keywords inside Debug windows

Visual Studio 2019 Updates

We can decide how and when to install Visual Studio 2019 updates. When we select **Tools | Options**, we will see the **Product Updates** field, as shown in the following screenshot:

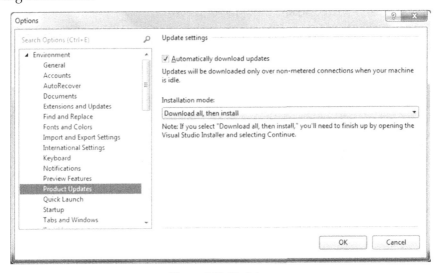

Figure 1.11: Updates

Requirements and prerequisites

In order to install or run Visual Studio 2019, the following minimum requirements must be met.

Supported Operating Systems

64-bit recommended for the following operating systems:

- Windows 10 (Home, Professional, Education, and Enterprise) version 1703 or higher
- Windows Server 2016 (Standard and Datacenter)
- Windows 8.1 (Core, Professional, and Enterprise) with Update 2919355
- Windows Server 2012 R2 (Essentials, Standard, Datacenter) with Update 2919355
- Windows 7 SP1 (Home Premium, Professional, Enterprise, Ultimate) with the latest Windows updates

Hardware

- 1.8 GHz or faster processor. Quad-core or better is recommended for Windows.
- 2 GB of RAM, but 8 GB of RAM is recommended. On virtual machines, 2.5 GB minimum is recommended.
- Minimum of 800MB up to 210 GB of available space on a hard disk, depending on the selected features installed. Installations typically require 20-50 GB of free space.
- A Solid State Drive (SSD) is recommended.
- Windows and Visual Studio 2019 can be installed on a solid-state drive (SSD) to improve performance.
- A video card that supports a minimum display resolution of HD Ready / Standard HD 1280 x 720 (720p). Visual Studio works best at a resolution of WXGA (Wide Extended Graphics Array) 1366 x 768 or higher.

Additional requirements

- Visual Studio 2019 must be installed using Administrator rights
- .NET Framework 4.5 is required in order to install Visual Studio
- Internet Explorer 11 or Edge
- Office 2010, Office 2013, or Office 2016 is required for Team Foundation Server 2019 Office Integration

- A processor that supports Client Hyper-V as well as Second Level Address Translation (SLAT) for Hyper-V Emulator support
- Windows 10 or Windows Server 2016 or Windows Server 2012 R2 in order to build Universal Windows Platform (UWP) applications
- 64-bit Windows for Xamarin.Android
- PowerShell 3.0 or higher

Visual Studio for Mac details had not been released at the time of writing this book.

Supported languages

Visual Studio is available in 14 different languages:

- English
- Chinese (Simplified)
- Chinese (Traditional)
- Czech
- French
- German
- Italian
- Japanese
- Korean
- Polish
- Portuguese (Brazil)
- Russian
- Spanish
- Turkish

Select the language we want in Visual Studio at the time of installation and Visual Studio Installer is available in the language we select.

Visual Studio 2019 Editions

Visual Studio 2019 comes in various flavors as follows:

- Visual Studio 2019 Preview
- Visual Studio Community
- Visual Studio Professional
- Visual Studio Enterprise

Visual Studio 2019 Preview

Usually the Preview contains more than one iterations, but in Visual Studio 2019's case, it contains three Previews, each containing its own new changes. Preview 2 contains fixes for Preview 1 as well as some new features. Preview 3 contains fixes for Preview 2 and some new features and is seen as the final Edition before the actual product launch.

Visual Studio 2019 Preview 1

Visual Studio 2019 Preview 1 was released on 04 December 2018 and included the following new features:

Area	New features
IDE	The following are the new features with respect to IDE: • Visual Studio Live Share enables us to collaborate easily with others and is installed by default. • A new Start window enables us to open and start projects faster. • The New Project dialog box features an improved search experience and filters to create projects faster. • The shell provides a more modernized look and feel thanks to a small facelift. • Our code has more vertical room. • Document indicator enables us to check and maintain our code's issues. • The IDE appears sharper regardless of our display configurations because of improved support for monitor awareness.
Performance	The following are the new features with respect to performance: • Solution Filter files enable us to choose which projects should be loaded when a Solution is opened. • Task Status Center shows Solution load progress. • Improved typing performance. • Stepping Speed and Branch switching speed improvements.

Debugging	The following are the new features with respect to debugging: • Search keywords inside the Watch, Autos, and Locals windows while debugging. • Custom Visualizer • Format specifiers' dropdown inside the Watch, Autos, and Locals windows.
Source Control	The following are the new features with respect to source controls: • Azure DevOps focuses on developer's workflows. • Pull Requests for Visual Studio integrates Pull request Reviews in Visual Studio. • Stores changes temporarily while working on another task.
Web	The following are the new features with respect to web: • Added support for working with .NET Core 3.0 projects. • Snapshot debugger for apps running on Azure Kubernetes, Virtual Machines and Virtual Machine Scale Sets. • Visual Studio Kubernetes Tools enable us to develop container applications for Kubernetes.
Xamarin	The following are the new features with respect to Xamarin: • New Property panel for `Xamarin.Forms` controls. • Improvements to `Xamarin.Android` incremental build performance. • Improved Android Emulator. • IntelliCode for `Xamarin.Forms` XAML.
UWP (Universal Windows Platform)	The following are the new features with respect to UWP: • Package Creation Wizard allows us to submit directly to the Microsoft Store. • The Windows Application Packaging project can now produce MSIX packages via the help of .NET Core.

Table 1.1: Visual Studio 2019 Preview 1 features

Visual Studio 2019 Preview 2

Visual Studio 2019 Preview 2 was released on 23 January 2019 and included the following new features:

Area	New features
Installation	Choose how and when to install Visual Studio 2019 Updates.
IDE	The following are the new features with respect to IDE: • Tag-based search. • Easily accessible Recent Project Templates list. • Code Cleanup fixers can be saved as a profile. • New Notifications experience. • The Extensions and Updates dialog allows us to see the status of our extensions with tags indicating Trial, Paid or Preview. • Azure App Service features have been removed from the Server Explorer Window and have now moved to the Cloud Explorer Window.
Performance	The following are the new features with respect to performance: • Ability to load larger .NET Core projects. • Improved performance of IntelliSense. • New Build All command making use of CMake.
Debugging and diagnostics	The following are the new features with respect to debugging and diagnostics: • Hot path highlighting. • Debug our JavaScript applications in the IDE.
Web	The following are the new features with respect to web: • Publish profile summary enhancements for all apps. • On publishing an app to Azure App Service, a new section will be available. This section is called Dependencies. Dependencies allow us to associate Azure Storage and Azure SQL resources with app service instances. • Better console app for .NET Core tooling.

Container Tools	The following are the new features with respect to container tools: • Streamlined single-projects. • Supports the latest ASP.NET and .NET Core images.
Xamarin	The following are the new features with respect to Xamarin: • `Xamarin.Forms` 4.0 project template. • Improved performance for Xamarin projects. • d8/r8 support for `Xamarin.Android`. d8 produces and compiles smaller and faster `dex` files. R8 shrinks and minifies Java `bytecode` to `dex` code. • Faster deployment. • Initial support for constraint layouts in the `Xamarin.Android` designer.

Table 1.2: Visual Studio 2019 Preview 2 features

Visual Studio 2019 Preview 3

Visual Studio 2019 Preview 3 was released on 13 February 2019 and included the following new features:

Area	New features
IDE	The following are the new features with respect to IDE: • The dotnet format global tool allows us to apply code style preferences from the command-line. • We can browse, sign in, and one-click clone and connect to hosted repositories from Azure DevOps straight from the new start window. • We can install extensions for other source control hosts in order to view repositories owned by us or our organization.
Debugging and diagnostics	The following are the new features with respect to debugging and diagnostics: • Data Breakpoints for .NET Core 3.0 breaks when a specific object's property value changes. • The Search Deeper function in the Autos, Locals, and Watch windows enables us to quickly select how deep we want our initial and subsequent searches to be.

Extensibility	The following are the new features with respect to extensibility:
	• VSIX Projects now include an `AsyncPackage`.
	• An empty VSIX Project template is now included.
	• The Extensions and Updates dialog indicates whether an extension is Free, Paid, or Trial.
	• NuGet package Microsoft.VisualStudio.SDK.
Web	The following are the new features with respect to web:
	• We will be able to re-supply publish credentials for an existing Azure functions publish profile.
	• Several Visual enhancements during the creation of a new ASP.NET application.
UWP (Universal Windows Platform)	The following are the new features with respect to UWP:
	• Deployment to Windows Mobile devices is no longer supported in Visual Studio 2019.

Table 1.3: Visual Studio 2019 Preview 3 features

Visual Studio 2019 Community

The Community Edition of Visual Studio 2019 is free. However, it does not have all the features that the Professional and Enterprise Editions have. Visual Studio Community 2019 is a fully-featured IDE that can be used for creating applications for Android, iOS, Windows, plus web applications and cloud services.

Visual Studio 2019 Professional

Visual Studio 2019 Professional includes professional developer tools and services for individuals or small teams. The Professional Edition includes everything a professional developer needs to build desktop applications, web applications as well as mobile applications.

Visual Studio 2019 Enterprise

Visual Studio 2019 Enterprise is an integrated solution for teams of any size with demanding scale and quality needs. It includes all the features Visual Studio has to offer. We can take advantage of all the debugging and testing tools such as Coded UI Testing, Xamarin Inspector, Code Coverage, and Live Unit Testing.

Integrated Development Environment (IDE) Comparison

Let us compare the Community, Professional, and Enterprise Editions.

The features might still change after the time of writing.

The following table shows the available features in each Edition of Visual Studio 2019:

Features	Community	Professional	Enterprise
To be used by individual developers	Y	Y	Y
To be used for classroom learning	Y	Y	Y
To be used for academic research	Y	Y	Y
To be used for contributing to open source projects	Y	Y	Y
Has development platform support	Y	Y	Y
Has live dependency validation			Y
Includes architectural layer diagrams			Y
Includes code clone			Y
Includes peek definition	Y	Y	Y
Ability to do refactoring	Y	Y	Y
Provides one-click web deployment	Y	Y	Y
Includes dependency graphs and code maps	Y	Y	Y
Multi-Targeting for applications	Y	Y	Y
Code map debugger integration			Y
Includes .NET memory dump analysis			Y
Ability to do graphics debugging	Y	Y	Y
Provides static code analysis	Y	Y	Y
Includes performance and diagnostics hub	Y	Y	Y
Ability to do live unit testing			Y
Test case management			Y
Web load and Performance testing			Y
Code coverage			Y
Lab management			Y
Provides coded UI testing			Y
Microsoft test manager			Y

Ability to do unit testing	Y	Y	Y
Embedded assemblies			Y
Xamarin inspector			Y
Xamarin profiler			Y
Remoted iOS simulator for Windows	Y	Y	Y
Share code with Xamarin	Y	Y	Y
Native iOS and Android UI designers	Y	Y	Y
Xamarin.Forms	Y	Y	Y
Xamarin instant player	Y	Y	Y
PowerPoint storyboarding	Y	Y	Y
Code review	Y	Y	Y
Task suspend/resume	Y	Y	Y

Table 1.4: Supported Features

Installation options

Visual Studio 2019 provides many options to install. It all depends on our space, time and requirements. The more we select, the longer the installation will run. Installation time has been reduced drastically since Visual Studio 2017, and Visual Studio 2019 is even faster.

At the time of writing, an ISO version was not available.

We can select anyone option, which is explained in the following sections.

Windows

The following options are available for installing Visual Studio 2019 on Windows:

- **.NET desktop development:** We can create **Windows Presentation Foundation (WPF)** applications and Window Forms applications. Windows Presentation Foundation is a graphical system by Microsoft for displaying user interfaces in Windows applications. Windows Forms allow us to create powerful Windows-based applications.

- **Desktop development with C++:** Create applications using Win32 APIs and the Windows SDK in C++.

- **Universal Windows Platform development:** With Windows 10, the Universal Windows Platform was launched. This is a common application platform that can run Windows 10. This includes Internet of Things (IoT), Mobile, Xbox, HoloLens, Surface Hub and PCs, and laptops.

Web and cloud

The following options are available for installing Visual Studio 2019 for web and cloud:

- **ASP.NET and web development:** We can create web applications with ASP. NET. Wecan design the pages through either the Design view, or HTML, CSS and JavaScript code. Then, we can add C# code at the backend for business logic or data access. ASP.NET MVC Applications can also be created with this workload. ASP.NET MVC is a web application framework that implements the **model–view–controller (MVC)** pattern. It is a design pattern that decouples the user-interface (view), data (model), and application logic (controller). With the MVC pattern, requests get routed to a controller (application logic) that is responsible for working with the model (data) to perform actions or retrieve data. The controller (application logic) chooses the view to display, and then provides the view model (data). The view renders the page, based on the data that in the model. In *Chapter 9: ASP.NET Tools* we will cover ASP. NET MVC in detail.

- **Azure development:** Azure allows us to build, debug, deploy and manage scalable multi-platform apps and services easily.

- **Python development:** Python is a programming language best suited for working in Data Analytics, Test Automation, and Machine Learning. Visual Studio 2019 enables us to program in Python and includes the necessary Python tools.

- **Node.js development:** Node.js is a JavaScript framework created for server-side scripting specifically. Visual Studio includes tools that aid in creating decent Node.js projects.

- **Data storage and processing:** The data storage and processing workload provides the tools to develop queries against databases, data warehouses and on-premises or Azure data lakes. It supports SQL, U-SQL (Unified SQL), and Hive.

- **Data science and analytical applications:** The Data Science and Analytical Applications workload joins the strengths of R, Python, and F# with their respective runtime distributions.

- **Office/SharePoint development:** The Office/SharePoint development workload provides all the tools we need in order to extend Office and SharePoint.

Mobile and gaming

The following options are available for installing Visual Studio 2019 for mobile and gaming:

- **Mobile development with .NET:** We can build native iOS, Android, and **Universal Windows Platform (UWP)** apps using C# and Xamarin.

- **Game development with Unity:** We can create 2D and 3D games and interactive content with the Unity engine.

- **Mobile development with C++:** We can create and build native C++ apps for Android and iOS.

- **Game development with C++:** We can create games that run on Windows, Xbox.

Other toolsets

The following options are available for installing Visual Studio 2019 for Extension development or Linux development:

- **Visual Studio extension development:** We can create extensions for Visual Studio using Visual Basic, C++, or C#.

- **Linux development with C++:** We can write C++ code for Linux servers, desktops, and devices.

- **.NET Core cross-platform development:** .NET Core is an open-source, general-purpose development platform. It supports Windows, macOS, and Linux and can be used to build cloud, device, and IoT applications.

Choose what to install

Currently, all the generally available editions can download the Community Edition Preview can be downloaded from **https://visualstudio.microsoft.com/vs/** and the preview can be downloaded from **https://visualstudio.microsoft.com/vs/preview/**

Download the Visual Studio by going to 2019 Community edition using the following link in our browser: **https://visualstudio.microsoft.com/thank-we-downloading-visual-studio/?sku=Community&rel=15#**

1. Once we have downloaded it, double click on the setup file. The following screenshot will be displayed:

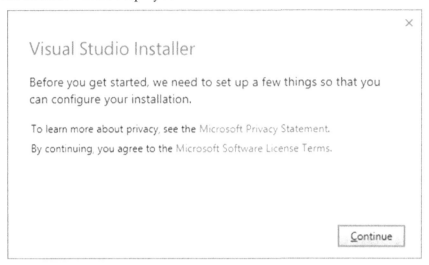

Figure 1.12: Start Visual Studio 2019 Installation

2. Click on **Continue**. The preceding screenshot displays the screen that will inform us that the installer is fetching and installing the necessary setup files. The following screenshot displays the screen once all files have been fetched and installed:

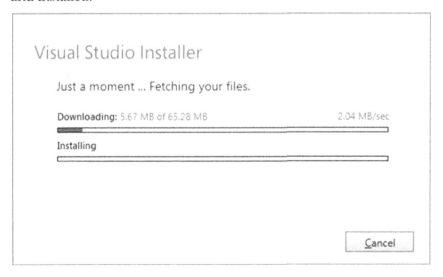

Figure 1.13: Installing Files

3. The Visual Studio Installer will then be displayed after the setup files have been installed with all the options, as explained in the previous section.

4. The following screenshot displays all the Windows **Workloads** available at the time of writing:

Figure 1.14: *Windows Workloads*

5. Web and Cloud Workloads include ASP.NET and Web Development, Python development, and Node.js development, as shown in the following screenshot:

Figure 1.15: *Web and Cloud Workloads*

6. Mobile and gaming workloads allows you to install options such as Unity (which is a very good platform for authoring good games) and .NET, as shown in the following screenshot:

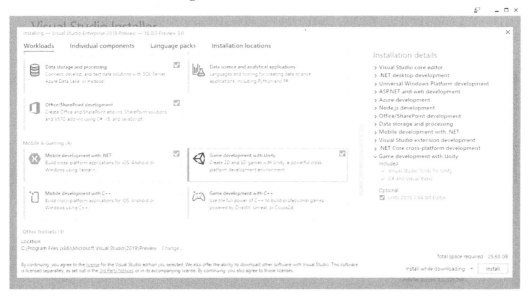

Figure 1.16: Mobile and Gaming Workloads

7. When you need to create extensions for Visual Studio or author code for Linux, the Other Toolsets Workload can be used, which is similar to the following screenshot:

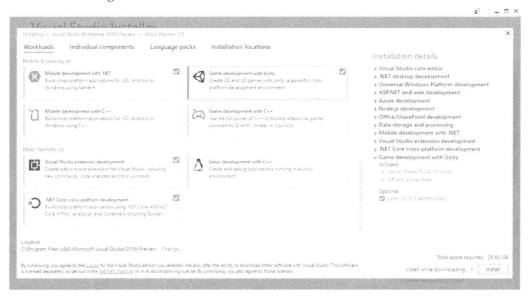

Figure 1.17: Other Toolsets

8. We can choose to install the options while downloading, or download everything first, and then install, as shown in the following screenshot:

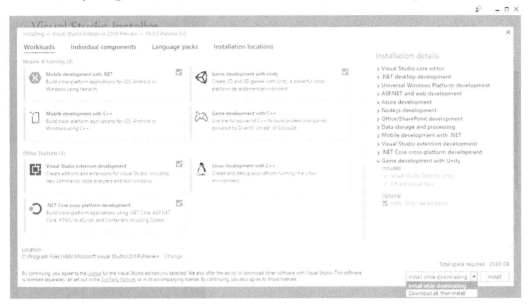

Figure 1.18: Installation Options

9. After we have made our selections on what to install, click on **Install**. A screen similar to the following screenshot will appear:

Figure 1.19: Install Visual Studio 2019

10. We can Pause the installation any time but we need to ensure that we have during the installation and continue at a decent later point of time. The installation time will vary depending on how many workloads you've selected and the internet connection speed. The following screenshot shows the final screen after everything has been installed, prompting us to restart our computer:

Figure 1.20: Installation Completed

Launching Visual Studio 2019

When launching Visual Studio 2019 for the first time, it will prompt us that the application is busy setting up our environment based on our theme choice, workload choices and its necessary settings. This may take some time. The following screenshot displays the waiting Visual Studio 2019 splash screen:

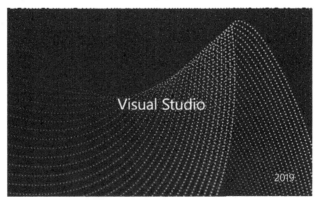

Figure 1.21: Visual Studio 2019 splash screen

Here, it is so much easier and quicker to get started on our current projects, as they are all displayed neatly. Starting a new project from scratch is also easier with the new template window allowing us to search and find our favorite templates quickly. You can refer to the following screenshot:

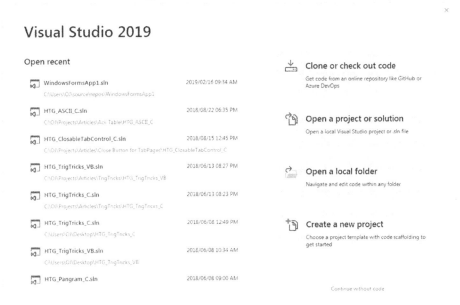

Figure 1.22: *Open Recent Project*

The **Create a new project** dialog box has a plethora of templates available for you to choose from. It is also much easier than before to search for templates:

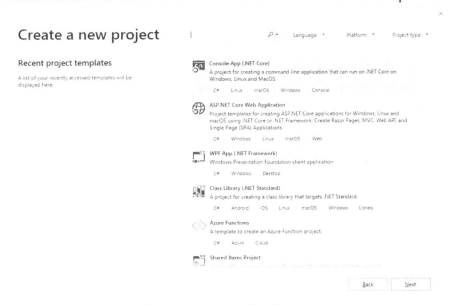

Figure 1.23: *Create a New Project*

The following screenshot displays the configuration screen of our project:

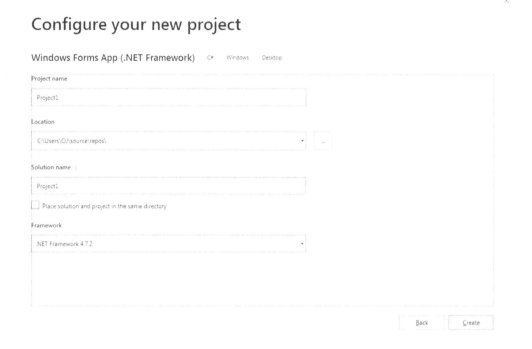

Figure 1.24: *Configure our new Project*

A new project will be created according to our specifications.

Conclusion

In this chapter, we were introduced to Visual Studio 2019. We learned about the different Editions of Visual Studio 2019: Preview, Community, Professional, and Enterprise, and their differences. We learned about the requirements needed to install Visual Studio 2019, how to install Visual Studio 2019, and what options are available to suit our needs. We learned about some new features such as the new project and open project dialog boxes and the debugging windows and how the new features can increase productivity. We explored the Visual Studio 2019 IDE and learned about some of the important windows such as the **Server Explorer**, **Toolbox**, and **Properties** window.

In the next chapter, we will delve deeper into the Visual Studio 2019 IDE and compare it systematically with mobile and web IDEs. We will also explore power tools and create Visual Studio Add-ons.

## CHAPTER 2

Digging into the Visual Studio 2019 IDE

The Visual Studio 2019 IDE is the most important tool at our disposal for creating programs. If the IDE is not up to scratch, our programs will not be up to scratch as simple as that. Knowing how to use Windows and the tools inside the IDE is crucial in order to be able to design and code properly.

In this chapter, we will learn about all the IDE windows and tools and how to use them. We will also compare all the IDEs with each other and learn about Extensions.

Structure

- The standard IDE Windows
- Comparing desktops, mobiles and web IDEs
- Visual Studio Add-ons
- IDE Productivity Power Tools

The standard IDE Windows

The abbreviation IDE means Integrated Development Environment. As the name implies, it is a development environment where you can develop, debug, and deploy any application. Integrated in IDE means you can develop in more than one programming language, as Visual Studio is capable of handling languages such as

Visual Basic.NET, C#, F#, JavaScript, and HTML. Visual Studio acts as a proxy for all these languages and a means of building complete modern-day applications, without sacrificing anything from another programming language.

Let us take a look at the standard Windows that are available in the Visual Studio 2019 IDE.

Menus

The main purpose of the menus is to provide easy navigation and control to the user inside Visual Studio. Some of the most common menu items are File, Edit, View, Debug, Tools, Help and more.

Toolbars

Toolbars provide quick access to frequently used commands.

Design window

The design window is usually the very first window that will be displayed, depending on the selected project type. If we select a **Control Library** project upon project creation, there will be no visible designer window, as a **Control Library** does not have an interface.

The designer window is where you create the UI (User Interface) for your project. You can add the desired controls from the toolbox to your form, or page, or mobile screen, and set their properties using the properties window.

In the event of having more than one page, screen, or form, each can be opened in its own tab, thus giving each equal space.

Data Sources

In *Chapter 1: Getting Started with Visual Studio 2019*, we briefly discussed the **Data Sources** window. Now, we will add a data source so that we can manipulate information from a database, or even a file! To see the broader picture, let us add a data source that connects to an Excel file. Start Visual Studio 2019 (as explained in *Chapter 1: Getting Started with Visual Studio 2019*) and create a new Windows Forms C# application. Once this is done, follow the following steps:

1. Open the **Data Sources** window. It is usually located on the left-hand side of the screen, as shown in the following screenshot (if the **Data Sources**

window is not shown, we can select the View menu, move to Other Windows, and select Data Sources, or by pressing the keyboard shortcut *Shift+Alt+D*):

Figure 2.1: Data Sources window

2. Click on the **Add New Data Source…** link. The **Data Source Configuration Wizard** dialog window will appear, as shown in the following screenshot:

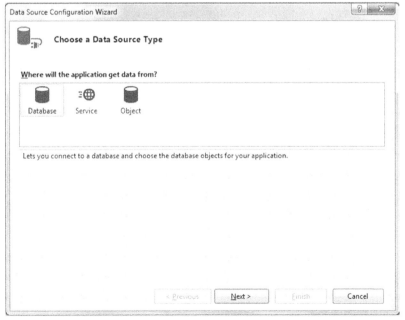

Figure 2.2: Add Data Source

3. Select **Database** and click on **Next**. It is important to understand that any file (well, most) if configured correctly can be used as a database. A database such as Microsoft Access or Microsoft SQL Server is known as a relational database. The reason for this is that all objects in the database are related; for example, an **Employee** database table can be related to a **Pension Fund** table. There are common items that can be used to link the related items.

Flat databases are generally files in plain-text form that can be read and manipulated, but it has a flat structure.

4. Select **Dataset** and click on Next>. The following screenshot displays the **Choose Database Model** window:

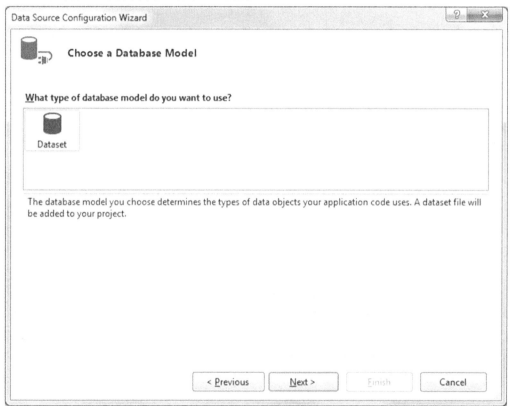

Figure 2.3: Dataset

A dataset is a set of data. Does it make sense, doesn't it? The purpose of a dataset is to hold whatever data is supplied. This gives us the opportunity to make use of the data in any of our programs on any of the platforms.

5. Obviously, we haven't supplied the database details or the dataset details. This is what the next step is for: **Choose Your Data Connection:**

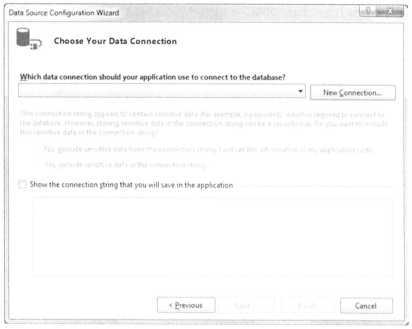

Figure 2.4: Data Connection

6. As the name implies, a data connection is a connection to a database. In this case, we need to supply the server where the database is located, the database name and the tables, views or queries from which the data will be provided. In our case, we will add a file as a database, as we need to keep things easy at this stage. Later on, we will perform more advanced data connections and tasks. To add a data connection, click on **New Connection**. The following screenshot shows the **Choose Data Source** window after the **<other>** option and a **Data provider** have been selected:

Figure 2.5: Choose Data Source

A data provider is a provider of data. This means it is a technology that allows you to access the desired data source. In this case, we select **NET Framework Data Provider for ODBC** (Open database Connectivity).

7. Click on **Continue**. In the next screen, we can select **MS Access Database** or **Excel Files**, as shown in the following screenshot:

Figure 2.6: Excel Connection String

8. Now, how do we connect an Excel file? Well, in this step, click on the **Build** button which will take us to a dialog box where we can select our desired Excel file as a data source.

9. Select the **Machine Data Source** tab and select **New**.

10. Select **User Data Source**, and click on the **Next>** button, as shown in the following screenshot:

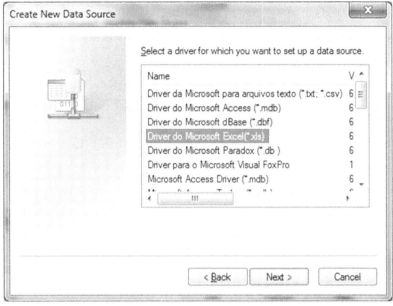

Figure 2.7: Create New Data Source

11. Select the **Driver do Microsoft Excel (*.xls)**, as shown in the preceding screenshot (*Figure 2.7*).

12. Click on the **Next>** button and then click on the **Finish** button.

13. Name the **Data source** and give a description.

14. Click on Workbook. Select the desired workbook in the displayed dialog boxes (which still look like the following screenshot – beats my why Microsoft hasn't upgraded them as well).

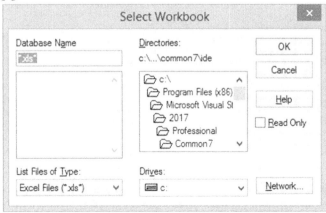

Figure 2.8: Windows 3.1 dialog box

15. Click on **OK** twice. This will bring you back to the **Add Connection** window again.

16. Click on the **Use user or system data source name** button.

17. Click on **Refresh**. Select the data source that was added and click on **OK**.

18. Click on **Next** twice and then click on **Finish**.

19. The data source now appears in the **Data Sources** window.

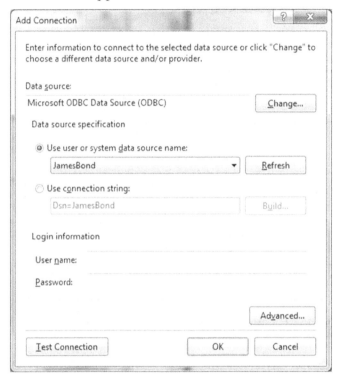

Figure 2.9: Added Data Source

After a few simple steps, our ODBC setup displays the Excel file we had selected. In the example, a file named `James Bond.xls` was selected.

Toolbox

The toolbox is probably the most important window at our disposal in the Visual Studio 2019 IDE. The toolbox is used to add controls to the Windows forms, mobile screens, or web pages. It is very simple to add a control; we need to simply double click on the desired control and it will be added to the form, page, or mobile screen. We can also simply drag a control from the toolbox to the form, page, or mobile screen.

Team Explorer

The **Team Explorer** window enables us to coordinate our code efforts with the other team members while working on a big software project. The **Team Explorer** window also allows us to manage the work that was assigned to single team members, the whole team, or certain projects.

Changes in code that were done during a particular period of time can be checked, thus becoming part of the final solution. By checking in code files, we can select the files we need to submit and the ones we are still working on. The following screenshot displays the **Team Explorer**:

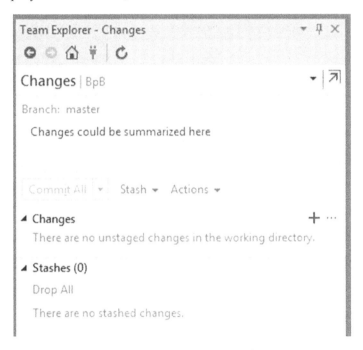

Figure 2.10: *Team Explorer Window*

Notifications

As the name implies, the **Notifications** window displays important notifications (such as important updates in Visual Studio 2019) from Microsoft that are related to Visual Studio 2019. The following screenshot displays notifications:

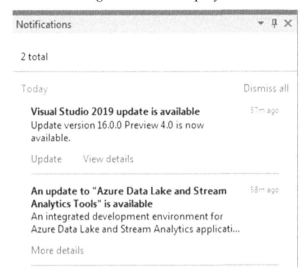

Figure 2.11: Notifications window

Cloud Explorer

The **Cloud Explorer** window in Visual Studio 2019 allows us to view our Azure resources and resource groups. We can inspect the properties of our Azure resources and perform diagnostics from within Visual Studio. The following screenshot displays the **Cloud Explorer** window:

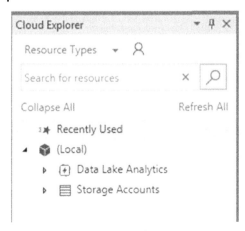

Figure 2.12: Cloud Explorer

Resource view

We can go to the **Resource** view window by clicking on the **View** menu and then selecting the **Other** windows. It displays all the project's resources. Now, what are resources? A resource is an item that can be added to the project; for example, pictures, files, and strings. These resources can be shipped with the project. To add a resource, open the project's **Properties** window by following the given steps:

1. Click on the **Project** menu item.

2. Select the Project Name (this is the project's name) **Properties**.

3. Select the **Resources** tab

4. Select the type of resource to be added (**Images**, **Strings**, **Files**, and more), as shown in the following screenshot:

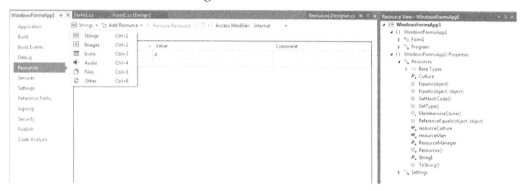

Figure 2.13: *Resources*

JSON outline

The JSON outline window displays the outline structure of a **JSON (JavaScript Object Notation)** file. JSON is a format in which data is sent from websites or mobile devices. It is very compact and has a small size, making it the optimal choice of transmitting data. This window can be reached by selecting View, Other Windows, JSON Outline). Here is an example:

```
{
  "FirstName": "Ockert",
  "LastName": "du Preez",
  "Gender": "Male",
  "Age": 40,
}
```

On the left-hand-side are the settings and on the right-hand-side are the values.

Project properties window

The Project Properties window enables you to set project-wide settings. We saw how to add resources to our projects, but that is not all we can do. On the **Application** tab, we can set the name of the program and the target .NET Framework.

With the **Build** page, we set the project build settings. The **Signing** tab allows us to add certificates to our project, and the **Publish** tab allows us to set publishing settings, especially for our web applications. The following screenshot displays the **Properties** window of an application:

Figure 2.14: *Project Properties*

Reference window

A reference is an external library we want to make use of in our project. This library can be self-built, or Microsoft supplied, or from any other third party. We can add references to our projects by following the given steps:

1. Select the **Project** menu.
2. Click on **Add Reference**.

3. Alternatively, we can right click on the **Solution Explorer** and select **Add Reference** there as well. The following screenshot is displayed on the screen:

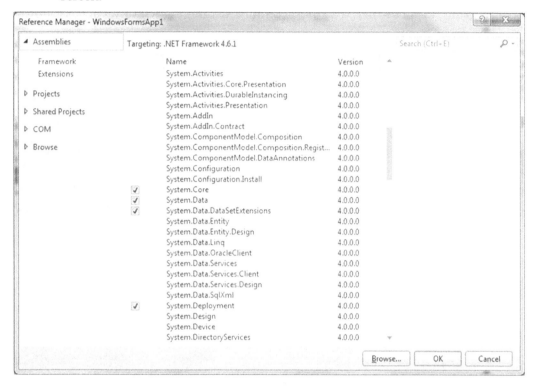

Figure 2.15: Reference

Code window

In *Chapter 1: Getting Started with Visual Studio 2019*, we briefly discussed the code window and now we will dive a bit deeper into it. As we know, the code window allows us to add the source code to our particular objects and their respective events. The following screenshot shows three aspects of the coding window. These dropdowns help us navigate through our code:

Figure 2.16: Coding Window Navigation

The left-most drop-down shows the projects a certain coding file belongs to, the middle drop-down box displays the classes in the current file, and the right-most drop-down displays the events.

Debugging window

Most debugging windows only appear when the project is running, unless they are docked to the side of the IDE. The most common debugging windows are as follows:

- Output window
- Quick Watch window
- Locals window

Output window

The **Output** window is very useful in determining what an object's current value is. When a breakpoint is set and the IDE enters the debugging mode, we can quickly display a value using the **Console.WriteLine** command. The current value of the object (i) is **23**, as shown at the bottom of the **Output** window in the following screenshot:

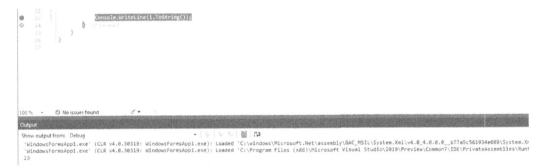

Figure 2.17: Output window

Quick watch

The benefit of the **QuickWatch** (by clicking on **Debug | QuickWatch**) window is that we do not need any extra effort or input in order to determine an object's value. We simply need to set a breakpoint, highlight the object by selecting it using the mouse, and then open the **QuickWatch** window. The value of **i** is **23**, as shown in the following screenshot:

Figure 2.18: QuickWatch

Locals

The **Locals** window is similar to the **QuickWatch** window, but the good thing is that it is not a separate dialog box; it can be docked as one of the IDE windows to see results quickly and easily. The following screenshot is an example of the Locals window:

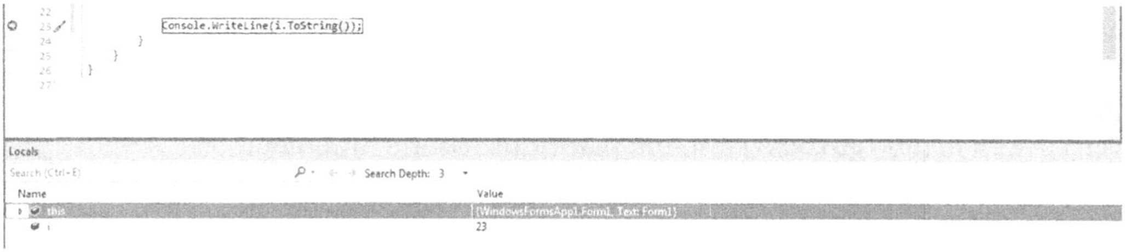

Figure 2.19: Locals window

Tasks List

The **Task List** window displays all the inactive or incomplete tasks. Let us take a look at the following code segment:

```
private void Button1_Click(object sender, EventArgs e)

    {

      //UNDONE: Complete this procedure

int I = 22;

      //TODO: Decrement I value

i++;

      //HACK: Display value in MessageBox

Console.WriteLine(i.ToString());

    }
```

The default tokens (TODO, HACK, and UNDONE) will be displayed in the **Task List** window, as shown in the following screenshot:

Figure 2.20: *Task List window*

Custom tokens can also be added as preferred.

The **Task List** window displays the tasks that need to be done, the name of the project, the file name, as well as the line number.

Comparing desktop, mobile and web IDEs

Most of the IDE's windows still function the same and there is not much difference for each project. For example, the **Solution Explorer** window will simply display different files and folders, depending on the project type. A big difference in the IDEs can be seen in the **Toolbox**. Different platforms require different tools.

For each platform, the **Toolbox** is divided into different sections.

Windows Forms

Windows Forms provides a **Graphical User Interface (GUI)** and allows us to write rich client applications for desktops, laptops, and tablet PCs. In order to design the GUI, we need tools specific to the Windows Forms platform, which are as follows:

- **All Windows Forms:** This toolbox section holds all Windows-related controls such as buttons, folder browsers, textboxes, and labels.

- **Common controls:** These are the controls that are most frequently used in Windows Forms projects. These include picture boxes, radio buttons, list boxes, and checkboxes.

- **Containers:** These controls can host child controls. Group boxes and panels are perfect examples as they can contain any controls inside them and act like their parents.

- **Menus and Toolbars:** These contain context menu strips, status strips, and tool strip controls.

- **Data controls:** These include datasets, data grid views, and charts.

- **Components:** These are special controls that usually do not have a visible interface, as they work in the background or unseen. These controls include background workers, image lists, error providers, and timers.

- **Printing:** It has printing controls.

- **Dialogs:** They contain common dialog controls such as font dialogs, save file dialogs, and color dialogs.

ASP.NET

ASP.NET is a server-side web application framework. As we need to create web applications, we cannot make use of controls designed specifically for Windows. We need proper controls, which will enable us to build content-rich web applications. The ASP.NET Toolbox is divided into different sections to help finding the right controls faster.

- **Standard:** The standard section in the ASP.NET Toolbox includes most of the tools that can be used to create decent web applications. These controls include AdRotator, Hyperlink, Button, and File Upload.

- **Data:** It controls data to work with and manipulates data. Data List, Grid View, Details View, and Sql Data Source are a few examples.

- **Validation:** Validation controls ensure that the data entered is correct. These include Range Validator and Required Field Validator.

- **Navigation:** Navigation controls include Menu and Site Map Path.

- **Login:** Login-related controls include Login, Password Recovery and Create User Wizard.

- **WebParts:** They include server widgets such as Catalog Zone and Editor Zone.

- **AJAX Extensions:** They enable us to work with AJAX.
- **HTML:** Standard HTML controls include text area, select, and the input controls.

Xamarin.Forms (mobile)

In order to create powerful Xamarin apps, the Xamarin toolbox supplies us with layouts, controls, and cells. The layouts are used to structure content on the pages and to host controls.The following is a breakdown of the Xamarin toolbox:

- **Controls:** In the controls section of the mobile toolbox, we can find all the basic building blocks to build a decent mobile application. These controls include Entry, Editor, Picker, and TimePicker.
- **Layouts:** Layouts are used to organize and structure our mobile app screens. Stack Layout enables us to put controls in a column format, Flex Layout gives us more versatility when designing screens and Scroll View supplies us with a scrollable view.
- **Cells:** The cells control section includes ImageCell, TextCell, and EntryCell.

.NET Core IDE

.NET Core is free and open-source. It is a managed computer software framework for the Windows, Linux, and macOS. It also is an open source, cross platform successor of .NET Framework.

Ensure that Visual Studio 2019 16.1 Preview 3 or newer is installed to be able to create .NET Core 3.0 projects. We will work with .NET Core 3.0 during the course of this book.

Visual Studio Code IDE

Visual Studio Code is a source-code editor developed for Windows, Linux and macOS. Visual Studio Code includes support for debugging, embedded Git control, syntax highlighting, intelligent code completion, snippets, as well as code refactoring.

We will work with Visual Studio Code during the course of this book.

Each of the IDEs has its own flavor and what better way to explore them, by doing a few exercises!

Desktop IDE

In *Chapter 1: Getting Started with Visual Studio 2019,* we learned how to create a new C# project. After the new C# Windows Forms project has been created, we make use of the **Toolbox** and **Properties** window to add the following controls to the form and set their properties:

Control	Property	Value
Label	Text	Username
Label	Text	Password
TextBox		
TextBox	PasswordChar	*
Button	Text	Log In
Button	Text	Cancel
Form	Text	Log In
	Size	300, 155

Table 2.1: Desktop controls

The design should resemble the following screenshot:

Figure 2.21: Windows Forms

Let us add some code to this small program using the following steps:

1. Double click on the **Log In** button. Then, add the following code:

```
private void Button1_Click(object sender, EventArgs e)
    {
if (textBox1.Text == "OJ" && textBox2.Text == "BpB")
    {
MessageBox.Show("Welcome Back!");
    }
else
```

```
        {
MessageBox.Show("Try Again.");


        }
    }
```

This code checks whether the values are of the two textboxes. If the Username is OJ and the `Password` is `BpB`, a welcoming message will appear on the screen, else a message will appear encouraging the user to try again.

2. Double click on the **Cancel** button and add the following code:

```
private void Button2_Click(object sender, EventArgs e)

    {
        textBox1.Text = "";

        textBox2.Text = "";

textBox1.Focus();

    }
```

The **Cancel** button clears all the entered text and returns the focus to the first textbox.

Now that we have explored the Windows Desktop Visual Studio IDE with the aid of a small project, let us do the same for a mobile project.

Mobile IDE

When creating a mobile application, we must ensure that we have installed the Xamarin workload while installing Visual Studio 2019. Applications that are built using Xamarin contain native user interface controls so that they look and behave the way the end users expect. Xamarin built apps have access to all the functionalities exposed by the underlying device, and they can make use of platform-specific hardware acceleration.

Follow the given steps to create a mobile application:

1. Create a new **Mobile App (Xamarin.Forms)** project. Click on **Next**.
2. Specify the project's name and location and then click on **Create**.

3. In the next box, select **Blank** from the template list and click on **OK**, as shown in the following screenshot:

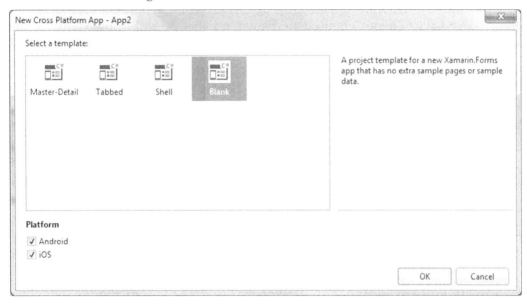

Figure 2.22: Cross Platform App

After the project has been created and loaded, we will see an entirely different design IDE.

4. Open the MainPage.xaml file and you will notice that coding similar to the following will appear:

```
<?xml version="1.0" encoding="utf-8" ?>

<ContentPage xmlns="http://xamarin.com/schemas/2014/forms"

        xmlns:x="http://schemas.microsoft.com/winfx/2009/xaml"

xmlns:local="clr-namespace:App2"

x:Class="MobileLogin.MainPage">

<StackLayout>

<!-- Place new controls here -->

<Label Text="Welcome to Xamarin.Forms!"

 HorizontalOptions="Center"

 VerticalOptions="CenterAndExpand" />

</StackLayout>

</ContentPage>
```

This is **XAML (Extensible Application Markup Language)**. XAML is a declarative language that describes the design of a page or mobile screen. In the preceding code segment, the XAML defines a `Content Page`. This page will host our current screen content. A `Stack Layout` is used to display a Label control in the centre of the screen.

There is a way to see the design of this page and that is to click on the encircled button, as shown in the following screenshot. The button beneath it switches back to the XAML code view:

Figure 2.23: XAML code view

We can make use of the **Toolbox** and **Properties** window to add the following controls to the form and set their properties:

Control	Property	Value
Label	Text	User Name
Label	Text	Password
Entry	Placeholder	Username
Entry	IsPassword	True
Button	Text	Login
Button	Text	Cancel

Table 2.2: Mobile controls

We can also add the XAML code manually to add controls to our page. This will take some getting used to and some learning:

```
<?xml version="1.0" encoding="utf-8" ?>

<ContentPage xmlns="http://xamarin.com/schemas/2014/forms"

        xmlns:x="http://schemas.microsoft.com/winfx/2009/xaml"

xmlns:local="clr-namespace:MobileLogin"

x:Class="MobileLogin.MainPage">
```

```
<StackLayout VerticalOptions="StartAndExpand">

<Label Text="User Name" />

<Entry x:Name="usernameEntry" Placeholder="Username" />

<Label Text="Password" />

<Entry x:Name="passwordEntry" IsPassword="true" />

<Button Text="Login" Clicked="OnLoginButtonClicked" />

<Button Text="Cancel" Clicked="OnCancelButtonClicked" />


<Label x:Name="messageLabel" />

</StackLayout>


</ContentPage>
```

The design should closely resemble to the following screenshot:

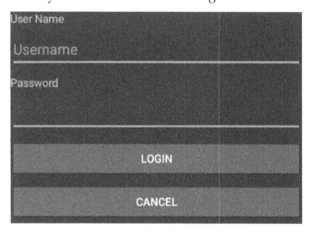

Figure 2.24: Mobile Design

Where do we add the code? Well, we need to still add our C# code to these buttons to work. In the **Solution Explorer**, search for the file named MainPage.xaml.cs and then open it by double clicking on it. This is where we can add the C# code for these objects.

Add the following lines of code to the Login and Cancel buttons:

```
void OnLoginButtonClicked(object sender, EventArgs e)
    {
```

```
if (usernameEntry.Text == 'OJ' && passwordEntry.Text == 'BpB')

    {

      messageLabel.Text = "Welcome Back";

    }

else

    {

      messageLabel.Text = "Try Again";

    }

  }


void OnCancelButtonClicked(object sender, EventArgs e)

    {

      usernameEntry.Text = "";

      passwordEntry.Text = "";

       usernameEntry.Focus();

    }
```

The code is the same as in the desktop project, except for the fact that the Welcoming and `Try Again` messages are displayed inside a label instead of a `Message Box`.

Web IDE

To create a web application, we need to create an ASP.NET web application project. ASP.NET is an open source web framework used for building web applications and services with .NET. After we select the ASP.NET web application project and click on **Next**, a new screen will appear prompting us to choose the type of the ASP.NET application. These types include:

- **Empty:** This template contains no content.
- **Web Forms (the one we will create):** This template provides a design surface, which we can use to host controls and our content.
- **MVC:** This enables us to create web applications using the MVC (Model-View-Controller) architecture.

- **Web API:** This enables us to create RESTful (Representational State Transfer) HTTP services.
- **Single Page Application:** This template enables us to create a JavaScript driven HTML5 application with the use of ASP.NET, Web API, CSS3, and JavaScript.

After the new ASP.Net web application is created, double click on one of the pages such as **Default.aspx**. This is usually the home page of a web application.

We need to get rid of the paragraphs and headings that are automatically created by the designer by deleting them. Then, we use the **Toolbox** and **Properties** window to add the following controls to the form and set their properties:

Control	Property	Value
LogIn	DisplayRememberMe	False
	LoginButtonType	Link

Table 2.3: ASP.NET controls

The design should closely resemble to the following screenshot:

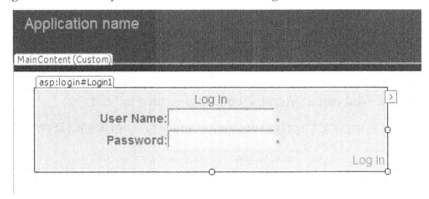

Figure 2.25: Web Login

The design window is split into three sections:
- The design view (which we have been working with)
- The split view displays the design view as well as the underlining HTML code.
- The source view shows the HTML code that makes your design.

HTML (Hypertext Markup Language) is the language used to create web pages. HTML elements are represented by tags (the elements between the <> signs) which identify pieces of content such as headings, paragraphs, tables, images, and so on. The code behind the Login design looks like the following:

```
<%@ Page Title="Home Page" Language="C#" MasterPageFile="~/Site.Master"
AutoEventWireup="true" CodeBehind="Default.aspx.cs" Inherits="WebLogin._
Default" %>

<asp:Content ID="BodyContent" ContentPlaceHolderID="MainContent"
runat="server">

<div class="jumbotron">

<asp:Login ID="Login1" runat="server" DisplayRememberMe="False"
LoginButtonType="Link" RememberMeSet="True" Width="412px">

</asp:Login>

</div>

<div class="row">

<div class="col-md-4">

</div>

</div>

</asp:Content>
```

The **Login** control is placed inside a DIV element, which is placed inside a Content element. For our application to do something, we must add the code to the C# class file. An easy way to do this is to navigate to the **LoggingIn** event in the **Properties** Window and double click on it. Else, we could search for the **.cs** file in the **Solution Explorer** as we did earlier. Add the code highlighted in bold.

```
protected void Login1_LoggingIn(object sender, LoginCancelEventArgs e)

    {
if (Login1.UserName == "OJ" && Login1.Password == "BpB")

    {

      Login1.TitleText = "Welcome Back";


    }

else

    {

      Login1.TitleText = "Try Again";

      Login1.UserName = "";

    }

    }
```

Although we have worked on three different platforms, the underlying C# code mostly remains the same. This may not always be the case, as this book shows examples that are not too complex (yet.)

Visual Studio 2019 Extensions

Extensions or Add-ins is a code package that can be run inside the Visual Studio 2019 IDE. Extensions provide new or improved Visual Studio features. This can be anything! From improving scrolling features to improving the IDE windows. There are literally thousands of Extensions available atthe Visual Studio Marketplace **(https://marketplace.visualstudio.com/).**

The Visual Studio Marketplace is an exclusive place for purchasing and renewing subscriptions, as well as for finding new extensions for Visual Studio and Visual Studio Code. Some extensions are free, whereas some are expensive. It all depends on the needs of the development team. Extensions can help improve our overall productivity.

Let us add some useful extensions to our Visual Studio 2019 IDE.

Finding and installing extensions

1. Navigate to **https://marketplace.visualstudio.com/**.

2. In the **Search** bar, type in RockMargin and press **Enter** or click on **Search**.

3. The result will be displayed. It shows a brief summary of the extension.

4. Click on RockMargin. This brings us to the **Download** page. This page gives a good description and details on how this extension works, as shown in the following screenshot:

Figure 2.26: RockMargin

5. Select **Download**. The VSIX file will be downloaded. The VSIX file is a compressed file, which holds all the necessary coding files that extends the functionality of the IDE.

6. Navigate to the file and double click on the VSIX file.

Image optimizer

Follow the same steps to search for an extension called Image Optimizer and install it, as shown in the following screenshot:

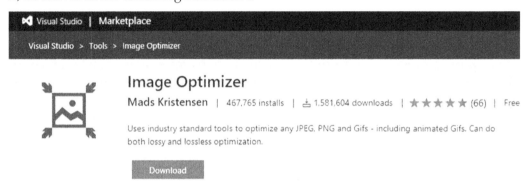

Figure 2.27: Image Optimizer

Follow the same procedure and add an extension named SmartPaster2019.

We can also use the extensions menu in the Visual Studio 2019 IDE to search for nice Extensions.

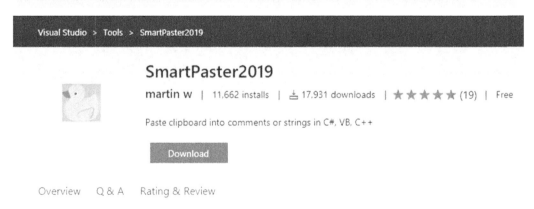

Figure 2.28: SmartPaster2019

Creating a very basic extension

The Visual Studio SDK needs to be installed before you can develop Extensions for Visual Studio 2019. It can be installed when Visual Studio 2019 is being installed for the first time or afterwards.

Let's create our very own extension, by using the next steps:

1. Create a new project and select VSIX as the template.

2. After the project is loaded, right click on the project node in **Solution Explorer**.

3. Select **Add**, **New Item**.

4. Expand the **Extensibility** node under **Visual C#**.

5. Choose from the available item templates (For our project, select **Custom Command**, as shown in the following screenshot (*Figure 2.29*)):

   - **Visual Studio Package**
   - **Editor Items**
   - **Command**
   - **Tool Window**
   - **Toolbox Control**

6. Click on **Add**, as shown in the following screenshot:

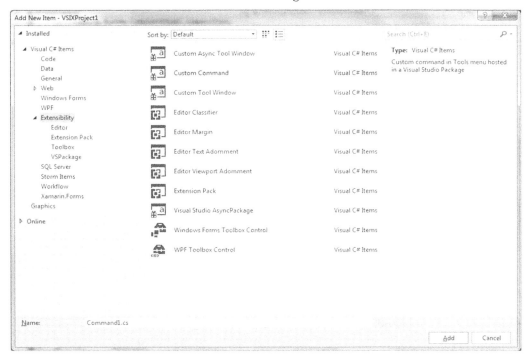

Figure 2.29: Extension

7. Double click on the `vsct` file. The code will open. Make sure to read the comments as well as they explain what is happening. The `vsct` file is where we can change the design of the objects and add objects.

8. Change the text of the button to `Click Me`, as shown in bold in the following code:

```
<Button guid="guidVSIXProject1PackageCmdSet" id="Command1Id"
priority="0x0100" type="Button">

<Parent guid="guidVSIXProject1PackageCmdSet" id="MyMenuGroup" />

<Icon guid="guidImages" id="bmpPic1" />

<Strings>

<ButtonText>Click Me!</ButtonText>

</Strings>

</Button>

</Buttons>
```

9. Open the `Command1.cs` file and modify the `Execute` procedure to the following:

```
private void Execute(object sender, EventArgs e)

    {

        ThreadHelper.ThrowIfNotOnUIThread();

        string message = "My first Extension";

        string title = "Extension Title";


        // Show a message box to prove we were here

VsShellUtilities.ShowMessageBox(

        this.package,

        message,

        title,

        OLEMSGICON.OLEMSGICON_INFO,

        OLEMSGBUTTON.OLEMSGBUTTON_OK,

        OLEMSGDEFBUTTON.OLEMSGDEFBUTTON_FIRST);

    }
```

10. Run the extension by clicking on the **Run/Start** button inside Visual Studio.

    A new instance of Visual Studio Experimental Instance will be spawned, but remember that this is just for testing the extension. It must be still installed and published properly.

    The running extension is shown next

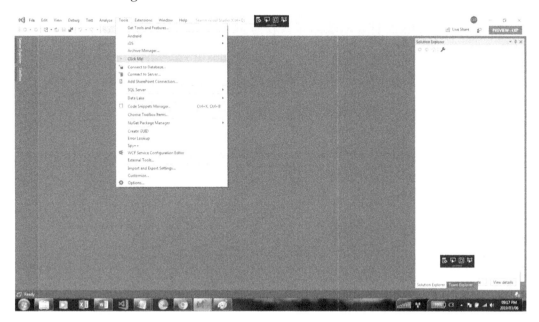

Figure 2.30: Test Extension

11. The preceding screenshot (*Figure 2.30*) displays the **Extension** in action. On the **Tools** menu, select Click Me!.

12. Click on it. A message box appears, as shown in the following screenshot:

Figure 2.31: Test extension result

IDE Productivity Power Tools

Productivity Power Tools 2017/2019 is an extension bundle installer from Microsoft DevLabs that will install its components individually. It contains the following extensions:

- **Align Assignments:** This extension enables us to align variable assignments.

- **Copy As Html:** This extension copies the text in the HTML format.

- **Double-click Maximize:** This extension maximizes and docks windows.

- **Fix Mixed Tabs:** This extension fixes tab spacing.

- **Match Margin:** This extension draws markers on the Visual Studio IDE scrollbars.

- **Middle-Click Scroll:** This extension allows us to scroll with the help of a click with the middle mouse button.

- **Peek Help:** This extension shows F1 Help inline in the code editor.

- **Power Commands for Visual Studio:** This is aset of useful extensions for the IDE.

- **Quick Launch Tasks:** This extension provides accessibility of frequent tasks.

- **Shrink Empty Lines:** This extension removes empty lines in the code editor.

- **Solution Error Visualizer:** This extension highlights errors and warnings inside the Solution Explorer.

- **Time Stamp Margin:** This extension adds a time stamp to the debug output. window.

Conclusion

In this chapter, we introduced the Visual Studio 2019 IDE. We learned about the difference between all the IDEs of Visual Studio 2019. We learned about extensions (what they are and how useful they can be) and how to create them. We also learned about the Productivity Power Tools.

In the next chapter, we will focus on IntelliCode and IntelliSense. We will explore the new JavaScript Intellisense and its AI capabilities for a better coding experience.

CHAPTER 3

Visual Studio 2019 IntelliSense

I n order to author proper code, we need proper tools to assist us. Tools such as IntelliSense and IntelliCode not only save our valuable coding time, but they assist us in conforming to the most popular coding standards as well.

In this chapter, we will learn about IntelliSense, how to install it, and its advancements and benefits. Then, we will move on to artificial intelligence in order to understand IntelliCode better. With IntelliCode, we will dive deep into its advantages and learn how to find and install it in Visual Studio 2019.

Structure

- IntelliSense
- Template IntelliSense Improvements in C++
- Artificial Intelligence (AI)
- IntelliCode Extension for Visual Studio 2019
- Advantages of using IntelliCode
- Installing the IntelliCode extension

IntelliSense

IntelliSense is an IDE tool that completes code; or we can say that it is a code-completion tool that assists us while we are typing our code. IntelliSense helps us add property and method calls using only a few keystrokes, keep track of the parameters we are typing, and learn more about the code we are using. IntelliSense is mostly language-specific.

IntelliSense includes the following features:

- **List members:** Usually, when a trigger character such as a period (.) in managed code such as C# and VB.NET or double colon (::) in C++ is pressed, a list of members from a type or namespace appears. As we type, the list filters to provide a proper camel case selection. We can make a selection by double clicking on the provided item or pressing the tab or space button. The member list also provides quick info, which means that if we hover our mouse over an item, we get an idea of the member's purpose and parameters.

  You can also invoke the list members feature manually by typing *Ctrl + J* and choosing **Edit | IntelliSense | List Members**, or by choosing the **List Members** button on the editor toolbar. To turn list members on (if it is off), navigate to **Tools | Options | All Languages** and deselect **Auto list members**.

  The following screenshot displays a list of string members that we may want to use such as **Length** (which gives us the length or rather the number of characters of the current string):

Figure 3.1: List Members

- **Parameter info:** Parameter info provides us with information on the number, names or the types of parameters required by a certain method, C++ template or a C# attribute generic type parameter. The bold parameter indicates the next required parameter while we are typing the function. In an overloaded function, we can simply use the up or down arrow keys to view information of different parameters for the function overloads.

When functions and parameters are annotated with XML documentation comments, the comments will display as parameter info. We can manually invoke parameter info by choosing **Edit | IntelliSense | Parameter Info**, by pressing *Ctrl + Shift + Space*, or by choosing the **Parameter Info** button on the editor toolbar.

The following screenshot shows the various parameters available for the Console. WriteLine command. In the following example, string format, which is in bold is the current parameter that needs to be input for the 19th overload:

Figure 3.2: Parameter Info

- **Quick info:** Quick info displays the complete declaration for any identifier in our code. As mentioned earlier, after we select a member from the **List Members** box, **Quick Info** appears on the screen. We can manually invoke quick info by first selecting the text then choosing **Edit | IntelliSense | Quick Info**, or by first selecting the text then pressing *Ctrl + I, Ctrl + K*, or by choosing the **Quick Info** button on the editor toolbar.

The following screenshot displays the quick info for the Console class:

```
Console.WriteLine(i.ToString());
```

class System.Console

Figure 3.3: Quick Info

- **Complete word:** Complete word completes the rest of a command, object, variable, or function name after sufficient characters have been entered to disambiguate the term.

We invoke complete word by choosing **Edit | IntelliSense | Complete Word**, or by pressing *Ctrl + Space*, or by choosing the **Complete Word** button on the editor toolbar.

Template IntelliSense Improvements in C++

In C++, a function template defines a family of functions and a class template defines a family of classes. IntelliSense for these templates were only introduced in Visual Studio 2017 15.8 Preview 3 with the inclusion of the template bar.

In Visual Studio 2019, Template IntelliSense has improved a great deal with the inclusion of the following:

- Peek window UI and live edits
- Nested template support
- Default argument watermarks

Peek window UI and live edits

The Peek window UI allows us to do live edits and it integrates nicely into our workflow. The reason why this is so important is that when clicked on the edit button on the template bar, a modal box would pop up. Because of this, making live changes were impossible and difficult. Now, as we type template arguments, IntelliSense updates in real time, thus enabling us to see how the arguments may affect our code.

Nested template support

The template bar would only appear at a top-level parent template. Now, it includes support for nested templates.

Default argument watermarks

If there is a default argument present, the textbox inside the peek window gets automatically populated with it, or else a different argument can be specified.

Artificial Intelligence (AI)

Artificial Intelligence (AI) or **Machine Intelligence** is simply put as intelligence demonstrated by machines. This means that we can teach machines to do certain tasks, or we can program the machines so that they are able to learn things themselves.

Now why are we talking about AI instead of IntelliSense and IntelliCode? The answer is simple. The IntelliCode Extension for Visual Studio 2019 is able to learn how you code and what your preferences are. This speeds up coding as IntelliCode already knows what you want to do and how.

IntelliCode Extension for Visual Studio 2019

The IntelliCode Extension for Visual Studio 2019 is a tool that enhances our software development efforts with the help of AI. IntelliCode helps developers and teams find issues faster and focus on code reviews. Visual Studio IntelliCode improves developer productivity using features such as contextual IntelliSense, code formatting and style rule inference. It combines existing developer workflows with machine learning to provide an understanding of the code and its context.

IntelliCode extensions are available in Visual Studio and Visual Studio Code, C++, C#, and XAML in Visual Studio and Java, TypeScript/JavaScript, and Python in Visual Studio Code.

IntelliCode is available at the Visual Studio Marketplace **(https://marketplace. visualstudio.com/items?itemName=VisualStudioExptTeam.VSIntelliCode).**

The preview edition of IntelliCode can be found at the above link. At the time of writing, the live version was not available.

Advantages of using IntelliCode

Using IntelliCode has the following advantages:

* Assisted IntelliSense
* Recommendations for your types based on your code (C#)
* Inferring code style and formatting conventions
* Find issues faster
* Focused code reviews

Assisted IntelliSense

IntelliCode saves our time by putting what we are most likely to use at that point in time at the top of the completion list. Thanks to its built-in AI following recommendations on common practices used by thousands of developers in thousands of open source projects.

Recommendations for your types based on your code (C#)

IntelliCode can learn patterns from our code so that it can make recommendations for types that are not in the open source domain such as your own utility classes.

Do not worry, the service keeps the trained models secured so that they cannot be accessed by those we do not choose to share our models with.

Inferring code style and formatting conventions

Visual Studio IntelliCode dynamically creates an .editorconfig file from codebase to define our coding styles and formats.

EditorConfig

EditorConfig helps us to maintain a consistent coding style while working with multiple developers on the same project with different editors and IDEs. An EditorConfig project consists of a file format that defines coding styles and plugins that enable editors to read the file format and adhere to defined styles.

The following code is an example of what an .editorconfig file looks like in Visual Studio. To understand the file and identify core features in a better way, it is broken up into three coding segments.

The core EditorConfig options and .Net coding conventions handle the general settings for the editor. These settings are applied to all .NET languages in the IDE:

```
# To learn more about .editorconfig see https://aka.ms/editorconfigdocs

###############################
# Core EditorConfig Options   #
###############################

root = true

# All files

[*]

indent_style = space

# Code files

[*.{cs,csx,vb,vbx}]

indent_size = 4

insert_final_newline = true

charset = utf-8-bom

###############################
# .NET Coding Conventions     #
###############################
```

```
[*.{cs,vb}]

# Organize usings

dotnet_sort_system_directives_first = true

# this. preferences

dotnet_style_qualification_for_field = false:silent

dotnet_style_qualification_for_property = false:silent

dotnet_style_qualification_for_method = false:silent

dotnet_style_qualification_for_event = false:silent

# Language keywords vs BCL types preferences

dotnet_style_predefined_type_for_locals_parameters_members = true:silent

dotnet_style_predefined_type_for_member_access = true:silent

# Parentheses preferences

dotnet_style_parentheses_in_arithmetic_binary_operators = always_for_
clarity:silent

dotnet_style_parentheses_in_relational_binary_operators = always_for_
clarity:silent

dotnet_style_parentheses_in_other_binary_operators = always_for_
clarity:silent

dotnet_style_parentheses_in_other_operators = never_if_
unnecessary:silent

# Modifier preferences

dotnet_style_require_accessibility_modifiers = for_non_interface_
members:silent

dotnet_style_readonly_field = true:suggestion

# Expression-level preferences

dotnet_style_object_initializer = true:suggestion

dotnet_style_collection_initializer = true:suggestion

dotnet_style_explicit_tuple_names = true:suggestion

dotnet_style_null_propagation = true:suggestion

dotnet_style_coalesce_expression = true:suggestion

dotnet_style_prefer_is_null_check_over_reference_equality_method =
true:silent
```

```
dotnet_prefer_inferred_tuple_names = true:suggestion

dotnet_prefer_inferred_anonymous_type_member_names = true:suggestion

dotnet_style_prefer_auto_properties = true:silent

dotnet_style_prefer_conditional_expression_over_assignment = true:silent

dotnet_style_prefer_conditional_expression_over_return = true:silent

###############################
# Naming Conventions          #
###############################

# Style Definitions

dotnet_naming_style.pascal_case_style.capitalization            =
pascal_case

# Use PascalCase for constant fields

dotnet_naming_rule.constant_fields_should_be_pascal_case.severity =
suggestion

dotnet_naming_rule.constant_fields_should_be_pascal_case.symbols  =
constant_fields

dotnet_naming_rule.constant_fields_should_be_pascal_case.style    =
pascal_case_style

dotnet_naming_symbols.constant_fields.applicable_kinds            = field

dotnet_naming_symbols.constant_fields.applicable_accessibilities  = *

dotnet_naming_symbols.constant_fields.required_modifiers          = const
```

Code segment 1: C# settings are obviously more than Visual Basic.NET so the next coding segment shows the C# coding conventions that we can change:

```
###############################
# C# Coding Conventions        #
###############################

[*.cs]

# var preferences

csharp_style_var_for_built_in_types = true:silent

csharp_style_var_when_type_is_apparent = true:silent

csharp_style_var_elsewhere = true:silent
```

```
# Expression-bodied members

csharp_style_expression_bodied_methods = false:silent

csharp_style_expression_bodied_constructors = false:silent

csharp_style_expression_bodied_operators = false:silent

csharp_style_expression_bodied_properties = true:silent

csharp_style_expression_bodied_indexers = true:silent

csharp_style_expression_bodied_accessors = true:silent

# Pattern matching preferences

csharp_style_pattern_matching_over_is_with_cast_check = true:suggestion

csharp_style_pattern_matching_over_as_with_null_check = true:suggestion

# Null-checking preferences

csharp_style_throw_expression = true:suggestion

csharp_style_conditional_delegate_call = true:suggestion

# Modifier preferences

csharp_preferred_modifier_order =
public,private,protected,internal,static,extern,new,virtual,abstract,

sealed,override,readonly,unsafe,volatile,async:suggestion

# Expression-level preferences

csharp_prefer_braces = true:silent

csharp_style_deconstructed_variable_declaration = true:suggestion

csharp_prefer_simple_default_expression = true:suggestion

csharp_style_pattern_local_over_anonymous_function = true:suggestion

csharp_style_inlined_variable_declaration = true:suggestion
```

Code segment 2: Continuing with C#, the next coding segment follows the formatting rules for our C# code in the editor, and finally, the few Visual Basic.NET settings:

```
###############################
# C# Formatting Rules         #
###############################

# New line preferences

csharp_new_line_before_open_brace = all
```

```
csharp_new_line_before_else = true

csharp_new_line_before_catch = true

csharp_new_line_before_finally = true

csharp_new_line_before_members_in_object_initializers = true

csharp_new_line_before_members_in_anonymous_types = true

csharp_new_line_between_query_expression_clauses = true

# Indentation preferences

csharp_indent_case_contents = true

csharp_indent_switch_labels = true

csharp_indent_labels = flush_left

# Space preferences

csharp_space_after_cast = false

csharp_space_after_keywords_in_control_flow_statements = true

csharp_space_between_method_call_parameter_list_parentheses = false

csharp_space_between_method_declaration_parameter_list_parentheses =
false

csharp_space_between_parentheses = false

csharp_space_before_colon_in_inheritance_clause = true

csharp_space_after_colon_in_inheritance_clause = true

csharp_space_around_binary_operators = before_and_after

csharp_space_between_method_declaration_empty_parameter_list_parentheses
= false

csharp_space_between_method_call_name_and_opening_parenthesis = false

csharp_space_between_method_call_empty_parameter_list_parentheses =
false

# Wrapping preferences

csharp_preserve_single_line_statements = true

csharp_preserve_single_line_blocks = true

###############################

# VB Coding Conventions       #

###############################
```

```
[*.vb]
```

 # Modifier preferences

```
visual_basic_preferred_modifier_order =
Partial,Default,Private,Protected,Public,Friend,NotOverridable,
Overridable,MustOverride,Overloads,Overrides,MustInherit,NotInheritable,
Static,Shared,Shadows,ReadOnly,WriteOnly,Dim,Const,WithEvents,
Widening,Narrowing,Custom,Async:suggestion
```

Code segment 3: On close inspection, the file does not look too complicated! Luckily, the settings are properly named so that we are able to understand the setting's purpose. Most of the rules have the following format:

```
rule_name = false|true
```

We need to either specify true or false depending on our need for that setting. When we add an EditorConfig file to a project in Visual Studio, we can format the document by choosing **Edit | Advanced | Format Document** or pressing *Ctrl + K, Ctrl + D*.

Add an EditorConfig file to a solution or project

We need to follow the given steps to add an EditorConfig file to your solution or project:

1. Open a project or solution in Visual Studio.
2. From the menu bar, choose **Project | Add New Item**, or press *Ctrl + Shift + A*, or right click on the solution in the **Solution Explorer** window and select **Add| New Item**.
3. The **Add New Item** dialog box opens.
4. In the categories section on the left-hand side, choose **General**, and then choose the **Text File** template. In the **Name** text box, enter .editorconfig and then choose **Add**.
5. An .editorconfig file appears in **Solution Explorer** and it opens in the editor.
6. Edit the file as desired.

An easier way to add an EditorConfig file is to make use of the EditorConfig Language Service Extension, as explained as follows:

1. Navigate to the Visual Studio Marketplace at **https://marketplace. visualstudio.com/items?itemName=MadsKristensen.EditorConfig**
2. Select **Download**.
3. Double click on the VSIX file at your download location.

4. After the installation is complete, choose **Add | .editorconfig File** from the right-click menu of a solution, project, or any folder in **Solution Explorer**.

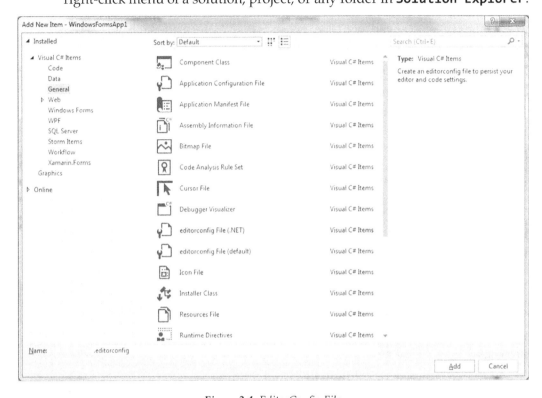

Figure 3.4: EditorConfig File

Find issues faster

Find issues faster by seeing issues in context. IntelliCode automatically scans our code when we commit or review our code. Visual Studio IntelliCode makes use of Artificial Intelligence to learn from the source code to spot misuse of variables, missed refactorings and irregular patterns among others.

Focused code reviews

Visual Studio IntelliCode acts as an extra pair of eyes on our code reviews. It highlights the changes which might require more attention based on factors like complexity, churn, and history.

Installing the IntelliCode extension

To install IntelliCode for Visual Studio, we follow the given steps:

1. Navigate to the marketplace **(https://marketplace.visualstudio.com/ items?itemName=VisualStudioExptTeam.VSIntelliCode).**

2. Click on **Download**, as shown in the following screenshot:

Figure 3.5: Download

3. Double click on the VSIX file. Click on **Install**, as shown in the following screenshot:

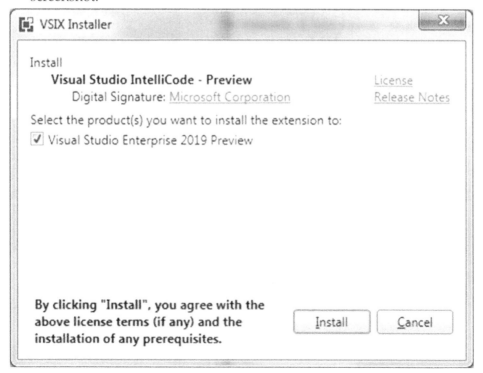

Figure 3.6: VSIX Install window

4. The following screenshot displays IntelliCode in action inside Visual studio 2019:

Figure 3.7: IntelliCode in action

To install IntelliCode for Visual Studio Code, follow the given steps:

1. Navigate to **https://marketplace.visualstudio.com/ items?itemName=VisualStudioExptTeam.vscodeintellicode**

2. Click the `Install` button, as shown in the following screenshot:

Figure 3.8: Visual Studio Code IntelliCode

3. If you do not have Visual Studio Code installed, the following screenshot will be displayed:

Figure 3.9: Install Visual Studio Code

4. If Visual Studio Code is not installed, we need to download Visual Studio Code from the following URL **https://code.visualstudio.com/download**:

Figure 3.10: *Download Visual Studio Code*

5. After the download is complete, launch the installer, as shown in the following screenshot:

Figure 3.11: *Install Visual Studio Code*

6. Return to the Visual Studio marketplace: **https://marketplace.visualstudio. com/items?itemName=VisualStudioExptTeam.vscodeintellicode**

7. Click on the `Install` button to install IntelliCode for Visual Studio Code.

8. Visual Studio Code will be launched and ask you to install IntelliCode and provide more details, as shown in the following screenshot:

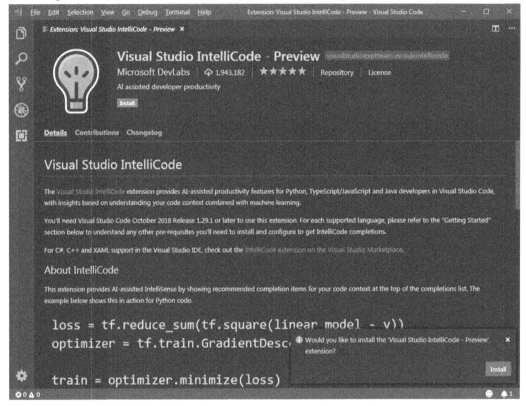

Figure 3.12: Visual Studio Code

9. Finally, click on the `Install` button.

Conclusion

This chapter has taught us how valuable the right tools are for our programming endeavors. If we have the right tools such as IntelliCode and IntelliSense, we can save time and be more productive as programmers. We learned how to install Visual Code in the event that it is not installed and also discussed AI.

In the next chapter, we will explore language and coding changes in the C# language and in general.

CHAPTER 4
Latest Features and Changes in C# 8.0

The C# language has been around for a very long time. It has kept on evolving over the years. Now with the advent of newer technologies such as IoT, the language had to adapt and grow to compensate for newer platforms.

However, in order to be able to adapt with the C# language, we have to ensure that first, we know the basics of the language, and then second, see what all the new features can do. This chapter explores the C# language as well as talks about its new features.

Structure

- The C# language
- Variables and constants
- Data types
- Arrays and collections
- Enums
- Selection statements
- Iteration statements
- New features in C# 8.0

Objective

The objective of this chapter is to first: make sure your C# skills are up to date, second: learn the new tricks of C# 8.0, and lastly, see where all the new changes fit in and how to practically use them.

The C# language

C# has come a long way since being shipped with the first version of the .NET Framework in the year 2000. Originally named **COOL (C-like Object Oriented Language)**, C# has morphed into one of the most popular and powerful programming languages in the world.

We need to understand what makes the language tick, before we can use it productively. Let us explore the common language concepts.

Variables and constants

A variable in programming terms is a named memory location in which you can store information. This information can be words (strings), whole numbers (integers), decimal numbers (floats), dates, yes/no values (Boolean), and so on. We will explain data types in detail a bit later.

A variable gets its value through a process called assignment and it looks like the following statement:

```
VariableName1 = Value;
```

Better examples follow:

```
VariableName2 = 2;
```

```
VariableName3 = "Hello!";
```

`VariableName2` now contains a value of `2` and `VariableName3` contains the string `Hello!`

The values stored inside the variables can be changed at any time. For example, the value inside the `VariableName2` variable can be changed to 50, 100, or 10000.

A constant's value cannot change after it has been assigned a value. Some perfect examples of constants are as follows:

Constant	Value
The number of months in a year	12
Minutes in an hour	60

Seconds in an hour	3600
Days in a week	7
Number of seasons in a year	4

Table 4.1: Constants

Whenever there is a value that might be repeated throughout code, it is always a good idea to convert that value into a constant.

Data types

A data type describes, as the name implies, the type of data that can be stored inside a variable or a constant. Without designating a data type, you cannot create a variable. The data type also determines how much space in memory needs to be set aside for a variable or a constant. Earlier in this chapter, we spoke about strings, Booleans, integers, and floats. These are just some of the few data types the C# language has.

The following table explains the type of values that can be stored as well as the size and range in memory the variable or constant will occupy:

Data type	Size in memory	Value
Boolean	Depends on implementing platform	True or False
Byte	1 byte	0 through 255
Char	2 bytes	Code points 0 through 65535
Date	8 bytes	0:00:00 AM on January 1, 0001 through 11:59:59 PM on December 31, 9999
Decimal	16 bytes	0 through +/- 79,228,162,514,264,337,593,543,950,335 (+/-7.9...E+28) with no decimal point 0 through +/- 7.92281625142643 375935439 50335 with 28 places to the right of the decimal
Double (double-precision floating-point)	8 bytes	-1.79769313486231570E+308 through -4.94065645841246544E-324 for negative values 4.94065645841246544E-324 through 1.79769313486231570E+308 for positive values

Integer	4 bytes	-2,147,483,648 through 2,147,483,647
Long (long integer)	8 bytes	-9,223,372,036,854,775,808 through 9,223,372,036,854,775,807
Object	4 bytes on 32-bit platform 8 bytes on 64-bit platform	Any type can be stored in a variable of type Object
SByte	1 byte	-128 through 127
Short (short integer)	2 bytes	-32,768 through 32,767
Single (single-precision floating-point)	4 bytes	-3.4028235E+38 through -1.401298E-45for negative values. 1.401298E-45 through 3.4028235E+38for positive values
String (variable-length)	Depends on implementing platform	0 to approximately 2 billion Unicode characters
UInteger	4 bytes	0 through 4,294,967,295
ULong	8 bytes	0 through 18,446,744,073,709,551,615
UShort	2 bytes	0 through 65,535

Table 4.2: Data types

Creating or declaring variables

In order to create a variable or constant and provide the necessary space in memory for it, we need to declare it. We can do it by supplying the data type first, then a decent name, and then optionally an initial value (known as initializing a variable or constant). Here is an example:

```
int Age;
```

The previous line of code creates an integer variable named Age. Let us take the example further:

```
int Age = 40;
```

The previous line of code creates the same variable, but it also gives it a starting value of 40. Age is a variable because its value can change. However, when we create a constant, its value cannot change during the course of the program. Here is an example:

```
const string FirstName;
```

```
const string LastName;
```

```
FirstName = "Ockert";

LastName = "du Preez";
```

Two constants are created in the preceding code segment and values are populated inside them. These values cannot change while the program is running. The moment you try to assign a new value to a constant, an error will be thrown.

Naming conventions

When naming an object, keep in mind that you are not allowed to use special characters or symbols in the object's name. Remember that names cannot start with a number as well. In general, there are two rules for capitalization in names. Following are the two popular variable naming conventions:

- CamelCase
- PascalCase

With CamelCasing, the first letter of an object or variable or constant starts with a small letter and every subsequent word in the name starts with a capital letter. With PascalCasing, the name starts with a capital letter and every subsequent word has a capital letter. Needless to say, names are not allowed to contain spaces.

Arrays and collections

The arrays and collections are known as grouping structures. Both arrays and collections are capable of holding more than one value; the only difference is how we want to make use of these values and how we want to refer to them.

Arrays

An array can hold multiple variables of the same type. These variables should be logically related to each other. The individual items of an array are called elements. Each array element has an index, which starts at 0 and ends at the highest element index value. The following code snippets are examples of an array:

```
#Declare a single-dimensional array and populate it with values.
        int[] ArrayName1 = new int[5];

        ArrayName1[0] = 0;

        ArrayName1[1] = 1;

        ArrayName1[2] = 1;

        ArrayName1[3] = 2;

        ArrayName1[4] = 3;
```

#Declare and set array element values populated with the first 5 Fibonacci numbers

```
int[] ArrayName2 = new int[] { 0, 1, 1, 2, 3 };
```

#Alternative syntax to set array element values with the first 10 Fibonacci numbers

```
int[] ArrayName3 = { 0, 1, 1, 2, 3, 8, 13, 21, 34, 55 };
```

The Fibonacci sequence in mathematics is the series of numbers: 0, 1, 1, 2, 3, 5,…The next number is the sum of the previous two numbers.

Jagged arrays and multi-dimensional arrays are beyond the scope of this book.

Collections

Another way to manage a group of similar information is by making use of collections. The arrays are usually the best options for creating and working with a fixed number of strongly typed objects. Collections are more flexible. They can grow and shrink dynamically as the needs of the application change. For the most common collections (such as the Hashtable class), we can assign a key to any object that was put into the collection so that we can quickly retrieve the object by using the key.

The following classes form part of the Collections namespace:

- ArrayList
- BitArray
- CaseInsensitiveComparer
- CaseInsensitiveHashCodeProvider
- CollectionBase
- Comparer
- DictionaryBase
- Hashtable
- Queue
- ReadOnlyCollectionBase
- SortedList
- Stack
- StructuralComparisons

Queues

When visiting a bank, a grocery store, or a fast food take away counter, we need to wait in a queue for service. The .NET queue class replicate this behavior in memory. The Queue class is what is known as a **FIFO** list (**First in, first out list**). This means that the first person in the queue will be helped first, and the last person will be helped last. With the items inside a queue, the first item in the queue will be processed first, and the last will be processed last.

The following example shows how to store values inside a queue by creating a Queue object and using its Enqueue method as follows:

```csharp
private Queue MyQueue = new Queue();

private void Button1_Click(object sender, EventArgs e)

{

  MyQueue.Enqueue("Item 1");

  MyQueue.Enqueue("Item 2");

  MyQueue.Enqueue("Item 3");

}
```

The following example shows how to remove items from a queue by looping through the Queue object and using its Dequeue method:

```csharp
private void Button1_Click(object sender, EventArgs e)

{

  while (MyQueue.Count > 0) {

    object obj = MyQueue.Dequeue();

    Console.WriteLine("from Queue: {0}", obj);

  }

}
```

Stack

The .NET Stack class can be compared to a stack of vinyl records, books, or papers on top of each other on a desk. A stack processes the last item first, and the first item in the stack last. This is what makes it a **LIFO** (**Last in, First out**) list.

The following example shows how to store values inside a stack by creating a `Stack` object and using its `Push` method:

```
private Stack MyStack = new Stack();

private void Button2_Click(object sender, EventArgs e)

{

  MyStack.Push("Item 1");

  MyStack.Push("Item 2");

  MyStack.Push("Item 3");

}
```

The following example shows how to remove items from a `stack` by looping through the `Stack` object and using its `Pop` method:

```
private void Button2_Click(object sender, EventArgs e)

{

  while (MyStack.Count > 0) {

    object obj = MyStack.Pop();

    Console.WriteLine("from Stack: {0}", obj);

  }

}
```

Hashtable

The `Hashtable` collection class enables us to store a collection of information that relates to a certain key. It is a collection of key and value pairs that get organized based on the hash code of each key.

The following example shows how to store values inside a `hashtable` by creating a `Hashtable` object and giving each item a value:

```
private Hashtable MyHashtable = new Hashtable();

private void Button3_Click(object sender, EventArgs e)

{

  MyHashtable.Add("Key1", "Value1");

  MyHashtable.Add("Key2", "Value2");

  MyHashtable.Add("Key3", "Value3");

}
```

The following example shows how to loop through the hashtable by iterating through each `DictionaryEntry` object in the `Hashtable`:

```
private void Button3_Click(object sender, EventArgs e)

{

  foreach (DictionaryEntry entry in MyHashtable)

  {

    Console.WriteLine("{0} = {1}", pair.Key, pair.Value);

  }

}
```

The other Collection types are beyond the scope of this book.

Enums

An enumeration is a list of named constants. Enums are value data types. By default, the first member of an enum has the value 0 and the value of each successive enum member is increased by 1. Keep in mind that enums cannot be used with the string data type, because strings are reference types and not value types. The following example shows how to create an enumeration using the enum keyword:

```
enum Day {

  Sunday = 0,

  Monday = 1,

  Tuesday = 2,

  Wednesday = 3,

  Thursday = 4,

  Friday = 5,

  Saturday = 6

};
```

We will make use of an enum by optionally creating a new variable and setting it to the desired enum item. We must also ensure that the correct data types and the necessary conversions are used; otherwise, an error would occur. Enums can hold any numeric value, and even if no value is supplied by the developer, it automatically assigns a numeric value to the items. This list starts at 0 and increments with each list item.

In the following code segment, the FirstDay variable is set to the value of Sunday inside the Day enumeration. This equals 0. LastDay equals 6. Because we are dealing with whole numbers here, we need to cast the enumeration value to the correct data type (usually of integer type) in order to store it inside the variables.

An example of casting variables to the correct data type is shown as follows:

```
private void Button4_Click(object sender, EventArgs e)
{
    int FirstDay = (int)Day.Sunday;
    int LastDay = (int)Day.Saturday;
    Console.WriteLine("Sunday = {0}", x);
    Console.WriteLine("Saturday = {0}", y);
}
```

Selection statements

A selection statement causes the program control flow to change depending on whether a certain condition is true or false. The condition is the expression we test for. We will briefly examine the if statements as well as the switch statement.

The if statement

An if statement determines which statement to run based on the value of a Boolean (true/false) expression.

In the following example, the if statement tests the value of the Age variable. If Age is equal to or greater than 40, a message will be displayed stating Old!. If the value is smaller than 40, a message will be displayed stating Young!:

```
int Age = 40;
if (Age >= 40)
{
    MessageBox.Show("Old!");
}
else
{
    MessageBox.Show("Young!");
}
```

In the following example, we test for more than one condition, which is the `Password`, and the program can branch in many different ways. All the passwords supplied to the `else if` statements are valid and will allow entry, whereas if the `Password` variable does not contain any of those values, the else statement kicks in and denies entry:

```
string Password = "BpB";

if (Password == "VB.NET")

{

  MessageBox.Show("Welcome!");

}

else if (Password == "C#")

{

  MessageBox.Show("Welcome!");

}

else if (Password == ".NET")

{

  MessageBox.Show("Welcome!");

}

else if (Password == "BpB")

{

  MessageBox.Show("Welcome!");

}

else if (Password == "OJ")

{

  MessageBox.Show("Welcome!");

}

else

{

  MessageBox.Show("No Entry!");

}
```

Switch

The next selection statement is the switch statement. In principle, it works in the same manner as an if statement with multiple else if clauses, but it is just simpler and easier to write. Here is the same example discussed previously, but using a switch statement:

```
string Password = "BpB";

switch (Password)
{
  case "VB.NET":
    MessageBox.Show("Welcome!");
    break;
  case "C#":
    MessageBox.Show("Welcome!");
    break;
  case ".NET":
    MessageBox.Show("Welcome!");
    break;
  case "BpB":
    MessageBox.Show("Welcome!");
    break;
  case "OJ":
    MessageBox.Show("Welcome!");
    break;
  default:
    MessageBox.Show("No Entry!");
    break;
}
```

A lot of less typing! Depending on the valid password, the entry will be given. If none of the cases matches the variable's value, the default clause will step in and display the No Entry message. We can make this even simpler! Seeing the fact that the same statement has to run if a valid password is supplied, we can do this as follows:

```
switch (Password)
{
  case "VB.NET":
  case "C#":
  case ".NET":
  case "BpB":
  case "OJ":
    MessageBox.Show("Welcome!");
    break;
  default:
    MessageBox.Show("No Entry!");
  break;
}
```

This saves even more time, as we can provide all the conditions, and then the common statement can be run.

Iteration statements

Iteration statements (loops) allow statements inside the loop to be repeated a number of times or until a certain condition becomes invalid. We can set the number of times the loop should repeat by explicitly stating it (as done with a for next loop), or we can have a condition determine the number of times the loop should repeat (as done with a while loop).

The for loop

The for statement executes its inner-statements a number of times, which are specified in the condition section of the for loop block. Let us see an example:

```
for (int i = 0; i < 5; i++)
{
  Console.WriteLine(i);
}
```

In the previous example, the for loop is supplied with an initializer, a condition, and an iterator. The initializer is the starting point for the loop. As in the previous example, an integer variable named i is set to 0. The condition is where i is checked if it is less than 5. If i is any number from 0 to 4, the loop will execute the statement or statements inside the for block. The iterator is the last part where i gets incremented by 1 with the use of the ++ operator.

The for loop, also known as a counter loop, cannot loop more than what was specified, but with the help of the continue, break and throw statements, we can exit it early.

The foreach loop

The foreach statement executes statements for each element in an instance of a type that implements either the System. Collections.IEnumerable or the System. Collections.Generic.IEnumerable<T> interfaces (such as the Hashtable we spoke about earlier on page 10 in the Hashtable section). It sounds more complicated than what it is. Here is a small example:

```
var lstFibonacci = new List<int> { 0, 1, 1, 2, 3, 8, 13, 21, 34, 55 };

foreach (int element in lstFibonacci)
{
    Console.WriteLine($"Element: {element}");
}
```

A list of Fibonacci numbers is created, and a for each loop is used to iterate through each of the list's elements to display them in the Console window.

The do...while loop

The do...while loop executes statements while a specified condition is true, or until the specified condition becomes false. The condition is re-evaluated after each iteration of the do loop. Very important to remember is that a do...while loop executes at least one time regardless of whether the condition is checked for true or false. This is because the checking only occurs after the loop has finished. Here is an example:

```
int i = 0;
do
{
    Console.WriteLine(i);
    i++;
} while (i < 5);
```

An integer variable is created. Inside the do...while loop the value of i is printed inside the `Console` window. The value of i is increased by 1 in each iteration. Lastly, the `while` condition tests the value of i. Be careful not to create an infinite loop. An infinite loop is a loop that does not exit. Why? Well, because the value being tested never changes. If we remove the part where i gets incremented, this do...while loop will never exit.

In order to exit a do...while loop, the `goto`, `return`, or `throw` statements can be used.

The while loop

The `while` loop executes statements while a specified condition evaluates to true. The condition is evaluated before each execution of the `while` loop, causing it to execute zero or more times. Let us see an example:

```
int i = 0;

while (i < 5)

{

  Console.WriteLine(i);

  i++;

}
```

An integer variable named i is created. The test for condition starts the `while` loop. If the condition is true, the statements inside the loop are executed. If the condition is initially false (i is equal to or greater than 5), the `while` loop will never be executed.

We can exit a while loop using the `goto`, `return`, or `throw` statements.

New features in C# 8.0

The C# language keeps evolving. It has to as the technology around it keeps evolving. In C# 8.0, there are quite a few new features. Let us explore them!

Features may change (become more when more info is available).

Pattern matching

A pattern tests whether a value has a certain shape and can extract information from that value when it matches. Pattern matching provides us with a more concise syntax for algorithms that test for matching values.

Yes, we can use the `if` and `switch` statements to test values and depending on whether the statements match, we can extract and use information from those values.

The new pattern matching syntax elements are extensions to statements such as `is` and `switch`. These new extensions combine testing a value as well as extracting that information.

Switch expressions

A `switch` statement usually produces a value in each of its case blocks. Switch expressions enable us to use more concise expression syntax. This means that there are fewer repetitive `cases` and `break` keywords. Here is a small example:

```
var (Operand1, Operand2, Operator) = (12, 75, "-");

var sum = Operator switch

{

  "+" => Operand1 + Operand2,

  "-" => Operand1 - Operand2,

  _ => Operand1 * Operand2

};
```

An object is created and it stores 12, 75, and the minus sign string. Next, a variable named sum is created and it will contain the answer of the **switch** expression. Because we have supplied the minus as the operator, the answer we will get would be -63 because 12 minus 75= -63. The default case inside the previous switch expressions has been replaced with the _ discard.

Property patterns

Property patterns enable us to match properties of the object that are being examined. In older days, we had to do quite a few tests to determine what a certain object's property values are. We mostly had to test if the object does contain a value and then interrogate its properties using a `switch` statement or an `if` statement, as follows:

```
var student = (Student)studentObject;

if (student != null)

{

  if (student.Name == "Ockert du Preez" && student.Age == 40)

  {

    Console.WriteLine($ "The Student : {student.Name} , Age {student.
Age}");

  }

}
```

The whole previous segment can be translated to the new way of interrogating properties, as follows:

```
if (student is Student {Name: "Ockert du Preez", Age: 40})

{

  Console.WriteLine($ "The Student: {student.Name} , Age {student.
Age}");

}
```

It does exactly the same, except for a lot less keystrokes and time.

Tuple patterns

A tuple pattern allows us to switch based on multiple values. Here is a small example of tuple patterns in C# 8.0:

```
public static string GetWinner(string Input1, string Input2)

=> (Input1, Input2) switch

{

  ("rock", "paper") => "Paper wins.",

  ("rock", "scissors") => "Rock wins.",

  ("paper", "scissors") => "Scissors wins.",

  ("paper", "rock") => "Paper wins.",

  ("scissors", "rock") => "Rock wins.",

  ("scissors", "paper") => "Scissors wins.",

  (_, _) => "Tie"

};
```

In the previous short example, multiple inputs are evaluated inside the switch expression and the output is provided depending on the matching tuple values.

Using declarations

A using declaration is a variable declaration that is preceded by the using keyword. This informs the compiler that the declared variable should be disposed at the end of the enclosing scope (when the using statement has completed).

```
static void WriteFile(IEnumerable<string> strLines)

{
```

```
using var swFile = new System.IO.StreamWriter("temp.txt");

foreach (string line in strLines)

{

  swFile.WriteLine(line);

 }

}
```

In the preceding example, the variable object named swFile is disposed as soon as the closing brace for the method is reached, which is the end of the scope in which swFile is declared.

Static local functions

Local functions can now have static modifiers added to them. This ensures that the local function does not reference any variables from the enclosing scope. In the following code, the local function InsideFunction accesses a variable named x, which is declared in the enclosing scope (EnclosingMethod). Therefore, InsideFunction cannot be declared with a static modifier. You can refer to the following example:

```
int EnclosingMethod()

{

  int x;

  InsideFunction();

  return x;


  void LocalFunction() => x = 0;

}
```

The following example contains a static local function. This is allowed because it does not access any variables in the enclosing scope:

```
int EnclosingMethod()

{

  int a = 6;

  int b = 8;

  return DoSubtraction(a, b);
```

```
static int DoSubtraction(int Operand1, int Operand2) => Operand1 -
Operand2;
}
```

Disposable ref structs

As we all may know, the C# compiler imposes many limitations on `ref structs` (structures that are referenced). This is to ensure that they will only be allocated on the stack. Some of the limitations include:

- Ref structs cannot be declared as a field of a class, normal `structs`, or a static field.
- Ref structs cannot be used as iterators, generic arguments and cannot implement an interface.
- Ref structs cannot be used as local variables in async methods.

In order to enable a `ref structs` to be disposed, it must have a `void Dispose()` method that is accessible. Here is an example:

```
class Program
{
  static void Main(string[] args)
  {
    using var student = new Student();
  }
}
ref struct Student
{
  public void Dispose()
  {
  //Code
  }
}
```

Because the `Dispose` method is in the public scope in the previous example, the `ref struct` is now disposable.

Nullable reference types

This feature has actually been around for a little while already, but some may not know about it. Any variable of a reference type is a non-nullable reference type. When a reference type variable gets a nullable value assigned to it, it throws an error because it cannot accept a null value. A null value means that the value is missing or unknown. In order to indicate that a variable may be null, you need to append the data type name with a ?to declare the variable as a nullable reference type and to ensure that it can contain a null value. The following example allows the `MiddleName` string variable to accept a null value, whereas the `FirstName` and `LastName` variables cannot accept null values:

```
class Student

{

  public string FirstName;    // May Not Be Null

  public string? MiddleName; // May Be Null

  public string LastName;     // May Not Be Null

}
```

Nullable contexts

Nullable contexts enable control for how the compiler interprets reference type variables. A nullable annotation context of any given line containing source code can be enabled or disabled. The nullable annotation context can be set for a project by using the Nullable element in your project `(.csproj)` file.

The possible settings for the nullable element are:

- **enable:** nullable annotation context and nullable warning context are enabled.

- **disable:** nullable annotation context nullable warning context are disabled.

- **safeonly:** nullable annotation context is enabled. nullable warning context is safeonly.

- **warnings:** nullable annotation context is disabled. nullable warning context is enabled.

- **safeonlywarnings:** nullable annotation context is disabled. nullable warning context is safeonly.

Asynchronous streams

An awesome new feature in C# 8.0 is async streams. In earlier versions of C#, the await keyword could only get a single result from an asynchronous method. Now in C# 8.0, await is now able to obtain a stream of results, thanks to asynchronous iterator interfaces and updates to the for each loop and the `yield` statement.

Here is an example:

```
public  static  async  System.Collections.Generic.IAsyncEnumerable<int>
GenerateFibonacci()
{
    int a = 0;
    int b = 1;
    for (int i = 0; i < n; i++)
    {
     int temp = a;
     a = b;
     b = temp + b;
     yield return a;
    }
}
```

`GenerateFibonacci` generates a new Fibonacci number. We are able to get an async stream because of the `IAsyncEnumerable` interface. The `yield return` statement returns successive elements in the asynchronous stream. Now, we can enumerate the sequence using the await for each statement:

```
await foreach (var fibo in GenerateFibonacci())
{
  Console.WriteLine(fibo);
}
```

Ranges and indices

Ranges and indices provide a short syntax for specifying subranges in arrays. We can specify an index from the end of an array. We can do this using the ^ operator. In an array, we can reference elements from the beginning by specifying its index. For example, `ArrayName[3]` means the element 3 *from the start.* Now, `ArrayName[^3]` means the element 3 *from the end.* Index 0 means *the beginning,* and `^0` means *the end.*

We can also specify ranges using the `..` operator. For example, `0..^0` specifies the entire range of the array: 0 from the start up to, but does not include 0 from the end.

Let us look at an example. The following array of `Months` contains annotations with its index from the start and from the end:

```
var Months = new string[]
{
  // start index    end index
  "Jan",      // 0                    ^12
  "Feb",    // 1                    ^11
  "Mar",    // 2                    ^10
  "Apr",      // 3                    ^9
  "May",    // 4                ^8
  "Jun",      // 5                ^7
  "Jul",      // 6                    ^6
  "Aug",      // 7                ^5
  "Sep"     // 8                ^4
  "Oct",      // 9                ^3
  "Nov",    // 10                  ^2
  "Dec"     // 11                  ^1
};
```

We can retrieve the last month with the `^1` index:

```
Console.WriteLine($"The last month is {Months[^1]}");
```

The following code creates a subrange with the `Months` `Apr`, `May`, and `Jun`. It includes `Months[3]` through `Months[5]`. The element `Jul` is not in the range:

```
var months = Months[3..6];
```

The following code creates a subrange with `Nov` and `Dec`. It includes `Months[^2]` and `Months[^1]`:

```
var lastMonths = Months[^2..^0];
```

Conclusion

This chapter has taught us a lot, newbies and professionals alike! We have gone through the basics of the C# language where we learned about all the language features in C#. We also took a look at the exciting new features of C# and saw how they can save our time with coding. We learned how to implement the new features in our programs.

In next chapter, we will learn about the new features of .NET Core 3.0. We will see what the .NET Framework 4.8 can do. Then, we will learn how to make default executables with .NET Core 3.0 and delve into the open-source world with WPF, Windows Forms, and WinUI.

Questions

Q. 1.   What is the difference between an array and a collection?

Q. 2.   What is the difference between the `for` loop and the `while` loop?

Q. 3.   Explain the term Asynchronous Stream.

Q. 4.   Explain the term Switch expression.

Q. 5.   What is the difference between a variable and a constant?

CHAPTER 5
What's New in .Net Core 3.0

The .Net Core 3.0 demonstrates the true power of an open source software. It allows us to combine the strengths of different platforms for different platforms. We can add the .NET framework 4.8 to improve the C# language in general and provide tools to make our lives as developers easier.

This chapter will delve into .NET Core 3.0 as a whole. We will learn about new developments in the open-source software fields, the new features of the .NET framework 4.8. We will learn how the installer has improved with MSIX, new tools and see how XML Islands will help us in creating one application for both WPF and Windows Forms. This is a very exciting chapter.

Structure

- The .NET Core 3
- Installing .NET Core 3.0
- The .NET framework 4.8
- The .NET platform dependent intrinsics
- Local .NET tools
- XAML Islands
- Cryptographic key import/export

- MSIX deployment for desktop apps
- Open -source WPF, Windows Forms, and WinUI

Objective

In this chapter, we will explore .NET Core 3.0 and all its new features. We will learn how to install .NET Core 3.0, XAML Islands and see how we can use them productively and learn about Cryptography changes in .NET Core. We will explore the new fun ways to deploy .NET Core apps. We will also take a look at the .NET framework 4.8 and see what is included in the new .NET framework.

.NET Core 3.0

The .NET Core is a free and open-source managed computer software framework for Windows, Linux, and macOS. .NET Core supports cross-platform scenarios such as ASP.NET Core web apps, command-line apps, libraries, and universal Windows platform apps.

The .NET Core 3.0 supports WinForms (Windows Forms), WPF (Windows Presentation Foundation) as well as ML .NET (Microsoft's open-source machine learning framework) and IoT (Internet-of-Things). It includes the Visual Basic .NET runtime, support for the Entity Framework 6, the .NET Framework 4.8, as well as support for the new C# 8.0 features talked about in *Chapter 4: Latest Features and Changes in C# 8.0.*

Installing .NET Core 3.0

Installing .NET Core 3.0 is quite easy. We need to perform the following steps:

1. Navigate to the following link and choose the desired .NET Core 3.0 version:

   https://dotnet.microsoft.com/download/dotnet-core/3.0

2. The following screenshot displays the contents of the .NET Installer webpage:

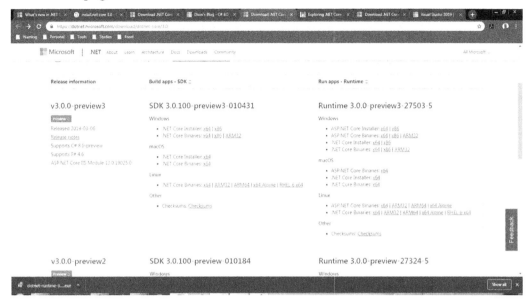

Figure 5.1: *.NET Core 3.0 download*

3. After it is downloaded, launch the installer, as shown in the following screenshot:

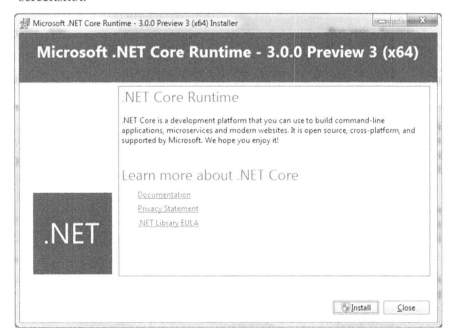

Figure 5.2: *Launch installing .NET Core 3.0*

4. The .NET Core 3.0 is now installed.

The .NET framework 4.8

Apart from the inclusion of the new C# 8.0 features, the inclusion of the .NET framework 4.8 into .NET Core 3.0 is probably the most important feature. We can expect the following improvements (and more) in the .NET Framework in the form of the .NET framework 4.8.

- **High DPI (dots per inch) improvements:** Every day the resolution of the displays is increasing to 4K (3840 x 2160 pixels or 4096 x 2160 pixels) and 8K (7680 × 4320 pixels) resolutions. The .NET framework ensures that our existing Windows Forms and WPF applications still look great on these displays.

- **Touch and UWP controls access: UWP (Universal Windows Platform)** contains new controls that take advantage of all the latest Windows features and touch displays. This means that we will not need to rewrite our apps to use these new controls and features.

- **Modern browser and media controls:** New controls are being added to replace the older controls that still make use of the legacy web and media technologies and are incompatible with the latest web changes or media outputs and codecs and formats.

- **Performance:** Apart from fixing small issues with the memory usage on the `AsyncLocal` and spin locks, a notable fix includes a fix that ensures `SqlDataReader.ReadAsync` performs asynchronously.

- **Deadlocks and race conditions:** Many of the core libraries of the .NET framework still harbor race conditions (race hazard) and deadlocks. A race condition occurs when a system attempts to perform two or more operations at the same time, but cannot because the system only allows the operations to be done in a proper sequence correctly. A deadlock, in concurrent computing, happens when each member of a group is waiting for another member, including itself to take a certain action, but neither takes an action. Concurrency-related issues are fixed in the .NET framework 4.8:

- Potential crash with concurrent calls to a new dynamic method in the **CLR (Common Language Runtime)**.

- Potential deadlock when calling the Dispose method on an EventSource in the CLR.

- `NetworkInformation.NetworkChange` deadlock when there is a lock around `NetworkChanged` listener and user's call back.

- Race condition in `AsyncResult` that closes a Wait Handle before the Set method is called in **WCF (Windows Communication Foundation)**.

The .NET platform dependent intrinsics

The .NET supports many platforms and hardware architectures. It ensures reasonable performance on different platforms and hardware configurations through .NET's runtime implementation.

APIs (Application Programming Interfaces) have been added to .NET Core 3.0 that allows access to performance-oriented CPU instructions such as the **SIMD (single instruction, multiple data)** and bit manipulation instruction sets for example. These instructions add big performance improvements in scenarios such as processing data efficiently in parallel.

Streaming SIMD Extensions (SSE) is an SIMD instruction set extension to the x86 architecture introduced in 1999 by Intel in their Pentium III series of CPUs. SSE originally added eight new 128-bit registers (XMM0 through XMM7). The AMD64 extensions from AMD added a further eight registers (XMM8 through XMM15), and this extension is then duplicated in the Intel 64 architecture.

Hardware intrinsics will be available in .NET Core 3.0. It will expose new namespaces, SIMD types, and classes representing different **ISA (Instruction Set Architectures).** The two most noteworthy namespaces are as follows:

- `System.Runtime.Intrinsics`: This namespace contains SIMD types, which abstract the underlying SIMD registers. This namespace also contains platform-agnostic functions that provide common vector operations.

- `System.Runtime.Intrinsics.X86`: This namespace contains classes representing different Intel ISAs (SSE, SSE2, SSE3, SSSE3, SSE4.1, SSE4.2, AVX, AVX2, FMA, LZCNT, POPCNT, BMI1, BMI2, PCLMULQDQ, and AES).

Platform dependent intrinsics guidelines

Platform dependent intrinsics should adhere to the following guidelines:

- Platform intrinsics should expose a specific feature that is not universally available on all platforms.

- If the functionality is common, it should be made platform independent.

- A platform intrinsic should be impactful.

- Platform intrinsics should solve a user problem.

- A way to determine if the current executing platform supports dependent functionality must be included.

- Running platform dependent APIs on a non-supporting platform must result in a `System.PlatformNotSupportedException`.

- The C# implementation of a platform intrinsic is recursive.

Local .NET tools

A .NET Core local tool is a special NuGet package that contains a console application. .NET Core 2.1 first introduced us to the global .NET Core tools, which are NuGet packages that are installed from the .NET Core **CLI (Command Line Infrastructure).** .NET Core global and local tools are framework-dependent applications (The application uses the version of .NET Core on the target system).

Local .NET tools are similar to global .NET tools, but associates with a particular location on disk. This enables per-project and per-repository tooling. Any tool that is installed locally is not available globally. Local .NET tools are also distributed as NuGet packages.

Local .NET tools needs a manifest file called `dotnet-tools.json` in the project's current directory. The `dotnet-tools.json` file defines the tools to be available in that folder and below it. If the manifest file has been created at the root of the repository, anyone cloning the code can restore and use the tools that are needed to successfully work with the code. An example of `dotnet-tools.json` manifest file is as follows:

```json
{
  "version": 1,
  "isRoot": true,
  "tools": {
    "dotnetHello": {
      "version": "1.1.1",
      "commands": [
        "Greet"
      ]
    },
    "dotnetBye": {
      "version": "1.0.78",
      "commands": [
        "Greet"
      ]
    }
  }
}
```

In the **JSON (JavaScript Object Notation)** file, we declared two tools, namely dotnetHello and dotnetBye, each containing a Greet command. This file can be edited manually, but it is always better to let it be generated automatically.

1. Ensure .NET Core 3.0 is installed before attempting the following exercise. If .Net Core 3.0 is not installed yet, the *Installing.Net Core* section in the beginning of the chapter explains how to install it

2. Create a new project.

3. Open the developer Command Prompt and add the next line that creates a new dotnet-tools.json file:

   dotnet new tool-manifest

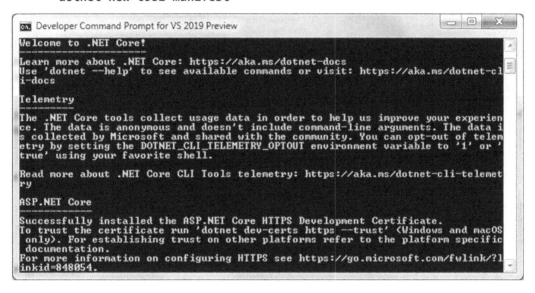

Figure 5.3: .Net Core developer Command Prompt

4. Add a new tool using the following command:

   dotnet tool install <packageId>

5. To get a list of all .Net global tools, enter the following command:

   dotnet tool list -g

6. Run a .Net tool with the following command:

   dotnet tool run <tool-command-name>

The Command Prompt may show tools or no tools, depending on if there are any installed, as shown in the following screenshot:

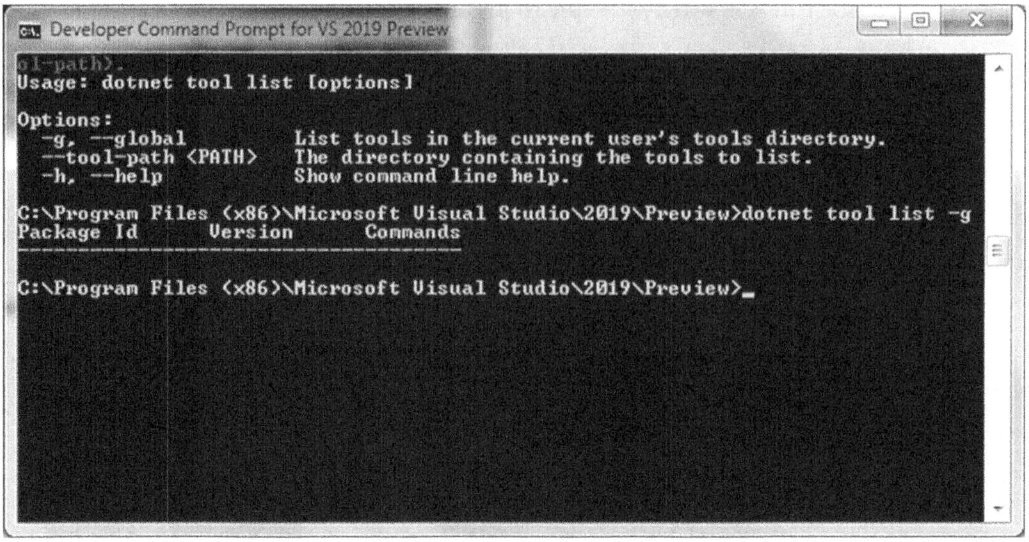

Figure 5.4: Tool list

Build Windows applications with .NET Core 3.0

With .NET Core 3.0, we can build Windows desktop applications by using either Windows Forms or WPF for Windows 10. WPF and Windows Forms will have modern controls as well as fluent styling via the use of XAML Islands.

XAML Islands

XAML (eXtensible Application Markup Language) Islands enables developers to use new pieces of UI from the UWP on their existing Win32 applications. The benefit of using XAML Islands is that it allows us to modernize our apps gradually.

This is possible because Windows 10 supports hosting UWP controls inside the context of a Win32 Process, with the help of two new system APIs, which are as follows:

- `WindowsXamlManager`
- `DesktopWindowXamlSource`

`WindowsXamlManager` has two methods: `Dispose` and `Initialize For Current Thread`. `Initialize For Current Thread` initializes the UWP XAML framework inside the current thread of the Win32 desktop app, thus creating the UWP UI in the Win32 desktop app.

`DesktopWindowXamlSource` is the instance of the Island content. The `DesktopWindowXamlSource` API renders and gets its input from an **HWND (Windows Handle),** so it needs to know to which HWND it will have to attach to. The programmer is responsible for sizing and positioning the parent's HWND. There is an easier option, which is to make use of the Windows community toolkit because it wraps these classes into an easy-to-use implementation for WinForms and WPF.

Any framework that exposes HWND is able to host an XAML Island. This means that we could theoretically have a Java or Delphi application hosting a Windows 10 UWP control, whether it is a simple button or a complicated custom control. With a wrapper for the HWND object, this is possible.

NuGet packages

The easiest way to use an Island inside our apps is to use the NuGet packages Microsoft provides. At the time of writing, the following NuGet packages were available.

- `Microsoft.Toolkit.Wpf.UI.XamlHost`: It provides the `WindowsXamlHost` class for WPF.

- `Microsoft.Toolkit.Wpf.UI.Controls`: It provides wrapper classes for WPF controls such as the `MediaPlayerElement` and `InkCanvas`.

- `Microsoft.Toolkit.Forms.UI.XamlHost`: It provides the `WindowsXamlHost` class for Windows Forms.

- `Microsoft.Toolkit.Forms.UI.Controls`: It provides wrapper classes for Windows Forms controls such as the `MediaPlayerElement` and `InkCanvas`.

In *Chapter 14: Mobile tools*, we will create our own NuGet Packages and publish them.

Windows community toolkit

We can integrate with XAML Islands using the Windows community toolkit. It is a collection of helper functions, custom controls, and app services. The Windows community toolkit can be used to build apps for any Windows 10 device, including PC, Mobile, Xbox, IoT, and even HoloLens.

The Windows community toolkit is available as a Visual Studio NuGet package for new or existing C# and VB.NET projects. **https://docs.microsoft.com/en-us/windows/communitytoolkit/getting-started.**

Alternatively, we can download the Windows community toolkit sample app in the Windows store by navigating to **https://www.microsoft.com/en-us/p/windows-community-toolkit-sample-app/9nblggh4tlcq?activetab=pivot:overviewtab.**

The Windows community toolkit sample app screen is shown as follows:

Figure 5.5: *Windows community toolkit*

Using the Windows community toolkit implementation, we can create and manage a `WindowsXamlManager` and a `DesktopWindowXamlSource` instance, a wrapper control called `WindowsXamlHost`. It also handles the loading of UWP types using a class called `UWPTypeFactory`. The `UWPTypeFactory` class creates a UWP XAML type instance from a WinRT type name.

Creating an app using XAML Islands

We have three options to create a Windows desktop app using XAML Islands and they are as follows:

- In the Developer Command Prompt, enter the following: `dotnet new wpf`.
- In the Developer Command Prompt, enter the following: `dotnet new winforms`.
- Open Visual Studio 2019, and choose any one of the new templates.

The new project types are mostly the same as the existing .NET Core projects, with a few extra additions. An example of the configuration for a WPF app may look like the following code:

```
<Project Sdk="Microsoft.NET.Sdk">

<Project Sdk="Microsoft.NET.Sdk.WindowsDesktop">

  <PropertyGroup>

    <OutputType>Exe</OutputType>

    <TargetFramework>netcoreapp3.0</TargetFramework>

    <UseWPF>true</UseWPF>

  </PropertyGroup>

</Project>
```

Here, the `Microsoft.NET.Sdk.WindowsDesktop` namespace is included, and the `UseWPF` setting is set to true. A Windows app looks similar to the following code:

```
<Project Sdk="Microsoft.NET.Sdk.WindowsDesktop">

  <PropertyGroup>

    <OutputType>Exe</OutputType>

    <TargetFramework>netcoreapp3.0</TargetFramework>

    <UseWindowsForms>true</UseWindowsForms>

  </PropertyGroup>

</Project>
```

The `UseWindowsForms` attribute is set to true. When both the frameworks are used, both the settings can be included:

```
<Project Sdk="Microsoft.NET.Sdk.WindowsDesktop">

  <PropertyGroup>

    <OutputType>Exe</OutputType>

    <TargetFramework>netcoreapp3.0</TargetFramework>

    <UseWPF>true</UseWPF>

    <UseWindowsForms>true</UseWindowsForms>

  </PropertyGroup>

</Project>
```

Cryptographic key import/export

Cryptography is the practice of techniques to secure communication from third parties. We use cryptography to construct protocols that prevent third parties and the public from reading private messages.

The .NET Core 3.0 supports the importing and exporting of asymmetric public and private keys without the need to use X.509 certificates.

All **RSA (Rivest–Shamir–Adleman), DSA (Digital Signature Algorithm), ECDsa (Elliptic Curve Digital Signature Algorithm)** keys support the X.509 certificate SubjectPublicKeyInfo format for public keys, and the PKCS#8, which is a standard syntax for storing private key information, `PrivateKeyInfo`, and PKCS#8 `EncryptedPrivateKeyInfo` format for private keys.

An example of a generated key may resemble the following:

```
1F-D1-82-34-F8-13-38-4A-7F-C7-52-4A-F6-93-F5-FB-6D-98-7A-6A-04-3B-BC-
35-8C-7D-FC-A5-A3-6E-AD-C1-66-30-81-2C-2A-DC-DA-60-03-6A-2C-D9-76-21-
7F-61-97-57-79-E1-62-45-62-C3-83-04-97-CB-32-EF-C5-17-5F-99-60-92-AE-B6-
34-6F-30-06-03-AC-BF-15-24-43-84-EB-83-60-EA-4D-3B-BD-D9-5D-56-26-F0-51-
CE-F3
```

MSIX deployment for desktop apps

MSIX is a new packaging format based on the `.msi` installer, `.appx`, installer, App-V, and `ClickOnce` installers. MSIX keeps the functionality of the existing app installer packages and installation files while enabling new and modern packaging and deployment features to Win32, WPF, and WinForm apps.

Prerequisites for MSIX

The following are the prerequisites for installing MSIX:

- Windows 10, version 1809, or above
- Participation in the Windows insider program
- A valid Microsoft account
- Administrator privileges on your PC

The tool can be downloaded from

https://www.microsoft.com/en-us/p/msix-packaging-tool/9n5lw3jbcxkf?activetab =pivot:overviewtab.

You will get the following screen:

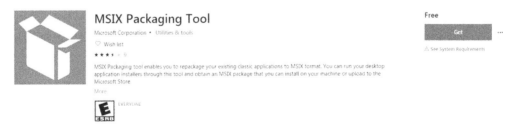

Figure 5.6: MSIX Tool on the Microsoft Store

Open-source WPF, Windows Forms, and WinUI

WPF, Windows Forms, and WinUI are now open source. An open-source software is a type of software in which the source code can be studied, changed, and distributed to anyone and for any purpose. .NET Core 3 adds support for building Windows desktop applications using WPF, WinForms, and the Entity framework 6. .NET Core 3 is open source and runs on Windows, Linux, macOS, and in the cloud.

Conclusion

This chapter was very exciting! We learned about XAML Islands and the new features of the .NET framework 4.8. We explored the world of installers as well as learned what intrinsics are and how they can be beneficial.

In the next chapter, we will explore built-in tools of Visual Studio 2019 and learn how we can use them.

Questions

Q. 1.   Explain the term .NET Core 3.0.

Q. 2.   Name three improvements in the .NET framework 4.8.

Q. 3.   What does API stand for?

Q. 4.   What is a .NET Core local tool?

SECTION II

Tools

Section II covers Tools for debugging and testing Windows, ASP.NET, Mobile and Azure Cloud applications.

CHAPTER 6
Built-in Tools

An IDE's real power is its containing tools. Without any decent tools, developing the project will take longer, and debugging the projects will be limited.

This chapter explores the built-in tool Visual Studio 2019 provides. We will learn about the various profiling tools that enable us to improve the application performance. We will take a look at the Live Share tool, which allows us to code simultaneously with other members of our team. Lastly, we will take a look at a new and improved Solution Explorer.

Structure

- Visual Studio Live Share

- Profiling tools

- Solution Explorer

Any decent IDE is nothing without its tools. Whether the tools are built-in or added on, they improve the hosting IDE. In Visual Studio 2019, there are numerous tools for sharing code edits and collaboration, emulators for mobile apps, code editing tools, cloud tools, and debugging tools. Let us take a look at some of the important tools.

Visual Studio Live Share

Visual Studio Live Share allows us to co-author and co-debug together with our peers. It also enables us to collaborate with our teammates as we type and review code. Live Share has several advantages, which are explained as follows:

- **Quick assistance:** Visual Studio Live Share enables us to get assistance instantly from our fellow peer or peers. If an issue such as resolving a bug or a mental block arises, Live Share can provide access to the project in question so that the issue can be resolved. By having Live Share, we can save a lot of time and effort by enabling people to help directly, instead of sending emails or calling back and forth.

- **Pair programming:** Pair programming involves two or more developers working together on a shared task. This increases team cohesion, product quality and enables the developers to share knowledge, irrespective of the proximity of all participants, role of each participant, the tasks as well as the duration of the tasks involved.

  Swarm or mob programming involves more than two developers working together on a shared task. This could be on an as-needed basis, or a full-time basis, with all the benefits and characteristics of pair programming.

- **Coding competitions and hack-a-thons:** Hack-a-thons and coding competitions are similar to mob programming apart from the tasks being short term and singular. Live Share helps a great deal here as the participants can work together quickly without being restricted to one keyboard and one screen. The time for adapting a new tool is also drastically shortened, as the tool is already familiar.

- **Developer streaming:** A new form of education is developer streaming. It is a streaming in which a developer live-streams a concept and shows the coding and practices involved. Live Share helps here as it can involve a lot more people and the lesson can become much more interactive.

  Interactive education and classroom lectures also benefit from Live Share because it allows more productivity and interaction between the fellow students and teachers.

- **Peer mentoring:** Live Share has a mode named Follow. This helps when introducing a new developer to a project's codebase, the technologies used and feature areas. The Live Share Follow mode allows the new developer to follow along with the person showing him or her with his or her personal IDE.

- **Team brown bag meetings:** A brown bag meeting is usually an informal meeting that occurs in the workplace at around lunchtime. The term brown bag is used because participants in the meeting bring their own lunches, which are sometimes packed in brown paper bags.

Team brown bags are similar to peer mentoring but presented to an entire team.

- **Code reviews:** Live Share can be used for adhoc code reviews, where direction and input can be sought and knowledge can be socialized across the team.

- **Technical interviews:** Live Share can be used to observe, in real time, how the potential candidates solve problems.

Profiling tools

Visual Studio profiling tools analyze performance issues in our applications. The profiling tools become available during a debugging session and can be found in the Diagnostic Tools window. In the event that the **Diagnostics Tools** menu option has been turned off, it can be shown by selecting: `Debug | Windows | Show Diagnostic Tools`. In this window, the various tools can be selected.

Visual Studio 2019 provides the following profiling tools:

- CPU usage
- Memory usage
- GPU usage
- Application timeline
- PerfTips
- IntelliTrace
- Network usage
- HTML UI responsiveness
- JavaScript memory

Let us explore these in more detail.

CPU usage

The CPU usage profiling tool shows the CPU time and percentage spent executing code in C#, Visual Basic, C++, and JavaScript apps. This tool can be run on an installed Microsoft Store app, an open Visual Studio project, or it can be attached to a running process on local or remote machines, or on a simulator or emulator, with or without debugging.

To use the CPU profiling tool, select **Debug | Performance Profiler**. A window will be shown listing all the profiling tools, as shown in the following screenshot. Select **CPU Usage**, and then select **Start**:

Figure 6.1: *Profiling tools*

By clicking on the little gear icon next to **CPU Usage**, Visual Studio 2019 opens up all the available settings for it, as shown in the following screenshot:

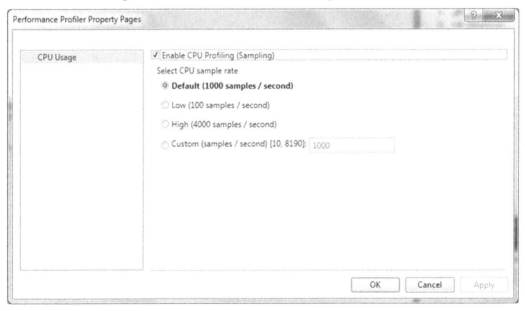

Figure 6.2: *CPU Usage settings*

The following screenshot shows the CPU profiler in action:

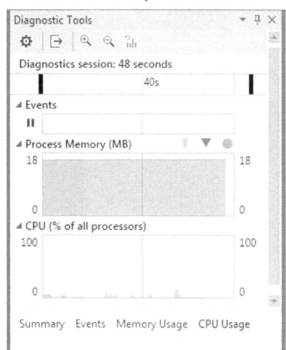

Figure 6.3: CPU profiler in action

Memory usage

The memory usage diagnostic tool finds memory leaks and inefficient memory. This tool can take snapshots of the managed and native memory heaps. The Visual Studio debugger controls how the execution of the application while investigating performance issues with the help of breakpoints, stepping, and break all.

To start collecting the memory usage data, set a breakpoint at the line where the investigation should start. Then, select **Debug | Performance Profiler**. The same screen as shown earlier appears. Select **Memory Usage**. The settings for the **Memory**

Usage profiler can be accessed by clicking on the little gear icon. The settings are displayed in the following screenshot:

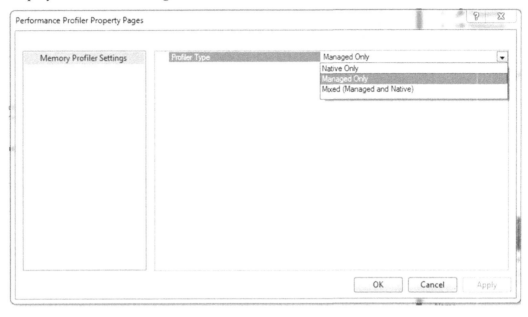

Figure 6.4: Memory usage settings

By clicking on **Start** on the profiler screen, the memory profiler will start analyzing the program, as shown in the following screenshot:

Figure 6.5: Memory profiler in action

GPU usage

The GPU usage profiling tool is used to understand the high-level hardware usage of Direct3D (low-level API used to draw lines, triangles and point per frame) applications. The GPU profiler helps us see if the application's performance is CPU-bound or GPU-bound.

To build DirectX desktop games, we need to perform the following steps:

1. Launch the Visual Studio installer.

2. Choose the **Game development with C++** workload under the **Mobile & Gaming** category, as shown in the following screenshot:

Figure 6.6: Game development

3. As explained in detail in *Chapter 1: Getting Started with Visual Studio 2019,* this workload will now be installed.

4. Install the **Universal Windows Platform development** workload using the same steps as mentioned earlier.

5. Once installed, create a new **DirectX** app by searching for the DirectX template in the **New Project** dialog box.

   C++ does not fall in the scope of this book. Any reference on DirectX apps can be found at

https://visualstudio.microsoft.com/vs/features/directx-game-dev/.

Using the GPU profiler tool

To see how easy it is to use the GPU Profiler, use these steps:

1. In the **DirectX** project, select **Debug**.

2. Select **Performance Profilers**.

3. Select **GPU Usage**.

4. Alternatively, select the little gear icon for more GPU profiler settings. The screen displayed is shown in the following screenshot:

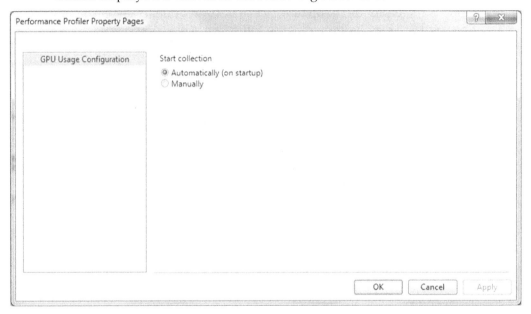

Figure 6.7: *GPU profiler settings*

Application Timeline

The **Application Timeline** profiling tool finds and fixes application-interaction related performance issues in XAML applications. It also improves the performance by showing a detailed view of the resource consumption of the applications. We can analyze the time spent by our the application for preparing its layout and rendering UI frames, servicing network and disk requests, application start-up, page load, and windows resize events.

In order to make use of the **Application Timeline** profiling tool, we need to perform the following steps:

1. Open an XAML application.

2. Click on **Debug**.

3. Click on **Performance Profiler**.

4. Select **Application Timeline** from the list of **Available Tools**, as shown in the following screenshot:

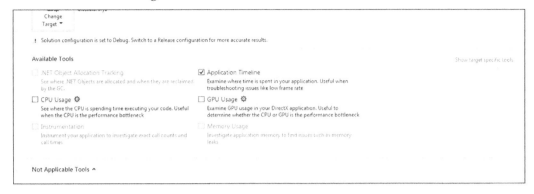

Figure 6.8: *Application Timeline*

PerfTips

Visual Studio debugger PerfTips help you to monitors and analyze the performance of applications while debugging. You need to keep in mind that the debugger can have a big impact on the performance of your application, albeit a good way of collecting important performance data.

The following screenshot displays the PerfTips in action. The **Diagnosti Tools** section in the window updates the used memory and CPU processing:

Figure 6.9: *Diagnostic tools*

IntelliTrace

IntelliTrace is included in Visual Studio Enterprise only and not in the Professional or Community editions. IntelliTrace records and traces the code's execution history by performing the following functions:

- Recording specific events in code
- Examining code, Locals Window data, and function call information
- Debugging difficult-to-find errors or errors that happen during deployment

Network usage

To analyze the network usage in UWP applications, we can use the Visual Studio Network diagnostics tool. This tool collects all the data of network operations performed using the `Windows.Web.Http` API/namespace.

HTML UI responsiveness

The UI responsiveness profiler for Universal Windows applications isolates problems such as responsiveness issues on the UI.If a UI is not responsive, the application may be slow and slow loading times for pages.

JavaScript memory

The JavaScript memory analyzer finds memory leaks in UWP applications built for Windows using JavaScript. The JavaScript memory analyzer helps you quickly find memory usage issues in applications.

Solution Explorer

The Solution Explorer in Visual Studio 2019 hosts the solution along with all its projects and each project's respective files. The Solution Explorer provides a nice tree structure where we can view the designer code files as well as the coding and design files quickly. It also lists all the references and other types of files added to it.

The following screenshot displays the **Solution Explorer** window:

Figure 6.10: *Solution Explorer*

A new feature that the Solution Explorer brings in Visual Studio 2019 is *solution filtering*.

Solution filtering

In *Chapter 1: Getting Started with Visual Studio 2019*, we briefly discussed solution filtering and solution filtering files, but we did not go into much detail. Solution filtering enables us to open a large solution but only load a few selective projects. It is common for large teams to have large solutions with many projects. Developers in this team do not always work on all the projects; they may work on a subset of projects whereas others may work on a different subset of projects. By filtering the solution, large solutions can be opened more quickly, as not all the projects have to be loaded.

Solution filtering provides the following benefits:

- We can get to the code faster by choosing the projects that need to be opened in a solution, thus saving our time.
- On reopening of a filtered solution, Visual Studio 2019 remembers the projects that were loaded when the solution was last opened, and only opens those.

- By creating a solution filter file, we can save the project-load configurations as well as share these configurations with teammates.

We need to perform the following steps to open a filtered solution:

1. Click on **File**.
2. Click on **Open**.
3. Then, click on **Project/Solution**.
4. In the displayed **Open Project/Solution** dialog box, select the solution, as shown in the following screenshot.
5. Mark **Do not load projects** checkbox before opening the project:

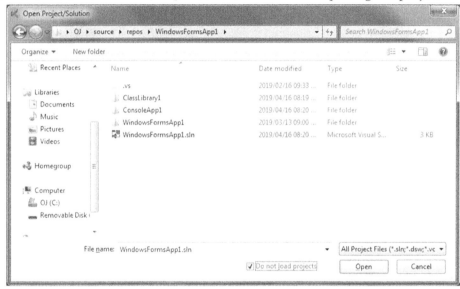

Figure 6.11: Open Project/Solution

6. Click on **Open**.
7. The solution will get loaded, but it will not load projects, as shown in the following screenshot:

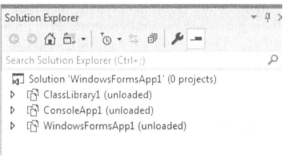

Figure 6.12: No projects loaded

8. When the solution has loaded, select the projects that you want to load (by pressing *Ctrl*) in the **Solution Explorer** window.

9. Right click on the project.

10. Click on **Reload Project**, as shown in the following screenshot (here, two projects were selected for reloading):

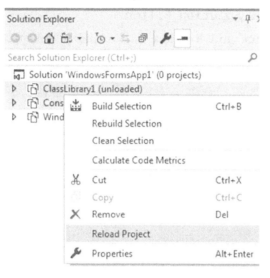

Figure 6.13: Reload Project

Showing and hiding unloaded projects

There are two ways to show unloaded projects in **Solution Explorer**, which are as follows:

- Right click on the solution in **Solution Explorer** and select **Show Unloaded Projects** or **Hide Unloaded Projects**.
- Toggle the **Show All Files** button in the **Solution Explorer**.

The following screenshot shows the loaded projects and the **Show all Files** button to show the hidden project:

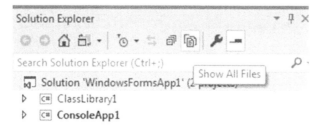

Figure 6.14: Loaded Projects

Solution filter files

We can share project-load configuration files by creating a solution filter file (with the extension .slnf). We need to perform the following steps:

1. Right click on the solution.

2. Select **Save As Solution Filter**.

3. Choose a name and location in the dialog box, which is similar to the following screenshot:

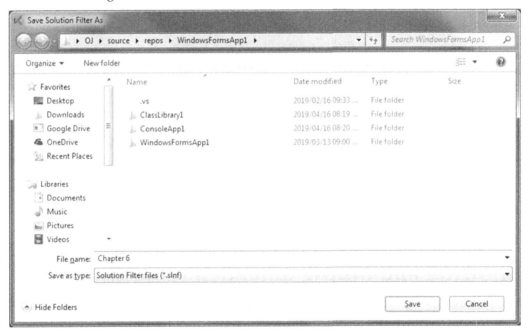

Figure 6.15: Save AsSolution Filter

The file is then added to the recent projects and solutions list, as shown in the following screenshot:

What would you like to do?

Open recent

Chapter 6.slnf	2019/04/16 08:43 PM	
C:\Users\O\source\repos\WindowsFormsApp1		
WindowsFormsApp1.sln	2019/04/16 08:26 PM	
C:\Users\O\source\repos\WindowsFormsApp1		
HTG_BinaryGap_C.sln	2019/04/15 09:30 PM	
C:\Users\O\source\repos\HTG_BinaryGap_C		
Project3.sln	2019/04/15 09:29 PM	
C:\Users\O\source\repos\Project3		
ClassLibrary2.sln	2019/04/15 09:29 PM	

Get started

Clone or check out code
Get code from an online repository like GitHub or Azure DevOps

Open a project or solution
Open a local Visual Studio project or .sln file

Open a local folder
Navigate and edit code within any folder

Figure 6.16: Recent List

Conclusion

In this chapter, we learned about the Tools section, which gave us an in-depth knowledge of the built-in tools Visual Studio 2019 provides. These tools will help us become more productive. We also learned about the profiling tools that enable us to investigate memory issues, CPU issues and many others so that we can ensure our apps are market ready and will not break unexpectedly.

In next chapter, we will explore the debugging tools in Visual Studio 2019 and how we can use them.

CHAPTER 7
Debugging Tools

The term *bug* has an interesting origin. At 3:45 pm on September 9, 1947, *Grace Murray Hopper* records the first instance of a bug being found in the *Harvard Mark II* computer's logbook. The actual bug was a moth that had been stuck between the relay contacts in the computer; hence, the term **bug**.

A bug in software is any error, flaw, failure, or fault in a computer program that causes the program to behave unintendedly or produce a wrong or unexpected result. Debugging is the process of finding and fixing bugs in a computer program. Interestingly, the term *debugging* was used (in 1945 in airplane engine testing) even before the first computer bug was found in 1947. Only in 1950, software developers started using the term bug.

In order to debug, we need debugging tools. In this chapter, you will learn about the awesome debugging tools Visual Studio 2019 has as well as their basic details.

Structure

- Code Cleanup
- Search bar on debugging windows
- Debugging in general
- Visual Studio 2019 remote debugging tools
- Code generation tools

Objective

This chapter focuses on the tools to help fixing program errors locally and remotely. It explores the next search features in the debugging windows to find values of objects quickly. The chapter also focuses on tools to help code better and faster.

Code Cleanup

In *Chapter 1: Getting Started with Visual Studio 2019,* we briefly discussed the *document health indicator.* The document health indicator enables us to check and maintain our code's issues. It works because of its Code Cleanup command. With Code Cleanup, we can identify and fix warnings and suggestions with one simple click of a button.

Code Cleanup formats the code and appliesall code fixes as suggested by its current settings and `.editorconfig` files. EditorConfig files, as discussed in detailin *Chapter 3: Visual Studio 2019 IntelliSense,* helps us to maintain a consistent coding style while working with multiple developers on the same project with different editors and IDEs. An EditorConfig project consists of a file format that defines coding styles and plugins that enable editors to read the file format and adhere to defined styles.

The health inspector can be accessed at the bottom of the code window, which is indicated by a little brush icon. The code window can be accessed by any of the following methods:

- Pressing *F7* anywhere in the design window
- Right clicking anywhere in the design window and selecting **View Code**
- Right clicking on the file in the **Solution Explorer** and selecting **View Code**

The document health inspector is shown in the following screenshot:

Figure 7.1: *Document health indicator*

There are two built-in profiles. One is pre-set, but can be edited. **Profile2** is initially empty but can be set at any time. In order to edit these profiles, we need to configure the Code Cleanup. The fixers available for the profiles might seem familiar to experienced Visual Studio users, as they are modeled after the text formatting options that isfound under **Tools | Options | Text Editor | C#** menu.

The following screenshot shows the configuration screen once **Configure Code Cleanup** has been selected from the menu:

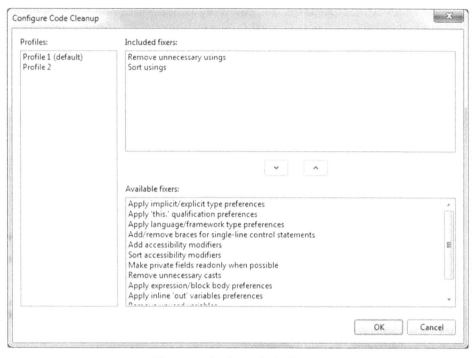

Figure 7.2: Configure Code Cleanup

The following screenshot shows the code formatting and refactoring options available in the C# code formatting **Options** screen:

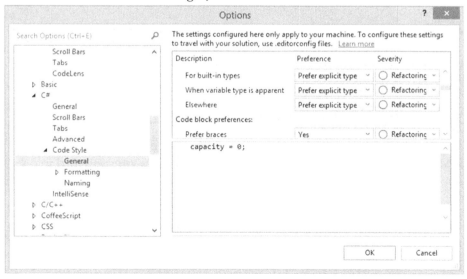

Figure 7.3: Code formatting options

Profile 1 includes the following two fixers:

- **Remove unnecessary usings:** It removes the usings that C# includes in code files by default. How does it know what is necessary and what is not? Well, when you look at a C# code file, you will find the usings at the top of the file. The namespaces included provide the functionality to make use of code that might not ordinarily exist in the code file. For example, when dealing with heavy math-oriented methods, the `System.Math` namespace should be included.

  By looking at the included namespaces, there might be faded lines in between, as shown in the following screenshot. These usings are unnecessary and can be removed:

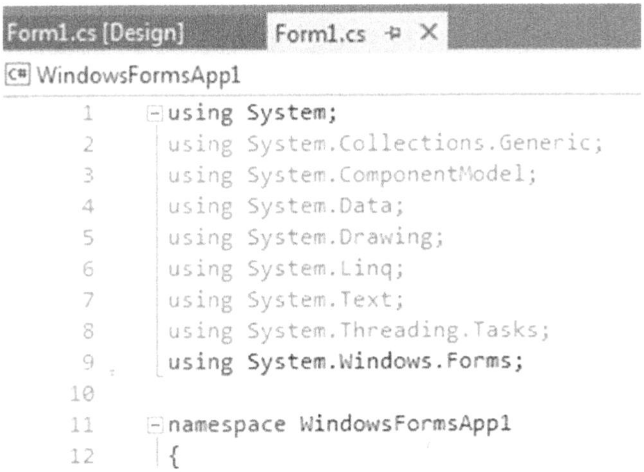

Figure 7.4: Unnecessary usings

- **Sort usings:** It improves the readability of the included namespaces and organizes them nicely. By running **Profile 1**, it will remove and sort usings.

Let us take a look at the other fixers available and see what we can do with them.

Apply implicit/explicit type preferences

The `Apply implicit/explicit type preferences` fixer converts every `var` variable to an explicit type, or the other way around. The `var` keyword in C# can be used instead of a type when declaring variables. This causes the compiler to simply infer the type of the variable.

A local variable implicitly typed with `var` is strongly typed, but the compiler still determines its type. The following two declarations are functionally equivalent:

```
var Age = 40; // Implicitly typed.
```

```
int Age = 40; // Explicitly typed.
```

Apply 'this.' qualification preferences

The **this** C# keyword appertains to the current instance of a class. The keyword **this** has the following uses:

- Qualify members hidden by similar names:

```
public class Student

{

private string FirstName;

private string LastName;

public Student(string FirstName, string LastName)

  {

     // Use this to qualify the members of the class

this.FirstName = FirstName;

this.LastName = LastName;

  }

}
```

- Pass an object as a parameter to methods:

```
GetMarks(this);
```

- Declare indexers:

```
publicint this[intparam]

{

get { return array[param]; }

set { array[param] = value; }

}
```

The **Apply 'this.' qualification preferences** fixer applies **this.** preferences where it is necessary.

Apply language/framework type preferences

The **Apply language/framework type preferences** fixer converts framework types to language types or vice versa.

Add/remove braces for single-line control statements

The `Add/remove braces for single-line control statements` fixer adds or removes curly braces from single-line control statements such as `if` and for. In the following example, both the `if` statements are similar:

```
if(condition)

{

  //Statement

}


if(condition)

  //Statement
```

Add accessibility modifiers

Access modifiers enable us to declare an object with certain accessibility. In C#, there are four access modifiers:

- `public`
- `protected`
- `internal`
- `private`

Although there are four access modifiers, there are six accessibility levels that can be specified, which are explained in the following table:

Access Modifier	Accessibility Level
public	No restrictions
protected	Containing class or derived types from containing class
internal	Current assembly
protected internal	Current assembly or derived types from containing class
private	Containing type or class
private protected	Containing class or derived types from containing class in current assembly

Table 7.1: Access modifiers

The **Add accessibility modifiers** fixer adds the missing accessibility modifiers wherever necessary.

Sort accessibility modifiers

The **Sort accessibility modifiers** fixer sorts accessibility modifiers nicely.

Make private fields read-only when possible

When fields are private and read-only, we cannotchange the value after the field's initialization. Private read-only fields can only be changed in the class' constructor or by the field's initialization. The make private fields read-only when possible fixer makes private fields read-only wherever possible.

Remove unnecessary casts

Casting is a method of converting values from one type to another. There are two types of casts, which are as follows:

- **Implicit casting:** The compilers cast the values automatically, if no loss of information occurs. Usually, this cast involves converting a smaller data type into a larger data type. For example:

  ```
  intSmallNumber = 2147483647; //2147483647 = Max positive value
  for 32-bit signed integer

  longBigNumber = SmallNumber; //long accepts the value, because it
  has a larger range
  ```

- **Explicit casting:** The developer specifies the type of casting with the risk of possibly losing data. For example:

  ```
  floatDecimalNumber = 1523647.87; //Specify floating point number

  intWholeNumber;

  WholeNumber  =  (int)DecimalNumber;  //Cast  Decimal  to  Integer
  resulting in: 1523647.
  ```

The **Remove unnecessary casts** fixer removes unnecessary casts wherever possible.

Apply expression/block body preferences

The **Apply expression/block body preferences** fixer converts expression-bodied members into block bodies or block bodies to expression-bodied members.

Apply inline 'out' variables preferences

In the earlier versions of C#, to use an out variable, we first declared a variable of the correct type, and then used it typically on the next line of code as an out parameter; for example:

```
DateTimeStartTime;

if (DateTime.TryParse(DateTime.Now.ToShortDateString(), out StartTime))

{

    // Use StartTime.

}
```

The **Apply inline 'out' variables preferences** fixes inline out variables wherever possible. The previous code segment now looks like:

```
if (DateTime.TryParse(DateTime.Now.ToShortDateString(), out
DateTimeStartTime))

{

    // Use StartTime.

}
```

Remove unused variables

The **Remove unused variables** fixer removes all variables that have notbeen used.

Apply object/collection initialization preferences

The object or collection initializers enable us to assign values to fields or properties of an object upon creation, without invoking a constructor and lines of assignments. For example:

```
Student student = new Student { Age = 40, Name = "Ockert" };
```

The **Apply object/collection initialization preferences** fixer uses object and collection initializers wherever possible.

Search bar on debugging windows

The **Watch**, **Autos** and **Locals** windows include a new search feature that enables us to find your variables and their properties quickly. With this new search feature, we can highlight and navigate to specified values, which are contained within the name, value, and type columns of the watch window.

Search and highlighting

When entering text in the search bar, the highlighting of matches currently expanded on the screen will occur.This gives youa faster alternativeto performing a large-scale search. The following screenshot displays the example of the search and highlighting feature:

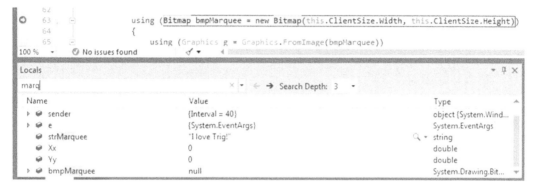

Figure 7.5: *Search and highlighting*

Search navigation

To commence searching in any of the **Watch** windows, you need to enter the query and press *Enter*, or, even easier, press the left (find next or *F3*) and right (find previous or *Shift+F3*) arrows. These search icons also navigate through each found match, as shown in the following screenshot:

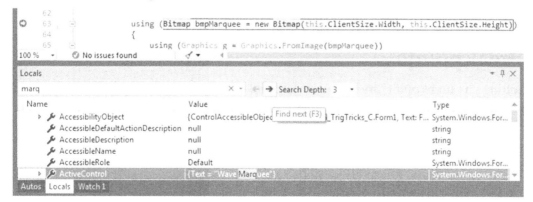

Figure 7.6: *Search navigation*

Search Depth

The debugging watch windows provide a **Search Depth** drop down to find matches nested deep into your objects, giving us the power to choose how thorough the search should be, as shown in the following screenshot:

Figure 7.7: Search Depth

Debugging applications

In Visual Studio 2019, when you debug your application, it means that you are running the application with the Visual Studio debugger attached. The debugger provides many ways and tools to see what the application's code is doing while it runs. This includes the following:

- Stepping through the code to look at the values stored in objects
- Watches on variables can be set to determine when values change
- Examine the execution path of the application's code

Breakpoints

Setting a breakpoint indicates to Visual Studio where it should suspend the application's running code so that the variables' values can be inspected, the behavior of memory can be determined, and whether or not a certain piece of code can be run.

To set a breakpoint, follow these steps:

1. Click on the left margin (or use the keyboard shortcut: *F9 / CTRL+F9*). A maroon dot `willappear`. This is the breakpoint, as shown in the following screenshot.

2. Start the program by clicking on the **Start** button.

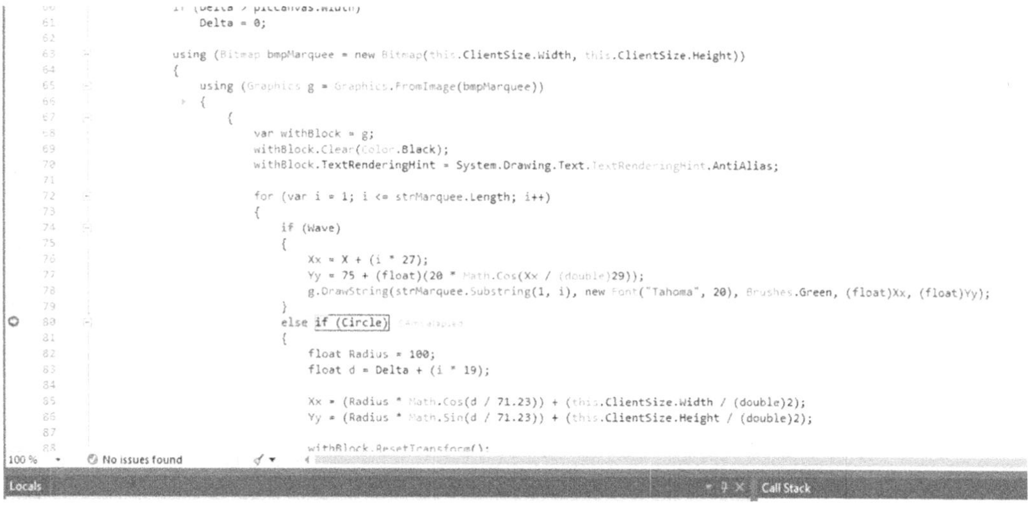

Figure 7.8: *Breakpoint*

Navigating code during the debug mode

We can navigate running code with the use of the following stepping commands:

- **Step into (F11):** The debugger steps through code statements one at a time. You can refer to the following screenshot:

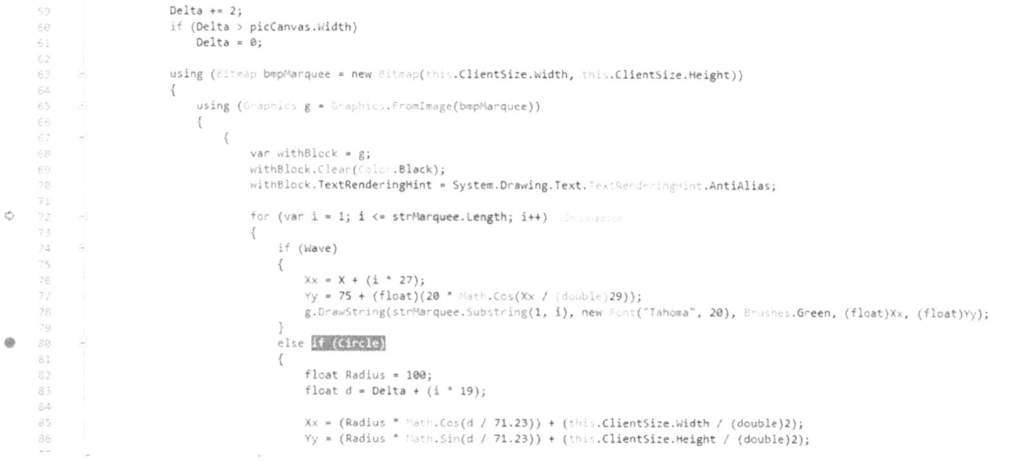

Figure 7.9: *Step into*

- **Step Over (F10):** The step over command steps over the execution of functions. This means that it will execute the function without pauses and only pause on the next statement after the function, as shown in the following screenshot:

```
using (Bitmap bmpMarquee = new Bitmap(this.ClientSize.Width, this.ClientSize.Height))
{
    using (Graphics g = Graphics.FromImage(bmpMarquee))
    {
        {
            var withBlock = g;
            withBlock.Clear(Color.Black);
            withBlock.TextRenderingHint = System.Drawing.Text.TextRenderingHint.AntiAlias;

            for (var i = 1; i <= strMarquee.Length; i++)
            {
                if (Wave)
                {
                    Xx = X + (i * 27);
                    Yy = 75 + (float)(20 * Math.Cos(Xx / (double)29));
                    g.DrawString(strMarquee.Substring(1, i), new Font("Tahoma", 20), Brushes.Green, (float)Xx, (float)Yy);
                }
                else (Circle)
                {
                    float Radius = 100;
                    float d = Delta + (i * 19);

                    Xx = (Radius * Math.Cos(d / 71.23)) + (this.ClientSize.Width / (double)2);
                    Yy = (Radius * Math.Sin(d / 71.23)) + (this.ClientSize.Height / (double)2);
```

Figure 7.10: Step over

- **Step out (Shift + F11):** The step out command continues to run the code and pauses the execution when the current function returns.

- **Step into specific:** The step into specific command steps into a specific field or property.

- **Run to cursor:** The run to cursor starts debugging and sets a temporary breakpoint on the current line of code where the cursor is, as shown in the following screenshot:

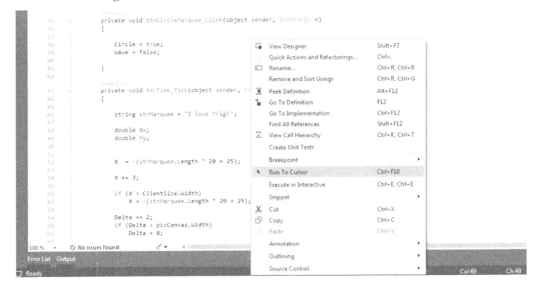

Figure 7.11: Run to cursor

Debug multiple processes

Visual Studio 2019 is able to debug a solution that has more than one process. It can switch between processes, break, step through sources, and detach from individual processes.

To debug multiple processes at the same time, you need to perform the following steps:

1. Right click on the solution in the **Solution Explorer**.
2. Select **Properties**.
3. On the **Properties** page, select **Common Properties**.
4. Select **Startup Project**.
5. Select **Multiple startup projects**.
6. Select **Start** from the **Action** list.
7. Click on **OK**.

You can refer to the following screenshot:

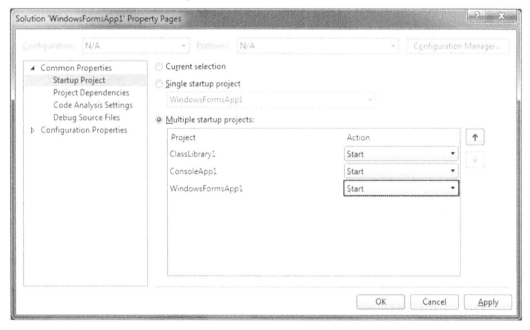

Figure 7.12: *Solution startup project properties*

Visual Studio 2019 remote debugging tools

We can debug Visual Studio 2019 applications that were deployed onto a different computer. In order to do this, we need to use the Visual Studio remote debugging tools. To debug applications that have been deployed onto a different computer, we need to follow these steps:

1. Download the remote tools.
2. Install and run the remote tools on the computer onto which the application was deployed.
3. Configure the necessary project(s) to connect to the remote computer from Visual Studio.
4. Run the application.

Download the remote debugging tools

Navigate to the following URL and download the tools according to the desired platform:

https://visualstudio.microsoft.com/downloads/?q=remote+tools#remote-tools-for-visual-studio-2019

Install and run the remote configuration wizard

After the remote tools have been downloaded, it needs to be installed and configured. The following screenshot shows the **Remote Tools** setup screen:

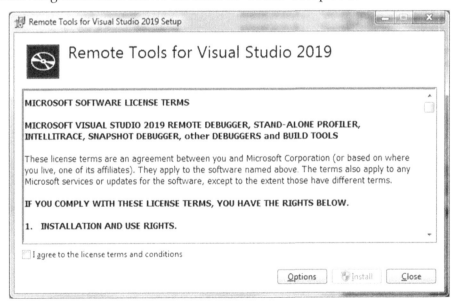

Figure 7.13: Remote debugging tools

The tools need to be configured. You need to find the **Visual Studio Remote Debugger Configuration Wizard** from the **Start** menu and run it.

The wizard opens and the following things need to be set:

- User account and password information
- The following networks for the firewall:
  - o Domain networks
  - o Private networks
  - o Informal or public networks
- When you click on the configure remote debugging button, the remote debugger window appears.

The **Remoted Debugger Configuration** wizard screen is displayed in the following screenshot:

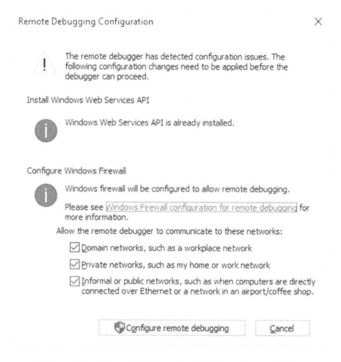

Figure 7.14: Remote Debugging Configuration window

1. Select at least one network type.
2. Click the **Configure remote debugging** button.
3. After the configuration is complete, the remote debugger waits for a connection.
4. Create a new project, or open the project which should be remotely debugged.
5. Right click the project in the **Solution Explorer**.
6. Select **Properties**.

7. Select the **Debug** tab.

8. Clear the text inside the `Working Text` folder.

9. Enter the name of the machine with the desired protocol in the Use remote machine textbox.

10. Ensure the `Use remote machine` is ticked.

11. Untick the `Enable native code debugging` textbox if necessary. The debug screen for the application to be debugged remotely is shown in the following screenshot:

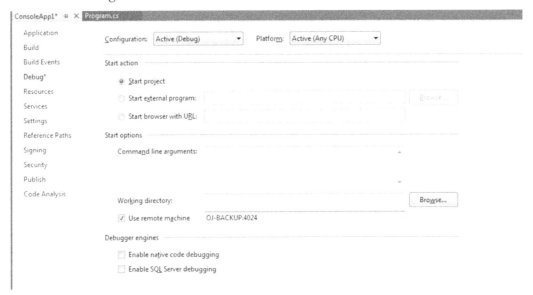

Figure 7.15: *Remote Debugging app settings for project*

12. Build the solution.

Code generation tools

Code Generation tools are not actually debugging oriented, but I thought it a good fit to speak about them here, as we are working with code already.

Visual Studio 2019 provides numerous ways that help generate, fix, and refactor code. We have spoken about refactoring earlier in this chapter and fixing is obviously debugging; so, let us concentrate on code generation tools. These include:

- Quick actions
- Code segments
- T4 text templates

Let us explore them in detail.

Quick actions

With quick actions, we can quickly refactor, generate, or modify code with a single action, usually a click. Quick actions can be used to do the following:

- Apply a code fix
- Suppress a code analyzer rule violation
- Apply a refactoring
- Generate code

Whenever a light bulb or screwdriver icon appears (or *Ctrl+ .* is pressed on a line of code), it means that there is a potential fix available for that line of code. This can be the fixing of a spelling error, or simply making the code more legible. The potential fix can be fixed with a click of the button. If you simply click on the lightbulb or screwdriver icon and a list of potential fixes will appear.

The following screenshot displays a light bulb icon enabling us to fix the spelling mistake:

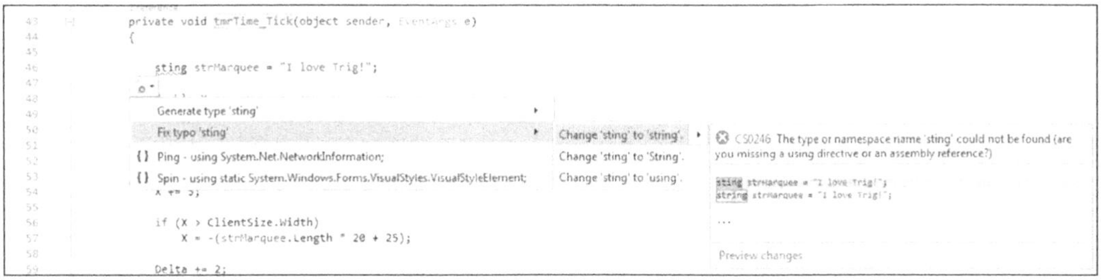

Figure 7.16: Light bulb icon

Code snippets

Code snippets are small blocks of reusable (commonly used) code that can be inserted in a code file. To insert a code snippet quickly, follow these steps:

1. Rightclick on the code editor.
2. Choose snippet.
3. Insert snippet.
4. Alternatively, press *Ctrl + K + X*.
5. Select the **Language** from the list.
6. Select the snippet from the list.

The following screenshot shows the code snippet menu in action:

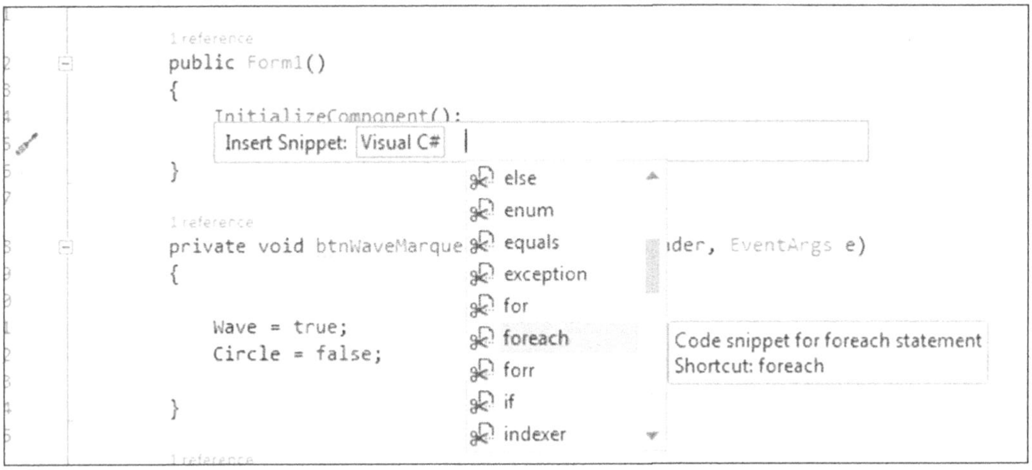

Figure 7.17: *Code snippet*

A T4 text template or pre-processed template is a combination of text blocks and control logic that can generate a text file. The logic is written as fragments of program code.

The followingare two types of pre-processed text templates:

- Design time
- Runtime

Design time T4 templates

Design-time T4 text templates generate program code in a Visual Studio project. To create a **Design-Time T4 Text Template**, performthe following steps:

1. Right click on the project in the **Solution Explorer**.
2. Choose **Add**.
3. Choose **New Item**.
4. In the **Add New Item** dialog box, select the **Text** template. The file already contains some code as shown next. We can now add to it.

The following is the Design-time T4 text template code:

```
<#@ template debug="false" hostspecific="false" language="C#" #>

<#@ assembly name="System.Core" #>

<#@ import namespace="System.Linq" #>

<#@ import namespace="System.Text" #>
```

```
<#@ import namespace="System.Collections.Generic" #>
```

```
<#@ output extension=".txt" #>
```

Runtime T4 text templates

We can generate text strings in our applications during runtime using runtime T4 text templates.

We need to perform the following steps to create a runtime T4 text template:

1. Right click on the project in the **Solution Explorer**.

2. Choose **Add**.

3. Choose **New Item**.

4. In the Add New Item dialog box, select the **Text** template.

5. Edit the .tt file to contain the text that needs to be generated by the application. For example:

   ```
   <#@ template debug="false" hostspecific="false" language="C#" #>
   ```

   ```
   <html>
   ```

   ```
   <body>
   ```

   ```
   <h1>Test T4 Output</h1>
   ```

   ```
   This is a test
   ```

   ```
   <table>
   ```

   ```
   <# for (int j = 1; j <= 10; j++)
   ```

   ```
       { #>
   ```

   ```
   <tr><td>Description <#= j #></td>
   ```

   ```
   <td>Value <#= j + j #></td></tr>
   ```

   ```
   <# } #>
   ```

   ```
   </table>
   ```

   ```
   </body>
   ```

   ```
   </html>
   ```

6. Save the `TextTemplate` file. On saving, a new class is created in the **Solution Explorer**. This file is named with the name of the `TextTemplate` file with the extension of CS. This file contains the output of the runtime T4 Text Template file:

```
<html>
<body>
<h1>Test T4 Output</h1>
This is a test
<table>
<tr><td>Description 1 </td>
<td>Value 2 </td></tr>
<tr><td>Description 2 </td>
<td>Value 4 </td></tr>
<tr><td>Description 3 </td>
<td>Value 6 </td></tr>
<tr><td>Description 4 </td>
<td>Value 8 </td></tr>
<tr><td>Description 5 </td>
<td>Value 10 </td></tr>
<tr><td>Description 6 </td>
<td>Value 12 </td></tr>
<tr><td>Description 7 </td>
<td>Value 14 </td></tr>
<tr><td>Description 8 </td>
<td>Value 16 </td></tr>
<tr><td>Description 9 </td>
<td>Value 18 </td></tr>
<tr><td>Description 10 </td>
<td>Value 20 </td></tr>
</table>
</body>
</html>
```

Conclusion

In this chapter, we learned about the code generation tools Visual studio 2019 provides. We also explored tools to help us clean up our messy code. Most importantly, we dived deep into debugging our programs properly and using the debugging tools to fix existing and potential future problems in applications, which exist on our local machines or on remote machines.

In next chapter, we will explore testing tools available as third-party tools in Visual Studio 2019

Questions

Q. 1. What is the purpose of the Code Cleanup command in the document health indicator?

Q. 2. Which debugging windows allow us to search object values quickly?

Q. 3. What is the difference between the step into and step over stepping commands?

Q. 4. Which tool can be used to setup and configure remote debugging?

Q. 5. Explain the term T4 text template.

CHAPTER 8
Testing Tools

Software testing is an ongoing process. It should be done during the building of an application as well as after the application has been built. Software developers usually create test scenarios for their logic. Normal users get involved. Dedicated software testers get involved. When everyone is happy with some program functionality, then only the next piece of functionality is tested.

Software testing does not only mean the testing of code. It involves testing the user interfaces on various platforms, testing the whole application on various platforms, and the ease of use of the user interface. The list is endless. There are many built-in debugging tools in Visual Studio that we discussed earlier, but now let us look at the testing tools available in Visual Studio and some third-party testing tools that are available.

Structure

- Unit testing in Visual Studio 2019
- Coded UI tests
- Selenium
- Appium

- Apache JMeter
- CloudTest
- Blazemeter
- Akamai

Objective

This chapter focuses on the tools to test our applications, regardless of the platform. These tests include normal coding tests, user interface tests as well as some speed tests.

Unit testing in Visual Studio 2019

Unit testing breaks down the functionality of any program into discrete and disparate testable behaviors that can be used to test as individual units. Visual Studio Test Explorer provides an efficient way to run our unit tests and view their results in Visual Studio 2019.

Visual Studio installs the Microsoft unit testing frameworks for managed and native code. Visual Studio makes use of the Microsoft unit testing framework to help us create unit tests, run these tests, and report the results of these tests.

Creating unit test projects and test methods

It is quick to generate a unit test project and unit test stubs by using code. Depending on the requirements, you can also create unit test projects and tests manually.

Create a unit test project and unit test stubs

To create a unit test project and unit test stubs, follow these steps:

1. Select the Namespace or method or type.
2. Right click.
3. Select `Create Unit Tests`.

4. The `Create Unit Tests` screen will appear, as shown in the following screenshot:

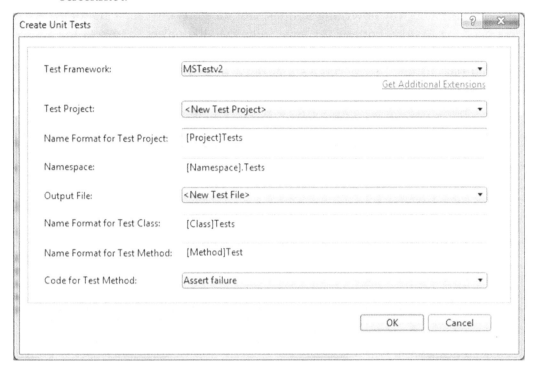

Figure 8.1: Create Unit Tests

5. Click `OK`

The unit test stubs are created in a new unit test project which includes all the methods in the class. This is shown in the next screenshot:

Figure 8.2: Test methods

Writing a small test

The most common way of writing unit tests for methods is to make use of the AAA (Arrange, Act, Assert) pattern. Arrange initializes the objects and sets the values of data that is passed to the test methods. Act invokes the test method with the arranged parameters. Assert verifies that the action of the test method behaves as expected.

By using the AAA pattern, a completed unit test method may end up like the next code sample:

```
namespace HTG_Maze_VB.Tests

{

    [TestClass()]

publicclassclsGameTests

    {

        [TestMethod()]

publicvoid GenerateTest(int intCols, Random rndRand)

        {

//Arrange

            List<Point> lstMaze = new List<Point>();

int intEmpty = (int)Math.Pow(intCols, 2);

            clsGrid.ptStart = new Point(rndRand.Next(0, intCols),
intCols - 1);

            clsGrid.Cells[clsGrid.ptStart.X][intCols - 1].blnSouth =
false;

//Act

            lstMaze.Add(new Point(clsGrid.ptStart.X, intCols - 1));

//Assert

            Assert.IsNull(clsGrid.ptStart.X, "X must have a value!");

            Assert.Fail("Failed");

        }

    }

}
```

Code sample 1

The Arrange part creates and initializes the necessary objects in order to do the test. The Act part does the physical action that needs to take place. Assert tests the action.

Test Explorer

The Test Explorer runs unit tests from Visual Studio or third-party unit test projects. We can also group tests into categories, filter the test list, and create, save, and run playlists of tests using the Test Explorer. Also, we can debug tests and analyze test performance and code coverage.

The next few steps displays the Test Explorer window and run a test

1. Click the Visual Studio **Test** menu
2. Select **Windows**
3. Select **Test Explorer**
4. Inside the Test Explorer, select **Run**. An example of this is displayed in the next screenshot:

Figure 8.3: Test Explorer window

Coded UI tests

Coded UI tests (CUITs) are functional tests of the **User Interface (UI)** controls. CUITs ensure that the whole application as well as its user interface is functioning correctly and properly.

> **Visual Studio 2019 will be the last version where Coded UI test will be available.**

Creating a Coded UI test

The following steps will guide you to create a Coded UI test:

1. Open Visual Studio 2019.
2. Click on **Tools**.
3. Click on **Get Tools and Features**.
4. Select the **Individual components** tab.
5. Scroll down to the **Debugging and testing** section.
6. Select the **Coded UI test** component, as shown in the following screenshot:

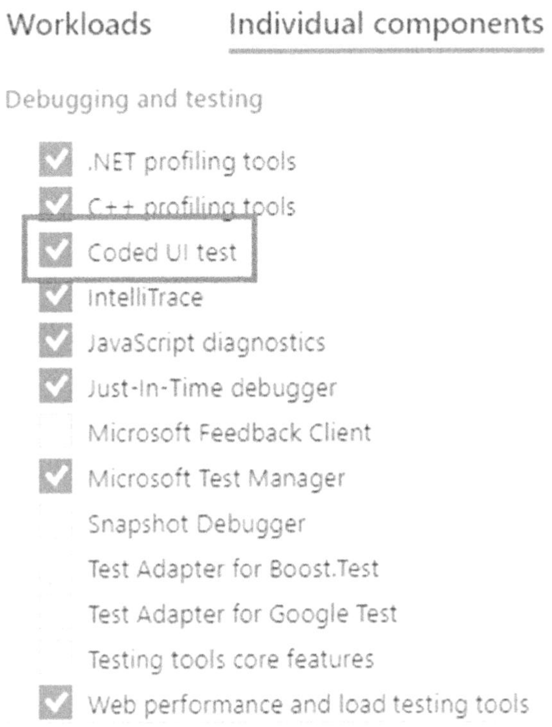

Figure 8.4: Coded UI test installer

7. Select **Modify**.

8. After the component is installed, select **File | New | Project**.

9. Search for and select the **Coded UI Test Project** template.

10. Right click on the project in the **Solution Explorer**.

11. Select **Add | Coded UI Test**.

12. Select **Record actions** in the **Generate Code for Coded UI Test** dialog box.

13. Click on Edit **UI map or add assertions**, as shown in the following screenshot:

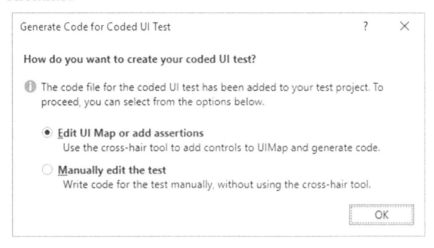

Figure 8.5: Generate Code for Coded UI Test dialog box

14. Click the **Record** button in the Coded UI Test Builder window.

15. To Add assertions, click the **Add** button in the Coded UI Test Builder window.

16. Choose a **control** in the running application.

17. In the list of properties that appears, select a **property**.

18. Right click.

19. Choose **Add Assertion**.

20. In the dialog box, select the **desired operator**.

21. **Close** the assertion window.

22. Choose **Generate Code**.

Now that we have had a look at Visual Studio 2019 testing tools, let's have a look at various other options for web testing, cloud testing and mobile testing. These are extensions that we can add to Visual Studio 2019, or run on their own.

Selenium

Selenium is an open source automated testing suite for cross-platform web applications. Selenium contains the following four components:

- Selenium IDE
- Selenium RC (Remote Control)
- WebDriver
- Selenium Grid

Let us explore Selenium's components one by one in the upcoming sections.

Selenium IDE

Selenium IDE (implemented as a Firefox Add-on or as a Chrome Extension) is an integrated development environment for Selenium tests. It organizes, records, edits, and debugs functional tests. It was previously known as **Selenium Recorder**.

Selenium IDE is quite easy to use and install as very little programming experience and an understanding of HTML is needed. It does however not support iteration and conditional operations.

To install it as a Firefox Add-on, follow any one of these methods:

Method 1:

1. Click on the menu on the right-hand side of the screen to open the Firefox menu, as shown in the following screenshot:

Figure 8.6: Firefox menu

2. Select **Add-ons** and thenclick on **Find more add-ons**.
3. Search for **Selenium IDE**.

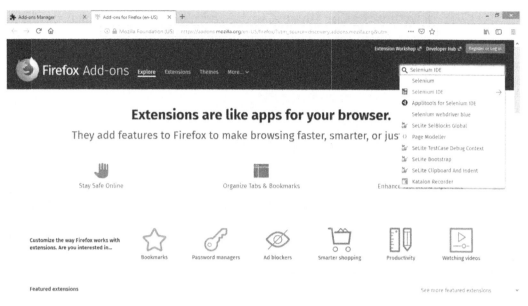

Figure 8.7: Selenium IDE

4. Click on the **Add to Firefox** button.

5. Give it the necessary permissions by clicking on **Add**.

Method 2:

1. Click on the little gear icon on the right-hand side of the screen, as shown in the following screenshot:

Figure 8.8: Gear icon

2. Click on **Extensions & Themes**, as shown in the following screenshot:

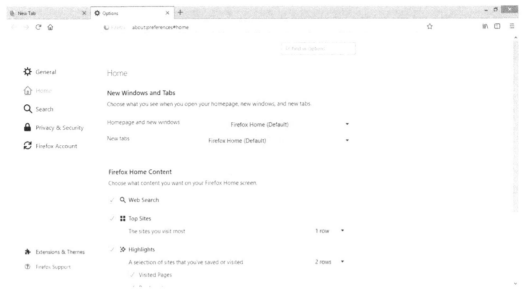

Figure 8.9: Extensions & Themes

3. Click on **Find more add-ons**.
4. Search for **Selenium IDE**.
5. Click on the **Add to Firefox** button.
6. Give it the necessary permissions by clicking on **Add**.

After the Selenium IDE Add-on has been added to Firefox, it will appear on the toolbar, as shown in the following screenshot:

Figure 8.10: Selenium IDE Add-On on toolbar

To add the Selenium IDE to Chrome, follow thegiven steps:

1. Navigate to the Chrome web store or the following URL: **https://chrome. google.com/webstore/search/selenium%20ide**
2. Search for **Selenium IDE**.

3. Click on the **Add to Chrome** button, as shown in the following screenshot:

Figure 8.11: Add to Chrome

4. Click on **Add Extension** to add it to Chrome.

Once added or opened, the Selenium IDE prompts for a name for a new project or a new test, or gives us the option to open an existing project.

If a project has been created, as shown in the following screenshot, we can fill in a few options. We can select a command (or action). We can set target pages and values:

Figure 8.12: Selenium IDE test project

Selenium RC

Selenium RC (Remote Control) is a test tool that enables us to write automated web application tests in any programming language against any HTTP/HTTPS website using any JavaScriptenabled browser.

Selenium RC has two parts, which is a server and the client libraries.The server receives commands via simple HTTP GET/POST requests from the program to be tested, interprets them, and then reports the results to the tested program. The client libraries provide the API that allows the commands to run.

Installing the Selenium RC server

The installation process is easy. Just follow these steps:

1. Navigate to download page: **https://www.seleniumhq.org/download/.**
2. Download the latest version. At the time of writing, the current version was 3.141.59.
3. Copy the file to the desired directory.

Running the server

To run the server, perform the following steps:

1. Open the Command Prompt.
2. Navigate to the location of the JAR file that was downloaded earlier.
3. Run the following command:

```
java -jar selenium-server-standalone-<version-number>.jar
```

Getting the client libraries to work

The following steps explain how to get the client libraries for Selenium to work:

1. Create a class library project in C# or VB.NET.
2. Download and install **NUnit** using the **NuGet Package Manager.**
3. Add references to the following DLLs:
   - nmock.dll
   - nunit.core.dll
   - nunit.framework.dll
   - ThoughtWorks.Selenium.Core.dll
   - ThoughtWorks.Selenium.IntegrationTests.dll
   - ThoughtWorks.Selenium.UnitTests.dll

4. Write the Selenium test in .NET.

5. Write a simple `main()` program or include NUnit in the project.

6. Run the server.

7. Run the test either from the IDE, the NUnit GUI, or the command line.

Selenium WebDriver

Selenium WebDriver (or Selenium 2) replaces Selenium RC. Selenium WebDriver accepts commands (similar to RC) and sends them to a browser. Unlike with Selenium RC, Selenium WebDriver does not need a special server to execute tests because WebDriver starts a browser instance directly and controls it.

Installing WebDriver

The easiest way to install WebDriver is to use NuGet (as explained in *Chapter 5: What's new in .NET Core 3.0*) to add the following repositories:

- WebDriver
- WebDriverBackedSelenium
- Support

WebDriver can also be downloaded from

http://selenium-release.storage.googleapis.com/index.html?path=4.0/.

Selenium Grid

Selenium Grid provides the ability to run tests on remote browser instances. With Selenium Grid, one server acts as the hub. This hub has a list of servers that provide access to WebDriver nodes or rather, browser instances.

Appium

Appium is an opensource automated testing tool for automating native, web, and hybrid applications on iOS, Android, and Windows desktop platforms. Appium supports Safari, Chrome, and the built-in Android browser. Appium is cross-platform. This allows us to write tests against multiple platforms using the same API and to reuse code between iOS, Android, and Windows test suites.

The easiest way to install Appium is to download and install Appium Desktop from **https://github.com/appium/appium-desktop/releases.**

The Appium desktop with the **Simple** tab selected is displayed in the following screenshot:

Figure 8.13: Appium desktop

All that is needed to start a basic default server is to click on the **Start Server** button and allow access if necessary.

The running server is displayed in the following screenshot:

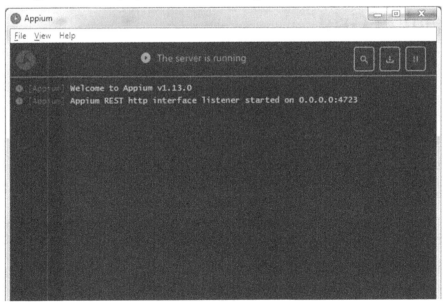

Figure 8.14: Running server

Apache JMeter

Apache JMeter is opensource. It is designed to load the test functional behavior and measure performance. Apache JMeter can be used to test performance on static and dynamic resources. It can simulate heavy loads on a server, a group of servers, or a network. It can load and performance test different servers and services like HTTP, HTTPS, SOAP, REST, and FTP.

To get started with Apache JMeter and Visual Studio, perform the following steps:

1. Create a free Azure DevOps account on **https://visualstudio.microsoft.com/team-services/**.

2. Create and name a new project, as shown in the following screenshot:

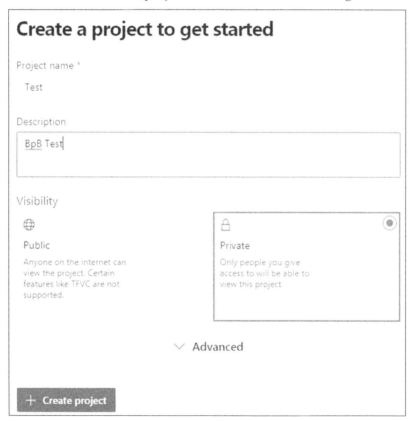

Figure 8.15: Test Project

3. Here, we can create **Boards**, **Repos**, **Pipelines**, **Test Plans** as well as **Artifacts**.

4. Click on **Test Plans**. This will produce a menu similar to the one shown in the following screenshot:

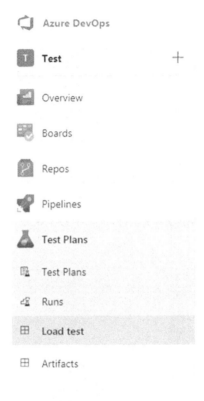

Figure 8.16: Test Menu

5. Select **Load test**.
6. Select **New | Visual Studio test**.
7. Browse for a Webtest file or Click on **OK**.
8. Select **Run**.

Blazemeter

BlazeMeter provides a quick way to find and fix performance bottlenecks. BlazeMeter is a tool that enhances abilities of Apache JMeter. BlazeMeter can run JMX scripts either in the cloud or from behind a firewall.

To get started with BlazeMeter, do the following steps:

1. Navigate to **https://a.blazemeter.com/app/**.
2. You can login, create a new profile, or sign up with your Google account.

3. Choose the type of **Test** to be created; for example, `Performance Test`, as shown in the following screenshot:

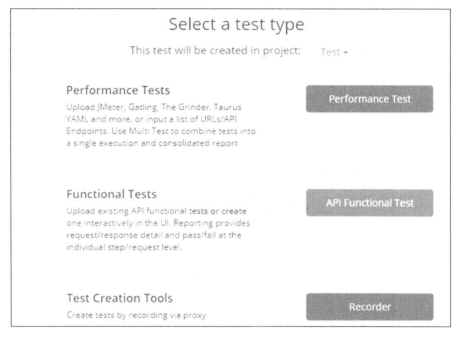

Figure 8.17: Type of test

4. Once the performance test is selected, a new screen appears where the scripts can be uploaded and the test can be run, as shown in the following screenshot:

Figure 8.18: Upload script

Akamai CloudTest

Akamai CloudTest is a highly scalable load-testing platform to help safely simulate large events in production with control, while producing a live analysis of what the site or app is capable of and drills down to the source of any performance bottlenecks.

To get started with Akamai CloudTest, perform the following steps:

1. Navigate to **https://www.akamai.com/us/en/products/performance/ cloudtest.jsp.**

2. Fill in the details in the requested form, as shown in the following screenshot:

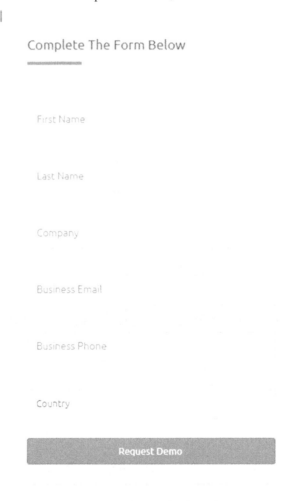

Figure 8.19: Akamai CloudTest demo

3. Click on the **Request Demo** button.

Conclusion

In this chapter, we explored testing tools. Testing tools ensure your applications are bug free and ready for distribution. We learned how to set up Coded UI. Then, we learned about Selenium, Appium, Apache JMeter, BlazeMeter, and Akamai CloudTest.

All the tools we explored covered all the areas in the programming spectrum. These included desktop apps, mobile apps, web apps as well as cloud apps.

In next chapter, we will explore ASP.NET tools in general and learn how they can be used to fix bugs and styling.

Questions

    Q. 1. The Selenium IDE can be installed on which two browsers?

    Q. 2. What does the Apache JMeter tool do?

    Q. 3. For which platform is Appium developed?

    Q. 4. Akamai CloudTest can help fix and find which problems?

    Q. 5. Which version of Visual Studio 2019 will be the last to include Coded UI?

SECTION III

Advanced Tools

Section III covers Advanced Tools for ASP.NET, Mobile devices, and Azure Cloud computing. In ASP.NET tools, we will learn about the various Web frameworks at our disposal to create proper Web applications. We will cover .NET Core 3.0 and talk about third-party tools and Extensions.

CHAPTER 9
ASP.NET Tools

In this chapter, we will learn about the various web frameworks at our disposal to create proper web applications. We will learn about .NET Core 3.0 and third-party tools and extensions. These extensions and tools include Blazor, which allows browsers to interpret C# natively: Amazon Cognito and Visual Studio Kubernetes for Cloud Services. We will also take a look at the web API.

Structure

- Web frameworks
- .NET Core 3
- Blazor
- ASP.NET Core Identity Provider for Amazon Cognito
- The Web API
- Visual Studio Kubernetes Tools

Objective

This chapter focuses on the tools to enhance our web applications where to find them, how to install them, and most importantly, how to make use of them.

Web frameworks

A web framework (or web application framework) is a framework that supports the development of web applications, web services, web resources, and web APIs. They provide a standard way to build and deploy web applications into the World Wide Web. They also automate the overhead associated with common activities by providing libraries for database access, supplying templating frameworks, and providing libraries for session management.

Although, there are numerous web frameworks available, we will discuss the three most popular frameworks.

ASP.NET MVC framework

ASP.NET MVC is a web application framework that implements the **model–view–controller (MVC)** pattern. It is a design pattern that decouples the user-interface (view), data (model), and application logic (controller). With the MVC pattern, requests are routed to a controller (application logic) that is responsible for working with the model (data) to perform actions or retrieve data. The controller (application logic) chooses the view to display, and then provides the view model (data). The view renders the page, based on the data that is in the model.

The ASP.NET MVC web framework is composed of the following three roles:

- **Model (or business layer):** Themodel corresponds to the data-related logic that the user will work with. The model represents the business logic and operations that it should perform. Along with the business logic, the implementation logic for persisting data should be encapsulated by the model.

- **View (or display layer):** The view represents the UI logic of an application. A view's responsibility is to present content via the user interface. It uses the Razor view engine to embed .NET code into HTML markup. The logic within a view should relate to presenting content and should be minimal.

- **Controller (or input control):** The controller is an interface between model and view components, which processes the business logic and interacts with the views. Controllers handle user interaction; work with the model, and select views to render. The controller is the entry point and selects the model types to work with and the views to render.

To create an ASP.NET MVC application, we need to perform the following steps:

1. Install Visual Studio 2019, as explained in *Chapter 1: Getting Started with Visual Studio 2019,* if necessary.

2. Install the ASP.NET and web development workload, as explained in *Chapter 1: Getting Started with Visual Studio 2019 if necessary.*

3. Create a new Visual Studio 2019 project.

4. Ensure that **ASP.NET Web Application** is selected. The following screenshot shows how it should look like when the **ASP.NET Web Application (.NET Framework)** is selected:

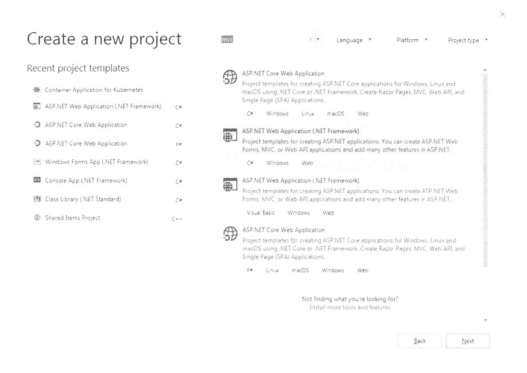

Figure 9.1: ASP.NET MVC Application

5. Click on **Next**. Specify the project details.

6. Click on **Create**.

7. Select **MVC**, and click on the **Create** button.

The **Solution Explorer** includes the model, views, and controller folders, and a HomeController.cs file, which looks like the following:

```
using System.Web.Mvc;

namespace WebApplication5.Controllers
{
  public class HomeController : Controller
  {
    public ActionResult Index()
```

```
    {

      return View();

    }

    public ActionResult About()

    {

      ViewBag.Message = "Your application description page.";

      return View();

    }

    public ActionResult Contact()

    {

      ViewBag.Message = "Your contact page.";

      return View();

    }

  }

}
```

DotNetNuke (DNN platform)

The DNN platform is a free, open source content management system. DotNetNuke (DNN) makes use of a three-tier architecture model with a core framework that provides support to the extensible modular structure.

The functionality of DNN can be expanded by adding third-party modules. It can be expanded from an existing module store, third-party authors, or through in-house development. A DNN skinning architecture provides a separation of presentation and content. This enables web designers to develop skins without requiring any development knowledge.

Using DotNetNuke

To get started with the DNN Platform, perform the following steps:

1. Navigate to **https://www.dnnsoftware.com/community/download**.
2. Select **Download**.

3. Extract the downloaded zipped files.

4. Create a directory in the `C:\inetpub\wwwroot\` folder called **DotNetNuke**.

5. Copy the contents of the extracted DNN INSTALL package to the `C:\inetpub\wwwroot\dotnetnuke\` folder.

6. Go to the properties of the `C:\inetpub\wwwroot\dotnetnuke\` folder by right clicking on it.

7. Click on the **Security** tab.

8. Give this account modify permissions on the folder.

9. Open the web server IIS Console: `start, run, INETMGR`.

10. Expand websites.

11. Expand the default website.

12. Right click on the `dotnetnuke` folder.

13. Click on **Convert to Application**.

14. Navigate to `http://localhost/dotnetnuke`.

15. Step through the installation wizard.

16. The default login accounts should be displayed.

MonoRail

MonoRail is an open source web application framework. MonoRail enforces a separation of concerns using a **model–view–controller (MVC)** architecture. MonoRail is inspired by Ruby on Rails Action Pack. It differs from the normal ASP. NET Web Forms development by enforcing a separation of concerns via the MVC architecture. It maps web requests to an action (a regular method on the controller). The controller invokes business services and controls the application's flow. After sending web responses to a client, the controller sets a view template to be rendered by putting the data in a **Property Bag**.

To download MonoRail, navigate to

https://github.com/castleproject-deprecated/MonoRail.

Vue.js

Vue.js is a framework for building user interfaces. Vue is incrementally adoptable. The core Vue library is focused solely on the view layer and is easy integrate with other libraries or existing projects. Vue is also capable of powering Single-Page Applications when used in combination with modern tooling.

Getting started with Vue.js and Visual Studio 2019

The next steps show how to install and make use of Vue.js and Visual Studio

1. Ensure that the Node.js development workload is installed, by selecting **Tools > Get Tools and Features**. This is shown in the next screenshot:

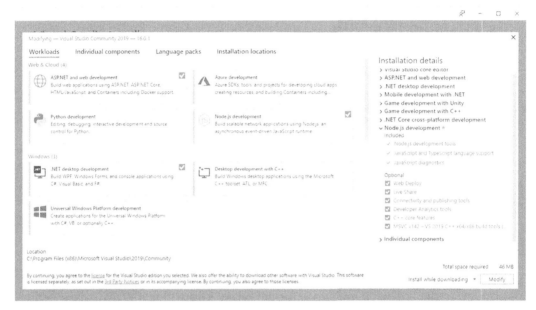

Figure 9.2: Node.js development workload

2. Download Node.js by navigating to

    https://nodejs.org/en/download/

3. Create a new project

4. In the Project type search box enter **Vue**. This will produce two templates, as shown next:

Figure 9.3: Vue Project templates

5. Select **Basic Vue.js Web Application**.
6. Select **Next**.
7. Fill in the project details.
8. Select **Create | Project | Add New Item**.
9. Select either **JavaScript Vue Single File Component** or **TypeScript Vue Single File Component** and select **Add**.
10. The main.js file is open in the code editor by default. Edit it to resemble the next code segment

```
import Vue from 'vue';

import App from './App.vue';


Vue.config.productionTip = true;


new Vue({

    render: h => h(App)
```

```
}).$mount('#app');
```

Open the `App.Vue` file and edit it to resemble the next code:

```
<template>
<div id="app">
<Home msg="BpB Vue.js Example" />
</div>
</template>

<script>
    import Home from './components/Home.vue';

    export default {
        name: 'app',
        components: {
            Home
        }
    };
</script>

<style>
</style>
```

11. **Run** the application.
12. If the Browser tells you that the page cannot be loaded, wait a little while as Node.js first needs to compile the application. After it has compiled the browser will show the following screen:

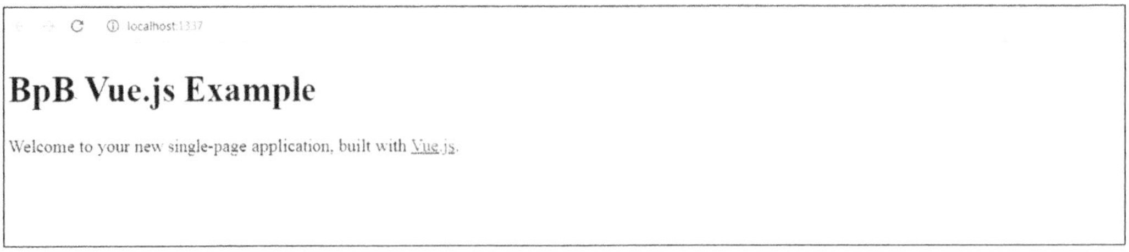

Figure 9.4: Vue example

React.js

React is a JavaScript library for building user interfaces. React is maintained by Facebook and a community of individual developers. It can be used as a base in the development of single-page or mobile apps, because of its ability to fetch rapidly changing data that needs to be recorded.

Getting started with React.js and Visual Studio 2019

The next steps show how to install and make use of React.js and Visual Studio:

1. Ensure that the Node.js development workload is installed, by selecting **Tools | Get Tools and Features**. This is shown in *Figure 9.2*.

2. Download **Node.js** by navigating to:

   https://nodejs.org/en/download/

3. **Create** a new project.

4. Select the **ASP.NET Core Web Application** template.

5. Click **Next**.

6. Enter the project details.

7. Click **Create**.

8. In the next screen, select React.js, as shown in the next screenshot:

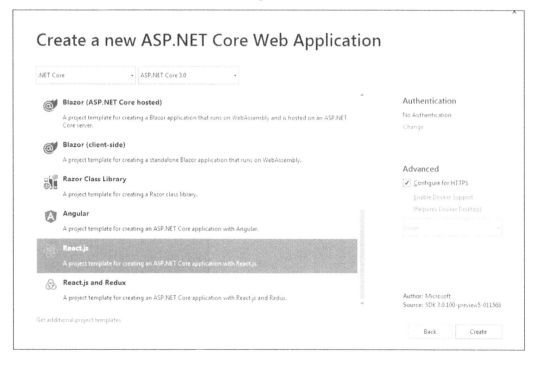

Figure 9.5: React.js

9. Select **Create**.

10. In the **Solution Explorer**, expand the `ClientApp` folder.

11. Expand the `src` folder.

12. Expand the **Components** folder.

13. Double click `Home.js` in the `Components` folder.

14. Edit it to look like the next code:

```
import React, { Component } from 'react';



export class Home extends Component {
  static displayName = Home.name;


  render () {
    return (
<div>
<h1>BpB React Example</h1>
<p>Welcome to your new single-page application, built with:</p>
<ul>
<li><a href='https://get.asp.net/'>ASP.NET Core</a> and <a
href='https://msdn.microsoft.com/en-us/library/67ef8sbd.
aspx'>C#</a> for cross-platform server-side code</li>
<li><a href='https://facebook.github.io/react/'>React</a> for
client-side code</li>
<li><a href='http://getbootstrap.com/'>Bootstrap</a> for layout
and styling</li>
</ul>
</div>
    );
  }
}
```

15. The browser will display a screen similar to the next screenshot:

Figure 9.6: *React example*

.NET Core 3

In *Chapter 5: What's new in .Net Core 3.0*, we discussed .NET Core 3.0, but here is a refresher.

.NET Core is a free and opensource managed computer software framework for Windows, Linux, and macOS. .NET Core supports cross-platform scenarios such as ASP.NET Core web apps, command-line apps, libraries, and Universal Windows Platform apps.

.NET Core 3.0 supports WinForms (Windows Forms), WPF (Windows Presentation Foundation) as well as supports ML.NET (Microsoft's OpenSource Machine Learning Framework), IoT (Internet-of-Things). It includes the Visual Basic.NET Runtime, support for Entity Framework 6, .NET Framework 4.8 as well as support for the new C# 8.0 features we talked about in *Chapter 4: Latest features and changes in C# 8.0).*

Blazor

Blazor is a web framework that enables us to write client-side web applications using C# via WebAssembly and Razor. This means that C# can run natively in all four major browsers: Firefox, Chrome, Safari, and Edge. **WebAssembly** applications are passed to the browser in a binary format that can run natively at a near-native speed. A Razor page is quite similar to the view component that ASP.NET MVC employs with the same syntax and functionality.

Getting started with Blazor and Visual Studio 2019

In order to get started with Blazor, we need the following:
- Visual Studio 2019
- .Net Core SDK 3.0 Preview (or later)

- The Blazor Extensions

- Blazor Templates

We have Visual Studio 2019, so all we need is the last three items in the list: the .NET Core SDK 3.0 Preview (or later), the Blazor extensions (which we can get from the Visual Studio Market Place) and the Blazor Templates. We will add them now.

Chapter 5: What's new in .Net Core 3.0, covered .NET Core 3.0 and how to download it. If the SDK for .NET Core is already installed, the steps pertaining to its download and installation can be skipped.

Setting up Blazor

In order to set up Blazor in its entirety, perform the following steps:

1. Navigate to **https://dotnet.microsoft.com/download/dotnet-core/3.0** to download .NET Core 3. The following screenshot displays the .NET Core 3 download screen. These options were available at the time of printing this book. More options may be reflected:

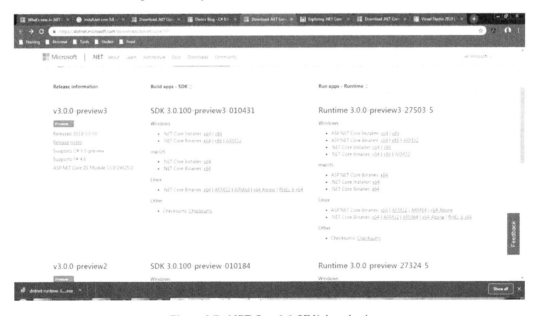

Figure 9.7: .NET Core 3.0 SDK download

2. After the download, launch the installer. An installer window similar to following screenshot will be displayed:

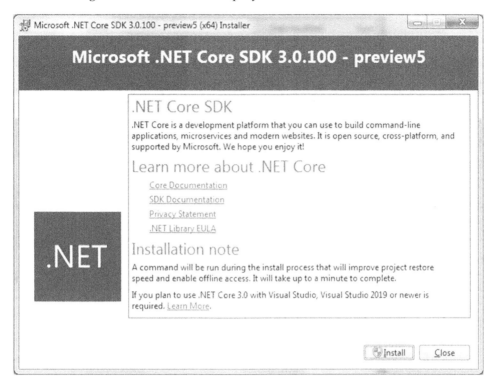

Figure 9.8: .NET Core 3.0 SDK Installer

3. Install it.

4. Open the developer Command Prompt and enter the following command:

```
dotnet new -I Microsoft.AspNetCore.Blazor.Templates::3.0.0-
preview5-19227-01
```

5. Wait until you get the confirmation that the Blazor templates have been installed. If you get the output similar to the following screenshot, it confirms that the Blazor templates have been installed:

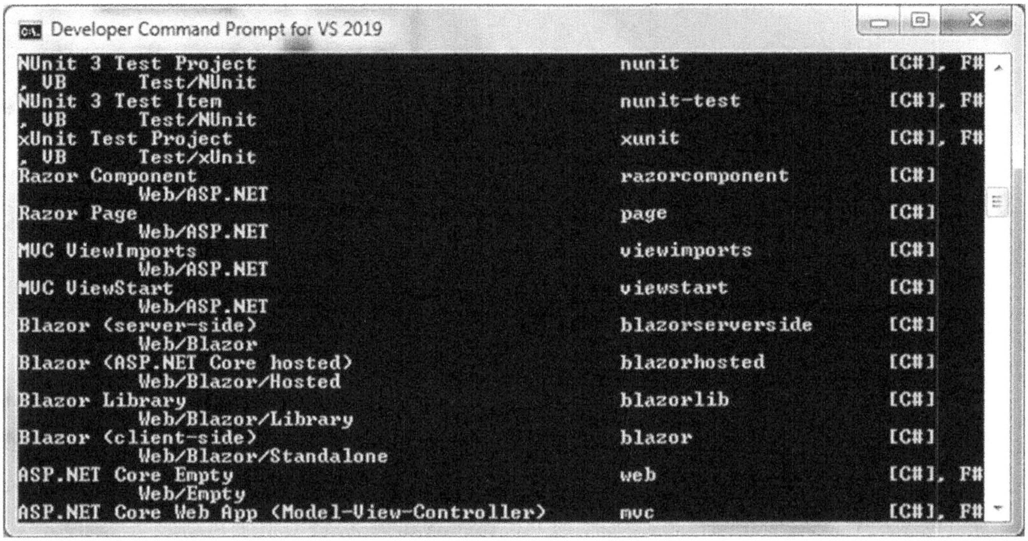

Figure 9.9: Blazor templates

6. To download Blazor, navigate to **https://marketplace.visualstudio.com/items?itemName=aspnet.blazor.**

7. Click on **Download** to download the Blazor extension.

8. Install the VSIX file.

9. Open Visual Studio 2019, and click on **Tools | Options.**

10. Select the projects and solutions node.

11. Click on **.NET Core**.

12. Check the box for Use **previews of the .NET Core SDK**, as shown in the following screenshot:

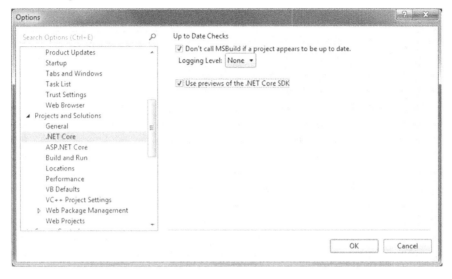

Figure 9.10: SDK options

13. Click on **OK**.

14. Create a new ASP.NET Core Web Application project (if the .NET Core cross-platform development workload has been installed).

15. Select **Blazor (client-side)**, as shown in the following screenshot:

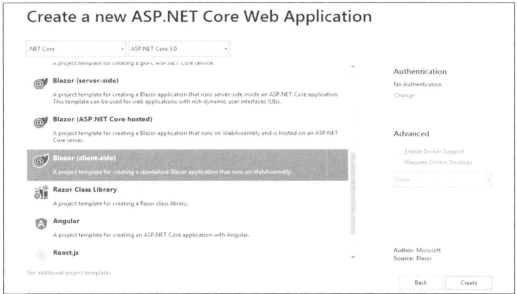

Figure 9.11: Blazor client side

16. Click on **Create**.

17. After the project loads, click on **Run**. The following screen will appear in the browser:

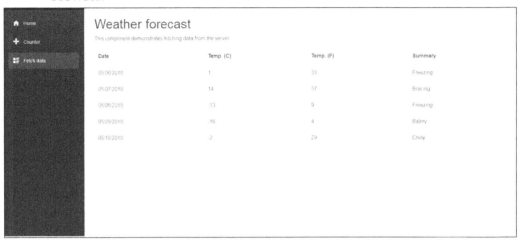

Figure 9.12: Blazor in action

18. In **Solution Explorer**, expand the Pages folder.

19. Open the FetchData.razor page to interrogate its code. The code in FetchData.razor is used to display the weather forecast in an HTML page. It reads the weather information from a JSON file, which is as follows:

```
@page "/fetchdata"

@inject HttpClient Http


<h1>Weather forecast</h1>

<p>This component demonstrates fetching data from the server.</p>

@if (forecasts == null)

{

<p><em>Loading...</em></p>

}

else

{

<table class="table">

<thead>
```

```
<tr>

<th>Date</th>

<th>Temp. (C)</th>

<th>Temp. (F)</th>

<th>Summary</th>

</tr>

</thead>

<tbody>

    @foreach (var forecast in forecasts)

    {

<tr>

<td>@forecast.Date.ToShortDateString()</td>

<td>@forecast.TemperatureC</td>

<td>@forecast.TemperatureF</td>

<td>@forecast.Summary</td>

</tr>

    }

</tbody>

</table>

}


@functions {

  WeatherForecast[] forecasts;

  protected override async Task OnInitAsync()

  {

    forecasts = await Http.GetJsonAsync<WeatherForecast[]>("samp
le-data/weather.json");

  }

  class WeatherForecast

  {
```

```
    public DateTime Date { get; set; }

    public int TemperatureC { get; set; }

    public int TemperatureF { get; set; }

    public string Summary { get; set; }

  }

}
```

ASP.NET Core Identity Provider for Amazon

We have been dealing with a lot of Microsoft-specific extensions and tools. Now, we will do something a bit different, just to show the true power and versatility of ASP.NET.

Cognito

Amazon Cognito supplies authorization, authentication, and user management for web and mobile applications. Users can sign in directly, or through a third party such as Amazon, Google, or Facebook.

Amazon Cognito consists of the following two main components:

- User pools
- Identity pools

User pools

In Amazon Cognito, a user pool is a user directory. Here, users can sign-into a web or mobile application.

User pools provide the following benefits:

- Sign-in and sign-up services
- Customizable web UI to sign in users
- Social sign-in with Google, Facebook, and Login with Amazon
- User directory management
- Multi-factor authentication (MFA)
- User migration via AWS Lambda triggers

Identity pools

With identity pools, users can obtain temporary AWS credentials in order to access AWS services like DynamoDB and Amazon S3. It supports anonymous guest users, and the following identity providers:

- Amazon Cognito user pools
- Social sign-in with Google, Facebook, and Login with Amazon
- OpenID Connect (OIDC) providers
- SAML identity providers
- Developer authenticated identities

Setting up and getting started with Amazon Cognito

The next steps shows how easy it is to set up Amazon Cognito

1. Create a new ASP.NET Core application.

2. Add the NuGet packages (*Chapter 5: What's new in .Net Core 3.0*) for the following:

   - `Amazon.AspNetCore.Identity.Cognito`
   - `Amazon.Extensions.CognitoAuthentication`

3. In the **Solution Explorer**, open the appsettings.json file.

4. Add the `UserPool` properties to the file:

```
"AWS": {

  "Region": "<Region ID comes here>",

  "UserPoolClientId": "<User Pool Client ID comes here>",

  "UserPoolClientSecret": "<User Pool Client Secret comes here>",

  "UserPoolId": "<User Pool ID comes here>"

}
```

5. Open the `StartUp.cs` file.

6. Remove any existing `ApplicationDbContext` references.

7. Add a call to `services.AddCognitoIdentity()`, as shown in the following code snippet:

```
public void ConfigureServices(IServiceCollection services)

{

  // Adds Amazon Cognito as Identity Provider

  services.AddCognitoIdentity();

  //Add Logic Here

}
```

8. Enable support for authentication:

```
public void Configure(IApplicationBuilder app, IHostingEnvironment env)

{

  // If not already enabled, you need to enable ASP.NET Core authentication

  app.UseAuthentication();

  //Add Logic Here

}
```

Web API

The ASP.NET Web **API (Application Programming Interface)** is a framework used for building HTTP services that can be consumed by browsers, mobiles, and tablets. It contains the ASP.NET MVC features such as routing, controllers, model binders, and dependency injection.

The ASP.NET Web API is the perfect platform for building RESTful applications using the .NET Framework. A RESTful application is an API that makes use of HTTP requests to GET, PUT, POST, and DELETE data.

The Web API supports the following features:
- Convention-based CRUD actions
- Responses have accept headers and HTTP status codes
- Supports text formats such as XML and JSON
- Supports OData automatically
- Supports self-hosting and IIS hosting
- Supports ASP.NET MVC features like routing and controllers

Creating a new Web API application

Perform the following steps to create a new Web API application:

1. Launch Visual Studio 2019.

2. Create a new **ASP.NET Web Application**.

3. Click on **Create**.

4. Select **Web API** from the list, as shown in the following screenshot:

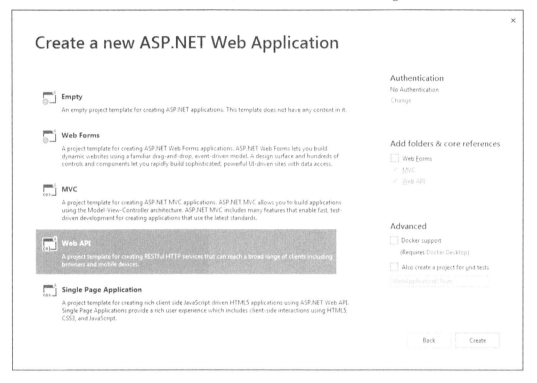

Figure 9.13: Web API

5. Click on **Create**.

6. The created views controller looks like the following:

```
using System.Collections.Generic;

using System.Web.Http;


namespace WebApplication5.Controllers

{

    public class ValuesController : ApiController
```

```
{
  // GET api/values
  public IEnumerable<string> Get()
  {
    return new string[] { "value1", "value2" };
  }

  // GET api/values/5
  public string Get(int id)
  {
    return "value";
  }

  // POST api/values
  public void Post([FromBody]string value)
  {
  }

  // PUT api/values/5
  public void Put(int id, [FromBody]string value)
  {
  }

  // DELETE api/values/5
  public void Delete(int id)
  {
  }
}
}
```

7. The created WebApiConfig file looks like the following:

```
using System.Web.Http;

namespace WebApplication5
{
  public static class WebApiConfig
  {
    public static void Register(HttpConfiguration config)
    {
      // Web API configuration and services

      // Web API routes
      config.MapHttpAttributeRoutes();

      config.Routes.MapHttpRoute(
        name: "DefaultApi",
        routeTemplate: "api/{controller}/{id}",
        defaults: new { id = RouteParameter.Optional }
      );
    }
  }
}
```

Visual Studio Kubernetes Tools

Kubernetes is an open source system that is a container orchestration system for applications. Kubernetes simplifies deployment and scaling operations of application containers. It runs on premises as well as in cloud providers such as **Azure Kubernetes Service (AKS)** for example.

Kubernetes defines a set of building blocks (also called *primitives*) that provide mechanisms for deploying, maintaining, and scaling applications based on memory, CPU or custom metrics.

Because of the Kubernetes API, Kubernetes is loosely coupled, so it is extensible to meet different workloads. The Kubernetes platform defines resources as objects. The central objects are as follows:

- **Pods:** A pod is composed of one or more containers that will be co-located on the host and can share resources. Each pod has a unique Pod IP address within the cluster, which allows apps to use ports without any risk of conflict. Pods define volumes such as a local disk folder or a network drive, and then expose it to the containers in the pod.

- **Services:** A Kubernetes service is a group of pods that work together. This group or set is defined by a label selector.

- **Volumes:** Filesystems in the Kubernetes Container provide short-term storage. A Kubernetes volume provides persistent (long-term) storage that exists for the entirety of the pod's life.

- **Namespaces:** A Kubernetes namespace is a way to partition managed resources to non-overlapping sets. These can be used in environments with users spread across multiple teams, or projects.

Installing Kubernetes

Installation of Kubernetes is quite easy. The following steps will guide you to install it:

1. Install Visual Studio 2019.

2. Install the ASP.NET and web development workload.

3. Ensure Visual Studio Tools for Kubernetes is installed.

4. Navigate to

   https://marketplace.visualstudio.com/items?itemName=ms-kubernetes-tools.vscode-kubernetes-tools.

5. Click on **Install**. The following screen should appear:

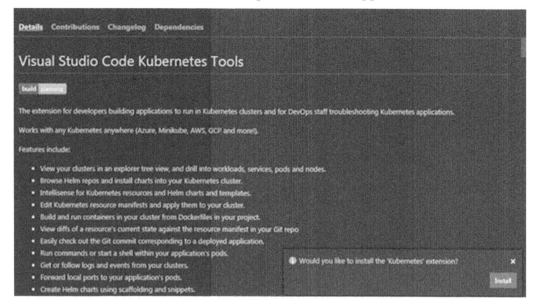

Figure 9.14: *Kubernetes*

6. Click on **Install** at the bottom right-hand corner of the screen. Kubernetes will be installed.

To create a Kubernetes Container application, perform the following steps:

1. Create a new Visual Studio 2019, C# project.

2. Search for the **Container Application for Kubernetes** template.

3. Once found, click on **Next**.

4. Then, enter the project details.

5. Click on **Create**.

6. Select **Web Application** on the next screen.

7. Click on **Create**.

8. The **Solution Explorer** window should resemble to the following screenshot:

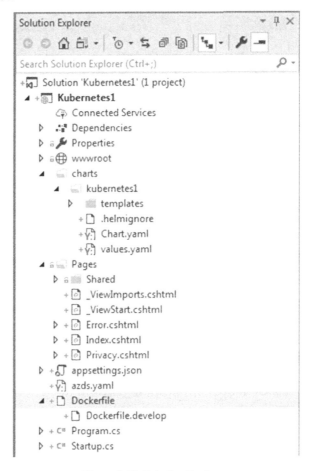

Figure 9.15: *Solution Explorer*

A few of the added files to the solution are as follows:

- `Dockerfile:` This allows us to generate a Docker container image to host a web application. Docker is a collection of **SaaS (Software-as-a-Service)** and **PaaS (Platform-as-a-Service)** services that employ operating-system-level virtualization for the development and delivery of software in standardized software packages, which are called containers.

- `Helm chart:` Helm manages Kubernetes applications. Helm charts define, install, and upgrade Kubernetes applications.

- `azds.yaml:` This YAML file contains the settings for Azure Dev Spaces. YAML (YAML Ain't Markup Language) is a simple, legible data-serialization language.

Conclusion

In this chapter, we explored ASP.NET and web tools. We learned how important it is to have several tools working together. We looked at the Web API and web frameworks. We also learned about the MVC web framework, which is the preferred framework to follow when developing websites. We also took a look at Cloud tools such as Kubernetes and Amazon Cognito.

In the next chapter, we will explore Mobile tools in .NET. We will also cover what they are, where to find them, and how to use them.

Questions

Q. 1.   Name three Web frameworks.

Q. 2.   What does Blazor enable us to do?

Q. 3.   Amazon Cognito consists of two main components. Name them.

Q. 4.   Name three Web API features

Q. 5.   Explain Visual Studio Kubernetes Tools.

CHAPTER 10
Mobile Tools

Mobile devices have become part and parcel of what we are. Phones are not just phones anymore; they are mobile computers. We can send emails and use social media with the touch of a finger. We can edit and take photos; we can listen to and record music and videos.

We have become so dependent on our phones, tablets, and smart watches that we cannot imagine life without them anymore. Perhaps, it is because the world has become so busy that we always need to be connected, or perhaps it is because we are always connected that the world has become so busy.

A mobile plays an essential role in the development scope.Because we use mobile devices to stay connected, we as programmers must use the best tools at our disposal to create the best possible mobile experiences for users. Users is the keyword here. We develop everything for the users, and when they are not happy, the app fails as simple as that.

We must also keep in mind that a company's website must look, feel and act in the same way as it does on a normal computer or laptop. Mobiles are not just about apps.

Structure

- JSON
- Xamarin
- DevExtreme
- Emulators and Simulators

Objective

In this chapter, we will learn about Mobile tools that we can use with Visual Studio 2019. We will learn about Xamarin and DevExtreme to create a nice experience for the user. We will touch on JSON and NuGet once again. JSON is the quickest and best way to deal with any data. Lastly, we will talk about Emulators and Simulators.

JSON

JSON **(JavaScript Object Notation)** is a lightweight format used for storing and transporting data from a server to a web page. JSON is quite easy to understand, as it is self-describing. The reason we are doing JSON here and now is because most of the data sent and received will be in JSON format, and the better you understand it, the easier it becomes to build apps properly. The following data types exist in JSON:

- **Number:** Any signed (positive or negative) decimal number that can contain fractions and the exponential *E* notation. This number may not contain non-numbers such as *NaN*.

- **String:** Any sequence of zero or more Unicode characters.

- **Boolean:** Either true or false.

- **Array:** An ordered list of zero or more values.

- **Object:** (also called a key) An unordered collection of name–value pairs.

- **null:** An empty value.

JSON structure

Objects inside a JSON document are enclosed between curly braces and make use of commas to separate the name and value pairs. The name is on the left side and the value is on the right side. In between is a colon. Arrays are enclosed with square brackets ([]) and make use of commas to separate each pair in the array.

The following code shows an example a JSON document:

```
{
  "FirstName": "Ockert",
  "LastName": "du Preez",
  "Age": 40,
  "Address": {
    "StreetAddress": "135 Danie Smal Street",
    "City": "Meyerton",
    "Province": "Gauteng",
    "Country": "South Africa"
    "PostalCode": "1960"
  },
  "PhoneNumbers": [
    {
      "Type": "Office",
      "Number": "012 345 6789"
    },
    {
      "Type": "Mobile",
      "Number": "987 654 3210"
    }
  ]
}
```

Without much trouble, a person is able to figure out what information has been sent in the previous example. Personal details such as `FirstName`, `LastName`, and `Age` are supplied. The `Address` is also supplied, but it is also broken up into sub-pieces (`StreetAddress`, `City`, `Province`, `Country`, and `PostalCode`). `Phone Numbers` is an array that holds two entities: one entity for the office number and another for the mobile number.

It gets more complicated, and the next topic will cover it.

JSON schemas

A JSON schema specifies a JSON-based format that defines the structure of JSON data for documentation, validation, and interaction control. A JSON schema provides a contract for JSON data that is required by a given application, and how this data can then be modified.

A JSON document being validated is called the **instance**; the document that contains the description is called the **schema**.

An example of a JSON schema looks like the following:

```
{
  "$schema": "http://json-schema.org/schema#",
  "title": "Student",
  "type": "object",
  "required": ["StudentID", "StudentName", "StudentMarks"],
  "properties": {
    "StudentID": {
      "type": "number",
      "description": "Student Identifier"
    },

    "StudentName": {
      "type": "string",
      "description": "Name of Student"
    },

    "StudentMarks": {
      "type": "number",
      "minimum": 0
    },

    "StudentSubjects": {
      "type": "array",
```

```
      "items": {

        "type": "string"

      }

    },

  }

}
```

The preceding JSON schema indicates that the `StudentID`, `StudentName`, and `StudentMarks` fields are required. `StudentSubjects` is not required. Although, it is specified later in the schema. The properties for each field are listed. These properties include the type of fields as well as the description of the fields. Lastly, the `StudentSubjects` field is supplied with its properties. It accepts an array of items of type string.

Now, we can use the precedings chema to test the validity of the following JSON code:

```
{

  "StudentID": 1,

  "StudentName": "Ockert",

  "StudentMarks": 99,

  "StudentSubjects": [

    "C#",

    "SQL"

  ]

}
```

This JSON data is passed through the JSON schema, and if it passes the validation, the data is accepted and can be used.

Combining multiple subschemas

A JSON schema includes keywords for combining subschemas. Combining subschemas allows a certain array value to be validated against multiple criteria at the same time.

The keywords to combine schemas are as follows:

- `allOf`

- anyOf
- oneOf
- not

Let us discuss the schema-combining-keywords:

- allOf: The allOf keyword validates the JSON data against all the subschemas. Keep in mind that when making use of the allOf keyword, it can be quite easy to create a logical impossibility. This means that two conflicting subschemas are created, thus causing the JSON data to always fail.

  The following code segment illustrates how to make use of the allOf keyword to create a combined schema:

```
{
  "allOf": [
{ "type": "string" },
{ "maxLength": 10 }
  ]
}
```

  This forces the supplied JSON array item to conform to its properties. The data must be a string and the maximum length of the supplied data is 10 characters. Any string longer than 10 characters will not be valid.

- anyOf: The anyOf keyword ensures that the supplied JSON array item is valid against any (at least one) of the subschemas. Here is an example of using anyOf:

```
{
  "anyOf": [
{ "type": "number" },
{ "type": "string" }
  ]
}
```

  The preceding code sample accepts either a number or a string.

- oneOf: When validating a JSON array item against oneOf, the supplied data must be valid against exactly one of the subschemas. Here are two examples (which tests for the same data):

Example 1:

```
{
  "oneOf": [
{ "type": "number", "multipleOf": 7 },
{ "type": "number", "multipleOf": 10 }
  ]
}
```

The supplied JSON data must either be a number, which is a multiple of 7. For example, 49,14, or a number that is a multiple of 10 such as 100 or 40.

Example 2 is a shorter version of Example 1:

```
{
  "type": "number",
  "oneOf": [
{ "multipleOf": 7 },
{ "multipleOf": 10 }
  ]
}
```

- not: The not keyword ensures that a given value validates when it does not validate against the supplied subschema. Here is an example:

```
{
  "not": {
    "type": "string"
  }
}
```

Any value supplied that is not of the string type will be accepted. Any string value that is supplied will not be valid.

Complex schemas

We can structure a JSON schema so that parts of it can be reused, instead of having to type the subschemas repeatedly. This is similar to writing a sub-procedure or method in C# that can be reused numerous times in a program. A simple example would be of clicking on the **Copy** button on a toolbar, or pressing *Ctrl* + *C*, or selecting edit and copy. Instead of writing the code three times, it can be written once and reused.

A complex schema can function in the same way. Here is an example of having to write repetitive subschemas in a JSON schema specification:

```
"HomeAddress": {
  "type": "object",
  "properties": {
    "StreetAddress": { "type": "string" },
    "City":          { "type": "string" },
    "Province":      { "type": "string" },
    "Country":       { "type": "string" }
  },
  "required": ["StreetAddress", "City", "Country"]
},


"WorkAddress": {
  "type": "object",
  "properties": {
    "StreetAddress": { "type": "string" },
    "City":          { "type": "string" },
    "Province":      { "type": "string" },
    "Country":       { "type": "string" }
  },
  "required": ["StreetAddress", "City", "Country"]
}
```

In the precedingcode segment, `HomeAddress` and `WorkAddress` have the exact same properties and expect the exact same data. This code can be shortened so that we can specify a section that can be reused.

Let us take a look at the following code segment example:

```
{
  "definitions": {
    "Address": {
      "type": "object",
      "properties": {
        "StreetAddress": { "type": "string" },
        "City":          { "type": "string" },
        "Province":          { "type": "string" }
        "Country":          { "type": "string" }
      },
      "required": ["StreetAddress", "City", "Country"]
    }
  }
}
```

It is customary to create a key in your JSON schema named definitions for reusable keys and properties. Now, to be able to reuse the `Address` key, we need to make use of the `$ref` keyword.

The following code shows the use of the `$ref` keyword:

```
{ "$ref": "#/definitions/Address" }
```

To improve on our preceding code segment, we can now simply do the following:

```
{
  "definitions": {
    "Address": {
      "type": "object",
      "properties": {
        "StreetAddress": { "type": "string" },
        "City":          { "type": "string" },
        "Province":          { "type": "string" },
        "Country":          { "type": "string" }
```

```
    },
    "required": ["StreetAddress", "City", "Country"]
  }
},


"type": "object",
"properties": {
  "HomeAddress": { "$ref": "#/definitions/Address" },
  "WorkAddress": { "$ref": "#/definitions/Address" }
}
}
```

Because Address is specified, we can reference it as many times as we need using the $ref keyword, as the preceding code segment shows.

Xamarin

Xamarin apps contain native user interface controls, which behave and look familiar and behave tothe endusers. These apps have access to the entire device's exposed functionality and they can leverage platform-specific hardware acceleration.

Xamarin is currently (at the time of writing this book) the only IDE that enables native Android, iOS, and Windows app development within Visual Studio 2019. Xamarin provides add-ins to Visual Studio 2019 that enables developers to build apps easily within the Visual Studio IDE using code completion and IntelliSense. Xamarin also has extensions within Visual Studio that support building, deploying, and debugging of Xamarin apps on a simulator or a directly on a device.

Installing Xamarin

To install Xamarin, follow the following steps:

1. Download any one of the Visual Studio 2019 suites from the Visual Studio page.

2. Start the installation.

3. Select the **Mobile development with .NET** workload from the installation screen, as shown in the following screenshot:

Figure 10.1: *Mobile development with .NET workload*

4. Click on the **Install** button atthe bottom right-hand corner of the screen.

Xamarin.Forms

Xamarin.Forms, a subset of Xamarin, is a cross-platform UI toolkit. This allows developers to create native user interface layouts that can be shared across platforms (Android, iOS, UWP). Xamarin.Forms allows you to share the business logic and data structures, and define the UI using common platform-independent controls.

Creating a Xamarin.Forms app

You need to perform the following steps to create a Xamarin.Forms application:

1. Select **File | New | Project**.
2. Choose **Mobile** from the **Project type** drop-down menu.

3. Select `Mobile App (Xamarin.Forms)`, as shown in the following screenshot:

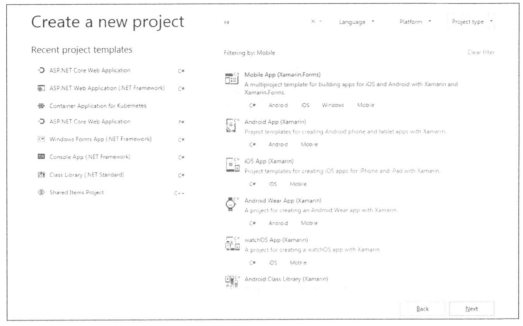

Figure 10.2: New Xamarin project

4. Click on **Next**. Enter the project details.
5. Click **Create**.
6. Click on the **Blank** project type.
7. Make sure **Android** and **iOS** check boxes are selected, as shown in the following screenshot:

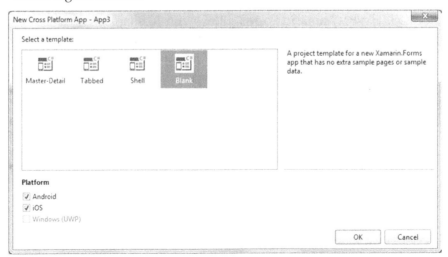

Figure 10.3: Blank Xamarin.Forms app

8. If necessary, accept the **Android SDK Licence**, as shown in the following screenshot:

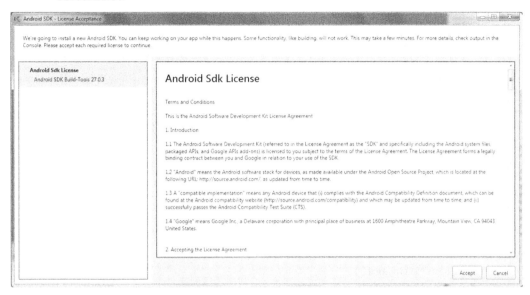

Figure 10.4: *Android SDK License*

9. After the project has loaded, open the `MainPage.xaml` file and edit it to look like the following code segment:

```
<?xml version="1.0" encoding="utf-8" ?>

<ContentPage xmlns="http://xamarin.com/schemas/2014/forms"

             xmlns:x="http://schemas.microsoft.com/winfx/2009/xaml"

             xmlns:local="clr-namespace:App3"

             x:Class="App3.MainPage">

<StackLayout>

<!-- Place new controls here -->

<Label Text="Welcome to Xamarin.Forms!"

       HorizontalOptions="Center"

       VerticalOptions="CenterAndExpand" />

<Button Text="Hello" Clicked="Button1_Clicked" />

</StackLayout>

</ContentPage>
```

10. Edit Main Page .xaml.cs to look like the following code segment:

```
using System.ComponentModel;

using Xamarin.Forms;


namespace App3
{
  // Learn more about making custom code visible in the Xamarin.
Forms previewer
  // by visiting https://aka.ms/xamarinforms-previewer
  [DesignTimeVisible(true)]
public partial class MainPage : ContentPage
  {
public MainPage()
    {
InitializeComponent();
    }
void Button1_Clicked(object sender, System.EventArgs e)
    {
      ((Button)sender).Text = $"Hello World!";
    }
  }
}
```

11. Click on the **Android Emulator** button to start it. The **New Device** setup dialog box may appear, which looks similar to the following screenshot:

Property	Value	Details
disk.dataPartition.size	800M	**disk.dataPartition.size**
hw.accelerometer	✓	
hw.audioInput	✓	Data partiton size.
hw.battery	✓	Default: 0
hw.camera.back	emulated	Specifies the size of the user data partition in bytes. If size is a simple integer, it specifies the size in bytes. You can also specify the size in kilobytes, megabytes, and gigabytes by appending K, M, or G to size. The minimum size is 9M and the maximum size is 1023G.
hw.camera.front	none	
hw.dPad	☐	
hw.gps	✓	
hw.gpu.mode	auto	
hw.keyboard	✓	
hw.lcd.density	420	
hw.lcd.height	1920	
hw.lcd.width	1080	
hw.mainKeys	☐	
hw.ramSize	1024	
hw.sdCard	✓	
hw.sensors.orientation	✓	
hw.sensors.proximity	✓	
hw.trackBall	☐	
sdcard.size	100M	

Name: My Device
Base Device: Nexus 5X
Processor: x86
OS: Oreo 8.1 – API 27
☑ Google APIs
☑ Google Play Store

Add Property   A new device image will be downloaded   Cancel   Create

Figure 10.5: New Device setup

12. The device will be setup and be created. It might take some time.

13. When the Emulator runs, it will display the little project that we created. It will show the button with the initial caption of Hello, and after you click on it, it will show HELLO WORLD!, as shown in the following screenshot:

Figure 10.6: Our Xamarin app in action

DevExtreme

DevExtreme is a suite of components for creating responsive web applications for touch devices and desktops. The DevExtreme suite includes UI components that can be used with jQuery, Angular, AngularJS, Knockout, ASP.NET MVC or ASP.NET Core, React, and Vue. These include the data grid, interactive charts, data editors, and navigation widgets.

Installing DeveExtreme

Perform the following steps to download and install DevExtreme:

1. Navigate to **https://js.devexpress.com/Download/**.

2. Click on the **Download Free Trial** button.

3. After the setup has downloaded, run the installer.

4. Choose between **Trial Installation** and **Registered Installation**. The trial installation carries an expiration date, whereas the registered installation does not. The following screenshot displays these options:

Figure 10.7: DevExtreme installation options

5. Ensure that Visual Studio 2019 is closed, and then select an option and continue with all the steps.

Emulators and Simulators

A simulator is a virtual environment that models or mimics real-world applications such as flying and driving. An emulator is a software that allows a computer software to function and behave identical to a certain software that is being emulated would.

Let us talk about simulators and emulators in a mobile programming environment. When an app needs to be tested, it can be tested by either connecting the physical device, or deploying the app to a physical device. Now, if there is no device available, what else can be done?

Differences between Simulators or Emulators to test apps

There are quite a few differences between simulators and emulators when it comes to testing mobile apps. The following table explains them in detail:

Simulators	Emulators
A simulator simulates the internal state of an object as close as possible to the internal state of an object.	An emulator emulates or mimics the outer behavior of an object.
Whenever a developer or testing team needs to test a mobile device's external behavior, simulators are preferable.	Whenever a developer or testing team needs to test the mobile device's internal behavior, emulators are preferable.
Simulators are usually written in high-level programming languages.	Emulators are usually written in machine-level assembly languages.
Simulators are difficult to use for debugging.	Emulators are more suitable to use for debugging.

Table 10.1: Differences between Simulators and Emulators

Visual Studio 2019 Android Emulator

A default emulator is installed when the Android SDK is installed, as shown previously in the Xamarin exercise we did earlier. The following screenshot shows the screen that pops up whenever the emulator is started by running the application.

This is the **Android Device Manager**, which is shown in the following screenshot:

Figure 10.8: Android Device Manager

The **Android Device Manager** displays various properties of the selected device. It shows the Android version, the processor, available memory, and its resolution. It is a nice feature where the emulator can be stopped and run independently.

Setting up a new device

Setting up a new device is quite simple. When you click on the **New** button, in the **Android Device Manager**, the **New Device** window will appear, as shown in the following screenshot. Here, the various properties of the device can be changed. Properties that are not normally available can also be added by selecting a property from the **Add Property** drop-down list, as shown in the following screenshot:

Figure 10.9: Add Property

Any of these properties can be added, and with the help of Xamarin, we can get even more access to native device properties.

Conclusion

In this chapter, we explored mobile tools. We explored JSON and JSON schemas and learned how powerful it is to send information from and to the web server. We also learned about Xamarin and DevExtreme, which can help us build native apps. Lastly, we learned how to test our mobile apps with emulators and simulators.

In the next chapter, we will explore Azure tools in .NET. In *Chapter 11: Azure Tools,*we will explore Azure, Azure SDK, Docker, and Azure IoT tools. It is a fun chapter!

Questions

Q. 1. Describe the term JSON schema.

Q. 2. What is the difference between a simulator and an emulator?

Q. 3. What is the difference between the `allOf` and `anyOf` JSON schema keywords?

Q. 4. Which tool do we use to install new Android devices to emulate?

Q. 5. What is DevExtreme?

CHAPTER 11
Azure Tools

Microsoft Azure is a cloud computing service designed for building, testing, deploying, and managing services and applications through managed data centers. Azure provides **platform as a service (PaaS), software as a service (SaaS), and infrastructure as a service (IaaS)**. It supports a variety of different programming languages, tools, and frameworks, both Microsoft-specific and third-party software.

Structure

- Internet of Things (IoTs)
- SAP on Azure
- Artificial Intelligence
- Azure DevOps
- Azure Blockchain Service

Objective

In this chapter we will cover all things related to Azure Cloud computing. These include IoTs, AI and Blockchain.

Internet of Things (IoTs)

The IoTs is the expansion of internet connectivity into physical devices and common everyday objects, such as kettles, TVs, fridges, and alarm systems - to name but a few. Devices embedded with electronics, internet connectivity, and sensors can communicate and interact with other devices over the Internet, and they can be remotely monitored and controlled.

Azure for IoT reduces complexity, lowers costs, and speeds up time to market. Azure for IoT is secure, open, and scalable and includes the following:

- **Azure IoT Hub:** Azure IoT Hub is a managed service that is hosted in the cloud, which acts as a central message hub for bi-directional communication between the devices and the IoT application. It is used to build IoT solutions with secure and reliable communications between IoT devices and a cloud-hosted solution backend. It supports numerous messaging patterns such as file upload from devices, device-to-cloud telemetry, and request-reply methods. It helps to build scalable and full-featured IoT solutions.

- **Azure IoT Edge:** Azure IoT Edge moves custom business logic and cloud analytics to devices so that organizations can focus on business insights and not data management. Analytics drives business value in IoT solutions. Azure IoT Edge contains three components, which are as follows:

    o IoT Edge modules which are containers that run Azure services, third-party services, or custom code.

    o The IoT Edge runtime that manages the modules deployed to each device.

    o A cloud-based interface that enables remote monitoring and managing IoT Edge devices.

- **Azure IoT Central:** Azure IoT Central is a fully managed SaaS solution to connect, monitor, and manage IoT assets at scale. It simplifies the initial setup of IoT solutions and reduces operational costs, the management and overhead of an IoT project.

- **Azure IoT solution Accelerators:** Azure IoT solution accelerators are complete, ready-to-deploy IoT solutions that implement common IoT scenarios. These include predictive maintenance, connected factory, remote monitoring, and device simulation. When deploying an Azure IoT solution accelerator, it includes all the required cloud-based services and any required application code.

- **Azure Sphere:** Azure Sphere is a solution for creating secured, connected MCU (Microcontroller) devices. It includes an operating system and an application platform which allows provides product manufacturers to create internet-connected devices that can be monitored, controlled, maintained, and updated remotely.

- **Azure Digital Twins:** Azure Digital Twins is an Azure IoT service that can create comprehensive models of the physical environment. It can create spatial intelligence graphs to model relationships and interactions between spaces, devices and people. With Azure Digital Twins we can query data from physical spaces rather than from many discordant sensors. It has the following capabilities:

  o The spatial intelligence graph which is a virtual portrayal of the physical environment

  o Digital twin object models which are predefined device protocols and data schemas

  o Multiple and nested tenants

  o Advanced compute capabilities

  o Built-in access control

  o Ecosystem

- **Azure Time Series Insights:** Azure Time Series Insights stores, visualizes, and queries large amounts of time series data generated by IoT devices. Time Series Insights has these functions:

  o It connects to event sources and parses JSON from messages and structures in clean rows and columns.

  o It manages the storage of data. It stores data in memory and SSDs for up to 400 days.

  o It provides visualization with the help of the Time Series Insights explorer.

- **Azure Maps:** Azure Maps provides developers powerful geospatial capabilities. It is an Azure One API compliant set of REST APIs for Maps, Search, Routing, Traffic, Mobility, Time Zones, Geolocation, Geofencing, Map Data, and Spatial Operations.

SAP on Azure

SAP on Azure solutions helps optimize **enterprise resource planning (ERP)** apps in the cloud, by using security features, reliability and the scalable infrastructure of Azure.

The SAP on Azure solutions includes:

- **SAP HANA:** SAP HANA on Azure handles transactions and analytics in-memory on a single data copy to accelerate business processes and gain business intelligence. It on Azure offers the following:

- o On-demand M-series virtual machines certified for SAP HANA with 4 TB scale.

- o Purpose-built SAP HANA instances with 20 TB scale on a single node.

- o Scale out SAP HANA capabilities up to 60 TB.

- o A 99.99 percent **service-level agreement (SLA)** for large instances in a high-availability pair.

- **SAP S/4HANA:** SAP S/4HANA is designed specifically for in-memory computing. It on Azure offers the following:

  - o Seamless connectivity for users accessing SAP Fiori-based applications whilst using Azure ExpressRoute.

  - o A 99.99 percent SLA for critical ERP instances.

  - o Backup for SAP S/4HANA and SAP B/4 HANA, with a low recovery-time objective.

  - o Certification of SAP S/4HANA running on SUSE Linux Enterprise and Red Hat Enterprise Linux servers.

- **SAP BW/4HANA:** SAP BW/4HANA/SAP BW on HANA on Azure collects and connects to any data in real time with next-generation data warehouses that are built on SAP HANA.SAP BW/4HANA/SAP BW on HANA on Azure offers the following:

  - o Optimization of SAP business warehouses and analytics environments.

  - o SAP business warehouse configurations that cannot fail.

  - o Flexible scaling.

  - o Certification that SAP BW/4HANA is running on SUSE Linux Enterprise and Red Hat Enterprise Linux.

- **SAP NetWeaver:** SAP NetWeaver on Azure offers the following:

  - o Agility for non-production environments.

  - o Cost-effective storage options.

  - o 99.9 percent availability for single VMs.

  - o SAP NetWeaver runs on Windows, SUSE Linux Enterprise and Red Hat Enterprise Linux.

- **SAP Business One:** SAP Business One provides more agility with on-demand VM infrastructures from Azure and it lowers non-production system costs via automation capabilities in Azure. It on Azure offers the following:

  - o 99.9 percent availability for single VMs.

  - o SAP Business One runs on Azure VMs.

- SAP Hybris: SAP Hybris on Azure offers the following:
  - o Business continuity via Azure Backup and Azure Site Recovery.
  - o 99.9 percent availability for single VMs.
  - o SAP Hybris Commerce Platform 5.x and 6.x runs on Windows Server, SQL Server and Oracle databases.
- SAP Cloud Platform: SAP Cloud Platform on Azure offers the following:
  - o Cloud Foundry for managing cloud environments.
  - o Co-locate applications using SAP ERP data.
  - o Fast application development by using Azure Event Hubs and Azure Storage.

Artificial intelligence (AI)

Artificial intelligence (AI) is intelligence demonstrated by machines, whereas humans and animals display natural intelligence. AI is also used to describe machines that mimic cognitive (the ability to acquire knowledge and understanding through thought, experience, and senses) functions that humans associate with other human minds.

AI can be grouped into three types of systems:

- **Analytical AI:** Analytical AI has cognitive intelligence characteristics; these include using learning based on past experience to make future decisions and generating cognitive representation of the world.
- **Human-inspired AI:** Human-inspired AI contains elements from cognitive and emotional intelligence such as the understanding human emotions and considering them in their decision making.
- **Humanized AI:** Humanized AI is self-conscious and is self-aware and has characteristics of all types of competencies such as cognitive, emotional, and social intelligence.

Microsoft AI platform

The Microsoft AI platform contains a suite of tools, such as the Bot Framework, Cognitive Services, and Azure Machine Learning that allow developers to infuse AI into applications and scenarios, thus enabling intelligent experiences for their users.

The Microsoft AI platform (powered by Azure) supplies a set of interoperable services, APIs, libraries, frameworks, and tools for developers. These include:

- **Cognitive Services:** The Cognitive Services API capabilities are organized into vision, speech, language, knowledge and search. The APIs leverages pretrained computer vision algorithms to recognize things such as landmarks, celebrities, face attributes, emotion, gender, and written words. Language capabilities analyze key phrases, recognize commands from users, perform translations as well as spell check.

- **Customized Computer Vision Models:** CustomVision.AI enables us to bring our own data, and use it to train your computer vision models.

- **Custom Machine Learning and Deep Learning Models:** Azure Machine Learning enables data scientists to build and manage models at scale. Data stores such as SQL, DB, CosmosDB, SQL Data Warehouse, and Azure Data Lake (ADL) then give access to the data that informs machine learning and deep learning models.

Azure AI

Microsoft Azure is a set of cloud services to help organizations meet their business challenges. AI is the capability of machines to imitate human behavior. With Azure AI, machines can comprehend speech, analyses images, make predictions using data, and interact in natural ways.

Azure AI is divided into three categories:

- Knowledge mining
- Machine learning
- API apps and agents

Knowledge mining

Knowledge mining is using Cognitive Search to find enterprise data with help of **Azure Search** and **Form Recognizer**. This data can be emails, text files, documents, PDFs, images, scanned forms, and so on.

Azure Search is a cloud search service with built-in AI capabilities that enriches all types of information to identify and explore relevant content. Form Recognizer applies machine learning to extract text, key-value pairs, and tables from documents.

Machine learning

Azure enables us to build, train and deploy machine learning models using **Azure Machine Learning, Azure Databricks** and **ONNX**.

Azure Machine Learning is a Python-based machine learning service with automated machine learning and edge deployment capabilities. Azure Databricks is an Apache Spark-based big-data service with Azure Machine Learning integration. ONNX is an open-source model format and runtime for machine learning which enables us to move between frameworks and hardware platforms.

API apps and agents

These include **Cognitive Services** and the **Bot Service**. Let's do a practical exercise utilizing a Cognitive Services API to detect a face or faces.

Use the next steps to create a free Azure account and subscribe to the desired Cognitive Services APIs:

1. Navigate to the following URL: **https://azure.microsoft.com/en-gb/ free/?WT.mc_id=A261C142F**

2. Click on the **Start for free** button as shown in the following screenshot:

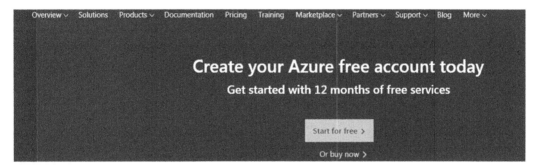

Figure 11.1: Start for free

3. Follow the prompts and fill in the desired information.

4. Navigate to the next URL to subscript to the Face API: **https://azure.microsoft. com/try/cognitive-services/?api=face-api**

5. Click on the **Subscribe** button. This adds the subscription and supplies all the keys and endpoints needed to create an app utilizing the API, as shown in the following screenshot:

Figure 11.2: Keys

Keep in mind that each App gets its own unique set of keys

6. Launch Visual Studio 2019.

7. Create a new **Console App (.NET Framework)**, as shown in the following screenshot:

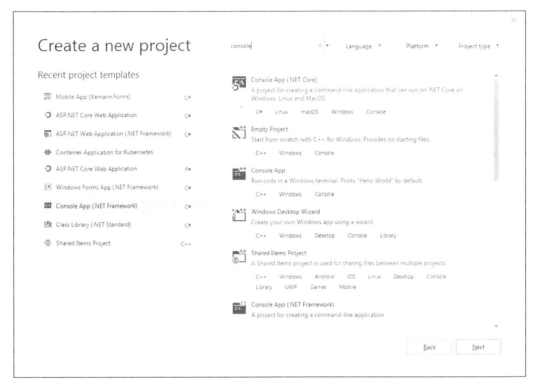

Figure 11.3: Console App

8. Click **Next**.

9. Supply a descriptive name and location for the project, click on **Create** button.

10. Add the necessary namespaces at the top of the Program.cs file, refer the following code snippet:

```
using System.IO;
using System.Net.Http;
using System.Net.Http.Headers;
```

11. Edit the Program.cs file to include the following code:

```
const string strKey = "YourKey";//"6e94db8d8df1405babec13d8f44627e7";
```

```
const string strInputURL = "https://westcentralus.api.cognitive.
microsoft.com/face/v1.0";

static void Main(string[] args)

{

  string strPath = "http://www.OJ.com/OJ.jpg";

  if (File.Exists(strPath))

  {

    try

    {

      AnalyzeImage(strPath);

      Console.WriteLine("\nProcessing.\n");

    }

    catch (Exception e)

    {

      Console.WriteLine("\n" + e.Message);

    }

  }

}

static async void AnalyzeImage(string strURL)

{

  HttpClient hcClient = new HttpClient();

hcClient.DefaultRequestHeaders.Add("Ocp-Apim-Subscription-Key",
strKey);

string strParam = "returnFaceId=true&returnFaceLandmarks=false" +

"&returnFaceAttributes=age,gender,headPose,smile,facialHair,
glasses,"+"emotion,hair,makeup,occlusion,accessories,blur,
exposure, noise";
```

```
        string uri = strInputURL + "?" + strParam;

    HttpResponseMessage hrmResponse;

    byte[] btData = GetBytes(strURL);

    using (ByteArrayContent content = new ByteArrayContent(btData))
    {
 content.Headers.ContentType=newMediaTypeHeaderValue("application/
octet-stream");

        hrmResponse = await hcClient.PostAsync(uri, content);

      string strResponse = await hrmResponse.Content.ReadAsStringAsync();

        Console.WriteLine(FormatOutput(strResponse));
    }
}

static byte[] GetBytes(string strURL)
{
    using (FileStream fsFile = new FileStream(strURL, FileMode.Open,
FileAccess.Read))
    {
        BinaryReader brReader = new BinaryReader(fsFile);
        return brReader.ReadBytes((int)fsFile.Length);
    }
}

static string FormatOutput(string strJSON)
{
    if (string.IsNullOrEmpty(strJSON))
        return string.Empty;
```

```
strJSON  =  strJSON.Replace(Environment.NewLine,  "").Replace("\t",
"");

    StringBuilder sbOutput = new StringBuilder();

    bool blnQuote = false;

    bool blnIgnore = false;

    int intOffset = 0;

    int intIndent = 4;

    foreach (char ch in strJSON)
    {
      switch (ch)
      {
        case '"':
          if (!blnIgnore) blnQuote = !blnQuote;
            break;
        case '\'':
          if (blnQuote) blnIgnore = !blnIgnore;
            break;
      }

      if (blnQuote)
        sbOutput.Append(ch);
      else
      {
        switch (ch)
        {
          case '{':
          case '[':
            sbOutput.Append(ch);
            sbOutput.Append(Environment.NewLine);
```

```
        sbOutput.Append(new string(' ', ++intOffset * intIndent));
      break;
    case '}':
    case ']':
      sbOutput.Append(Environment.NewLine);
      sbOutput.Append(new string(' ', --intOffset * intIndent));
      sbOutput.Append(ch);
      break;
    case ',':
      sbOutput.Append(ch);
      sbOutput.Append(Environment.NewLine);
      sbOutput.Append(new string(' ', intOffset * intIndent));
      break;
    case ':':
      sbOutput.Append(ch);
      sbOutput.Append(' ');
      break;
    default:
      if (ch != ' ') sbOutput.Append(ch);
      break;
    }
  }
}


  return sbOutput.ToString().Trim();
}
```

12. The code loads an image file from a supplied URL. It then analyses the image based on the parameters we supplied. Finally, it provides an output in JSON format.

13. The resulting output from the previous code may be similar to the following:

```
[
  {
    "faceId": "f6dde276-6421-44b4-8bdd-bc11c6dec812",
    "faceRectangle": {
      "top": 120,
      "left": 150,
      "width": 162,
      "height": 162
    },
    "faceAttributes": {
      "smile": 0.78,
      "headPose": {
        "pitch": 1.7,
        "roll": 2.3,
        "yaw": 3
      },
      "gender": "male",
      "age": 42.9,
      "facialHair": {
        "moustache": 0.7,
        "beard": 0.88,
        "sideburns": 0.06
      },
      "glasses": "sunglasses",
      "emotion": {
        "anger": 0.321,
        "contempt": 0.0,
    "disgust": 0.04,
        "fear": 0.02,
          "happiness": 0.495,
          "neutral": 0.023,
```

```
    "sadness": 0.0,
    "surprise": 0.005
},
"blur": {
    "blurLevel": "low",
    "value": 0.06
},
"exposure": {
    "exposureLevel": "goodExposure",
    "value": 0.78
},
"noise": {
    "noiseLevel": "low",
    "value": 0.15
},
"makeup": {
    "eyeMakeup": false,
    "lipMakeup": false
},
"accessories": [

],
"occlusion": {
    "foreheadOccluded": false,
    "eyeOccluded": false,
    "mouthOccluded": false
},
"hair": {
    "bald": 0.67,
    "invisible": false,
    "hairColor": [
        {
```

```
          "color": "brown",
          "confidence": 0.04
      },
      {
          "color": "black",
          "confidence": 0.87
      },
      {
          "color": "other",
          "confidence": 0.51
      },
      {
          "color": "blond",
          "confidence": 0.08
      },
      {
          "color": "red",
          "confidence": 0.0
      },
      {
          "color": "gray",
          "confidence": 1.0
      }
    ]
  }
  }
  }
]
```

Azure DevOps

Azure DevOps is a practice that unifies people, processes, and technology, development, and IT in five practices:

- Planning and tracking
- Development
- Build and test
- Delivery
- Monitoring and operations

While practicing DevOps different teams from different disciplines such as development, IT operations, quality engineering, and security, all work together.

Practicing a DevOps model

Teams across different disciplines follow the following phases through their delivery pipeline:

- **Plan and track:** Identify and track work visually by using practices such as Kanban boards and agile.

- **Developing:** Write code with the help of version control systems such as Git to integrate continuously to the master branch.

- **Build and test:** With an automated build process, the code is tested and validated immediately. This ensures that bugs are caught early in development.

- **Deploying:** By using continuous delivery practices, the final deployment to production is ultimately a manually controlled business decision.

- **Monitor and operate:** Once the app is live in production, monitoring delivers vital information about the app's performance and usage patterns.

Azure Blockchain Service

Blockchain is a transparent and verifiable system for exchanging values and assets. It is a shared, secure ledger of transactions distributed among a network of computers, instead of a single provider. Azure Blockchain Service simplifies the formation, management and governance of Blockchain networks so developers can focus on business logic and app development.

Now that we know more about the Azure Blockchain Service, let's create a managed ledger by using the following steps:

1. Use the steps explained previously to create an Azure account, if necessary, else sign in to the Azure portal by using this URL: **https://portal.azure. com/#home**

2. Select **Create a resource**.

3. Select **Blockchain | Azure Blockchain Service**, as shown in the following screenshot:

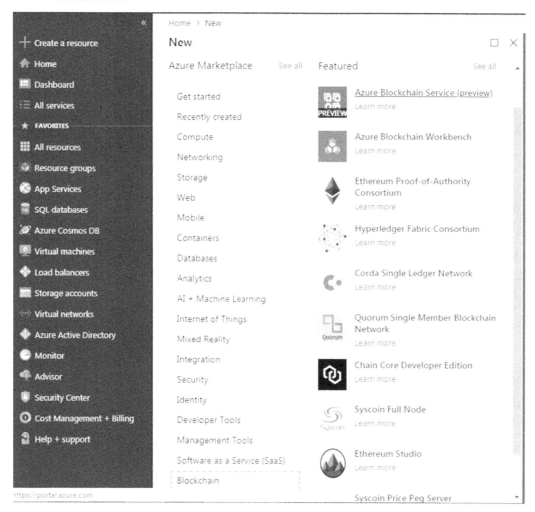

Figure 11.4: Azure Blockchain Service

4. Select **Start Free**, if necessary.

5. Fill in the necessary details of the Blockchain member, as listed in the following table:

Property	Value
Blockchain Member	A unique name between 2 and 20 characters, containing only lowercase letters and numbers
Subscription	A valid Azure subscription
Resource Group	A resource group name (existing or new)
Region	Consortium members location
Member Account Password	Used to encrypt the private key for the Ethereum account that is created for the member.
Consortium name	A unique Consortium name
Description	Consortium Description
Protocol	Quorum protocol
Pricing	Node configuration for the new service
Transaction node password	Password for the new member's default transaction node

Table 11.1: Blockchain Member Properties

6.   Select Create. The Blockchain member will be created.

Conclusion

In this chapter, we explored Azure tools. We explored Internet of Things in the Cloud, Blockchain, and Artificial Intelligence.

In the next chapter, we willexplore the world of IDE Extensions.

Questions

Q. 1.   Explain the term IoT

Q. 2.   Name three SAP on Azure solutions.

Q. 3.   What is knowledge mining?

Q. 4.   Explain the term Azure DevOps

Q. 5.   What is the Blockchain?

SECTION IV

Extensions

- IDE Extensions
- ASP.NET Extensions
- Mobile Extensions
- Azure Extensions

## CHAPTER 12

IDE Extensions

Extensions or Add-Ins are code packages that can run inside the Visual Studio 2019 IDE. Extensions provide new or improved Visual Studio features. This can be anything from improving on scrolling features, to improving the IDE windows.

Structure

- Preview label for Visual Studio Extensions
- GitHub
- Pull Requests for Visual Studio
- Microsoft Visual Studio Live Share
- Arduino IDE for Visual Studio
- Redgate SQL Change Automation Core

Objective

In this chapter we will learn about advanced Visual Studio Extensions. Extensions exist to make our lives easier. We will learn how to collaborate with team members through GitHub and Visual Studio Team Explorer. We will learn how to program computer boards with Arduino and have a quick look into the Redgate SQL Change Automation extension.

Visual Studio 2019 Extensions

As discussed in *Chapter 2: Digging into the Visual Studio 2019 IDE,* Extensions or Add-Ins are code packages that can run inside the Visual Studio 2019 IDE and provide new or improved Visual Studio features. This can be anything! From improving on scrolling features, to improving the IDE windows. There are literally thousands of Extensions available on the Visual Studio Marketplace: **https://marketplace.visualstudio.com/**

Visual Studio Marketplace is the exclusive place for purchasing and renewing subscriptions, as well as for finding new extensions for Visual Studio and Visual Studio Code. Some extensions are free, whereas some are expensive. It all depends on the needs of the development team. Extensions exist so that our productivity can be improved.

Preview label for Visual Studio Extensions

Extensions for Visual Studio 2019 are now marked with a Preview label next to it, on the Visual Studio Marketplace. This provides developers the freedom of identifying Extensions that are still actively being developed, and which might still contain some issues, to their customers. This also allows developers to get feedback from their users earlier, as they actively test out new code changes to improve the extension.

An example of an Extension with the Preview label included (at the time of writing this book) can be found here:

https://marketplace.visualstudio.com/items?itemName=ms-azuretools.vs-containers-tools-extensions

The next screenshot shows the Extension on the marketplace

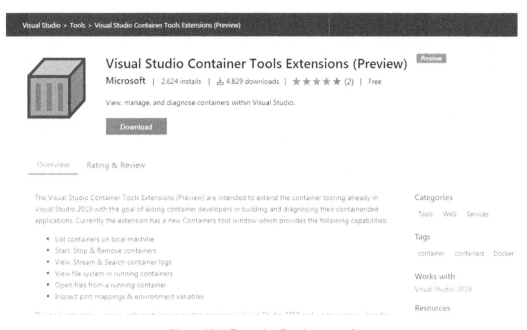

Figure 12.1: Extension Preview example

We have created extensions earlier in this book (in *Chapter 2: Digging into the Visual Studio 2019 IDE*), but here is a small refresher.

Creating a very basic Extension

Visual Studio SDK needs to be installed before you can develop Extensions for Visual Studio 2019. It can be installed when Visual Studio 2019 is being installed for the first time, or afterwards. Follow the following steps to create an Extension:

1. Create a new project and select VSIX as the template.

2. After the project has loaded, right-click the project node in **Solution Explorer**.

3. Select **Add | New Item.**

4. Expand the **Extensibility** node under **Visual C#**.

5. Choose from the available item templates (For our project, select **Custom Command**, as shown in the *Figure 12.2*):

    • Visual Studio Package

    • Editor Items

    • Command

    • Tool Window

    • Toolbox Control

6. Click on **Add** button.

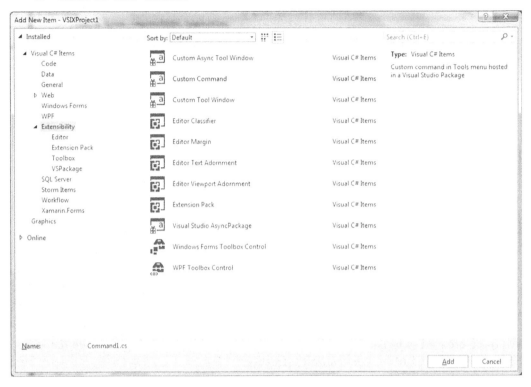

Figure 12.2: Extension

7. Double click the vsct file. The code will open. Make sure to read the comments as well as they explain what is happening. The vsct file is where we can change the design of the objects and add objects.

8. Change the text of the button to Click Me!, as shown in bold in the following code snippet:

```
<Button guid="guidVSIXProject1PackageCmdSet" id="Command1Id"
priority="0x0100" type="Button">

<Parent guid="guidVSIXProject1PackageCmdSet" id="MyMenuGroup" />

<Icon guid="guidImages" id="bmpPic1" />

<Strings>

<ButtonText>Click Me!</ButtonText>

</Strings>

</Button>
```

9. Open the `Command1.cs` file and modify the `Execute` procedure to the following:

```
private void Execute(object sender, EventArgs e)

{

ThreadHelper.ThrowIfNotOnUIThread();

string message = "My first Extension";

string title = "Extension Title";


    // Show a message box to prove we were here

VsShellUtilities.ShowMessageBox(

    this.package,

message,

title,

    OLEMSGICON.OLEMSGICON_INFO,

    OLEMSGBUTTON.OLEMSGBUTTON_OK,

    OLEMSGDEFBUTTON.OLEMSGDEFBUTTON_FIRST);

}
```

10. Run the Extension by clicking on the **Run/Start** button inside Visual Studio.

11. A new instance of Visual Studio Experimental Instance will be spawned, but, remember, this is just for testing the Extension. It still must be installed and published properly.

12. The following screenshot displays the Extension in action. On the **Tools** menu, select **Click Me**!:

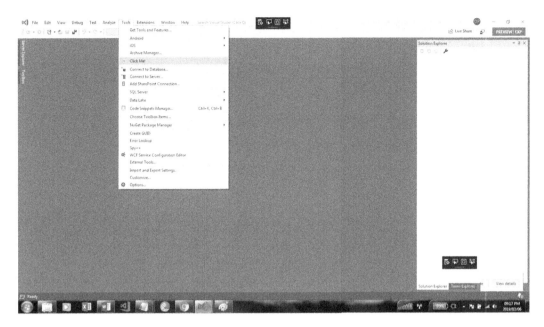

Figure 12.3: Test Extension

13. Click on it. A message box will appear, as shown in the following screenshot:

Figure 12.4: Test Extension Result

Add a preview label to an Extension

1. In the Extension's `.vsixmanifest` file, add the `<Preview>` element to the `<Metadata>` node, which is as follows:

```
<Metadata>
<Identity Id="GUID" Version="0.8" Language="en-US" Publisher="Name of Developer" />
<DisplayName>Extension Name</DisplayName>
```

```
<Description>Extension Description</Description>
<Icon>Resources\Icon.png</Icon>
<Preview>true</Preview>
</Metadata>
```

2. Navigate to Visual Studio Marketplace: **https://marketplace.visualstudio.com/**

3. Select Publish Extensions.

4. Fill in the required information.

5. Click **Create**.

GitHub

GitHub provides access control and collaboration features such as bug tracking, feature requests, task management, and wikis for every project. GitHub offers enterprise, team, pro, and free accounts (which are mostly used to host open-source software projects).

Creating a new repository

Use the following steps to create a new repository on GitHub:

1. Navigate to the next URL: **https://github.com/**

2. Sign into an existing account, or create a new one.

3. In the upper right corner, select the + sign, as shown in the following screenshot:

Figure 12.5: Create new repository

4. Select **Newrepository** option.

5. Enter the name and description for the repository, as shown in the following screenshot:

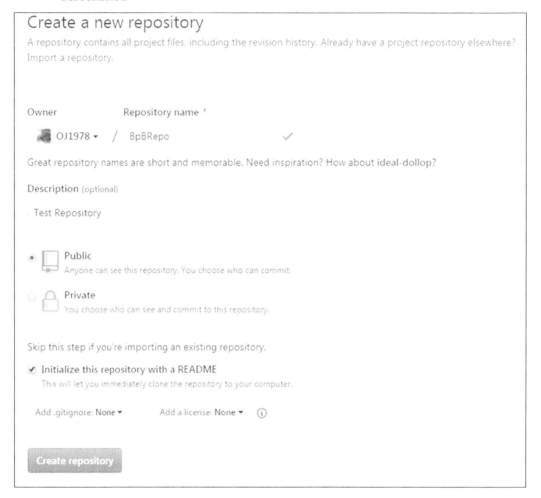

Figure 12.6: New repository properties

6. Click **Create repository**.

Forking a repository

A fork is simply a copy of a repository. Forking a repository allows developers to experiment with the repository without affecting the original project. Forks are mostly used to either propose changes (such as bug-fixes) to an existing project or to use the project as a starting point for another project.

Follow the following steps to fork a repository:

1. Navigate to any repository on GitHub. Luckily for us, GitHub has supplied a sample repository for us to use and experiment with!

2. Navigate to the **octocat/Spoon-Knife** repository **https://github.com/octocat/Spoon-Knife** as shown in the following screenshot:

Figure 12.7: *Example Repository to Fork*

3. Select **Fork** in the top-right corner.

This creates a fork to the repository, but doesn't actually give us the project files to experiment with. To do this, we have to **Clone or download** the repository.

Use the following steps to clone or download a repository:

1. Download and install a (using the default options) Git from the next URL if necessary: **https://git-scm.com/download/win**

2. Navigate to the **Fork** of the repository. This is usually found under repositories of the GitHub user's profile.

3. Select **Clone or download**, as shown in the following screenshot:

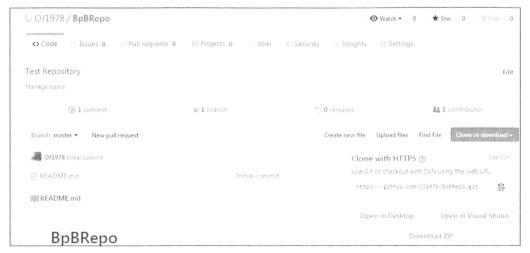

Figure 12.8: *Clone or download*

4. Click on the copy button (this is the button next to the URL in the **Clone with HTTPS** section).

5. Open Git Bash (assuming Git has been installed as explained earlier in this exercise)

6. Inside Git Bash type git clone.

7. Right click and paste the copied URL. It should look similar to the following command:

   ```
   $ git clone https://github.com/GITHUB-USERNAME/Spoon-Knife
   ```

8. Press *Enter*. A local clone will be created, as shown in the following screenshot:

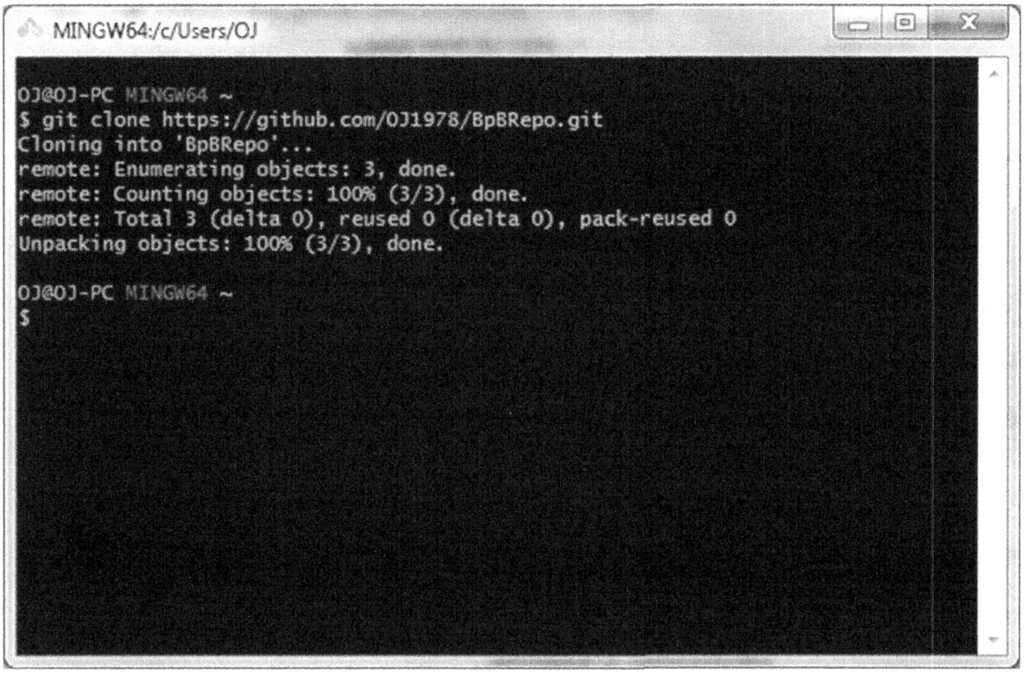

Figure 12.9: Git Bash

Another way to quickly download or clone a repository is to use the following steps:

1. Open Visual Studio 2019.

2. Click on the **Clone or check out code** button, as shown in the following screenshot:

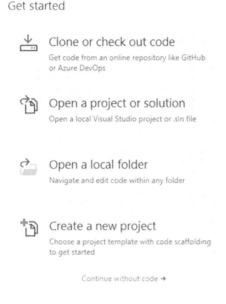

Figure 12.10: *Clone or check out code*

3. Enter the URL of the repository to be cloned.
4. Click **Clone**.

GitHub for desktop

GitHub for desktop provides a better experience when downloading or uploading repositories. Kit can be downloaded from here: **https://desktop.github.com/**

Pull Requests for Visual Studio

Pull requests let the main developer tell others about changes he or she pushed to a branch in a repository. Once a pull request is opened, developers can discuss and review potential changes with collaborators and add follow-up commits before the changes are merged into the base branch.

The Pull Requests for Visual Studio 2019 extension provides a set of code review tools for the Visual Studio IDE. With this extension we can:

- See a history of changes while coding
- Make live edits and set breakpoints

- Create new Pull Requests on Azure Repos

- Review and checkout Pull Requests from Azure Repos

- Add Likes

- Make comments over any span of code

- Use full markdown

Using the Pull Requests for Visual Studio Extension

Follow these steps to download and install the Pull Requests for Visual Studio extension:

1. Navigate to the following URL: **https://marketplace.visualstudio.com/items?itemName=VSIDEVersionControlMSFT.pr4vs**

2. Click **Download**.

3. Install the Extension by double clicking on the downloaded VSIX file.

Connect to an Azure Repo

The following steps explain how to connect to an Azure Repo:

1. Open **Team Explorer** and click the **Manage Connections** (the green plug) icon in the toolbar.

2. Click **Manage Connections | Connect to a Project**.

3. Sign in to an Azure account.

4. Select an **Azure Repo** from the list then click **Connect**. The following screenshot shows this box in action:

Figure 12.11:Connect to Azure Repo

5.   Click **Clone** in the **Team Explorer**.

Microsoft Visual Studio Live Share

Visual Studio Live Share enables developers to edit and debug with others collaboratively regardless what programming languages they're using or app types they're building. It allows developers to instantly their projects, debugging sessions, terminal instances, and local host web apps. It also allows developers to work together, while retaining their personal editor preferences.

Using Microsoft Visual Studio Live Share

Make use of the following steps to download, install and make use of Visual Studio Live Share:

1. Navigate to the following URL: **https://marketplace.visualstudio.com/ items?itemName=MS-vsliveshare.vsls-vs**

2. Download and install the Extension. The Live Share (as shown in the following screenshot) button will appear in Visual Studio 2019 afterwards:

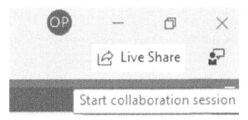

Figure 12.12: Live Share

3. Click **Live Share**.

4. Allow access for the Firewall, if necessary.

5. An invitation URL will be created, similar to what is shown in the following screenshot. Copy and send this URL to the required team members:

Figure 12.13: Invitation link

Arduino IDE for Visual Studio

Arduino is an open-source electronics platform. Arduino boards can read inputs such as light on a sensor, a finger on a button, or a Facebook post, and turn it into an output such as activating a motor or turning on an LED. We can tell an Arduino board what to do by sending instructions to the microcontroller on the board via the Arduino programming language.

Ensure that the Visual C++ Workload is installed as explained in *Chapter 1 - Getting Started with Visual Studio 2019:*

Installing Arduino IDE for Visual Studio

1. Navigate the VS Marketplace URL: **https://marketplace.visualstudio.com/ items?itemName=VisualMicro.ArduinoIDEforVisualStudio**

2. Download and install the Extension.

3. Run Visual Studio 2019.

4. Enter the details when prompted, as shown in the following screenshot:

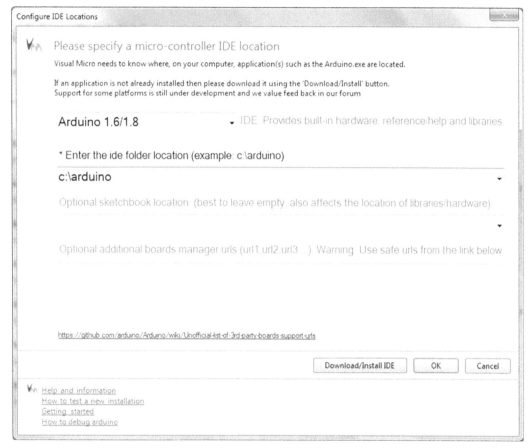

Figure 12.14: *Arduino options*

5. Click **OK**.

6. Select any of the Arduino projects, as shown in the following screenshot:

ar   × ▪ ▾   Language ▾   Platform ▾   Project type ▾

Single View App (iOS)

Single view application project for both iPhone and iPad. With storyboard support.

    F#   iOS   Mobile

Dynamic-Link Library with exports (DLL)

Build a .dll that can be shared between multiple running Windows apps.

Arduino Project

A new empty Arduino compatible project

Arduino Library Project

Add an Arduino compatible cross-platform library project then click "Add Reference" in any Arduino project to use the library. Include in the main code as a normal Arduino library. This project type does not build standalone. Requires VS2015 or above.

Arduino Shared Code Project

Add an Arduino shared project then click "Add Reference" in any Arduino project. The project code files are copied to temp during build and compiled alongside the main project code. Does not build standalone. Requires VS2015 or above.

Figure 12.15: Arduino projects

7. After the project has loaded, ensure that the correct Arduino IDE version is set and that a proper board and serial port are correctly selected. The following screenshot shows what it looks like when Arduino Uno on COM4 is used:

Arduino 1.6/1.8   ▾   Arduino/Genuino Uno   ▾   🔎 ⌄ COM4   ▾   🖳 Other▾ ⌄ ⚙ Add Library▾ Add Code▾ ⬆ ⓘ ⌄

Figure 12.16: Arduino Setup

8. Add the following code to play with an LED light:

```
// the setup function runs once when you press reset or power the board
void setup() {
```

```
pinMode(LED_BUILTIN, HIGH);

}


// the loop function runs over and over again until power down or
reset

void loop() {

digitalWrite(LED_BUILTIN, HIGH);

delay(1000);

digitalWrite(LED_BUILTIN, LOW);

delay(1000);

}
```

Redgate SQL Change Automation Core

Redgate SQL Change Automation Core is a migrations-first database development and deployment tool inside Visual Studio 2019. This enables us to:

- Prevent the database being a bottleneck
- Automate the deployment of database changes
- Manage database changes alongside application changes

Installing Redgate SQL Change Automation Core in Visual Studio 2019

Follow the following steps to install Redgate SQL Change Automation Core in Visual Studio 2019:

1. Download Redgate SQL Change Automation Core from this URL: **https://marketplace.visualstudio.com/items?itemName=vs-publisher-306627.RedgateSqlChangeAutomation**

Conclusion

In this chapter, we explored the world of Advanced IDE Extensions for Visual Studio 2019. We learned about GitHub and the importance of open-source computing and collaboration with other developers through GitHub and Visual Studio team Explorer. We saw how easy it is to work with programmable boards with Visual

Studio and the Arduino Extension. Lastly, we saw how the Redgate SQL Change Automation Core Extension can help us with our database oriented projects.

In the next chapter, we will explore advanced ASP.NET extensions including Web Compiler, Markdown Editor and a few third-party solutions.

Questions

Q. 1. What does forking a repository mean?

Q. 2. Explain the use of the Preview label for Visual Studio Extension

Q. 3. What is needed in order for the Arduino IDE for Visual Studio Extension to run on Visual Studio 2019?

Q. 4. What is a Pull Request?

Q. 5. Explain the use of the Redgate SQL Change Automation Core Extension.

## CHAPTER 13

ASP.NET Extensions

Extensions or Add-ins are code packages that can run inside Visual Studio 2019 ASP.NET. Extensions provide new or improved Visual Studio features for web applications.

Structure

- Markup Language
- Markdown
- Markdown Editor
- Web Compiler
- Web Accessibility Checker
- ASP.NET core VS Code Extension Pack

Objective

In this chapter, we will explore the world of advanced ASP.NET Extensions in Visual Studio 2019. We will learn about the markdown editor extension as well the markdown language in general. Next, we will have a look at the web compiler extension, and several other web languages such as LESS, JSX, Stylus, and SASS.

We will learn about the importance of web accessibility, to provide a better webexperience for everyone.

Markup language

A markup language is a programming language that makes use of tags to define elements within a document. Markup is human-readable and contains standard words, instead of a typical programming syntax. The most common markup languages are HTML and XML.

Markdown

Markdown is a light-weight markup language with a plain text formatting syntax. It can be converted to many output formats. Markdown is commonly used for writing messages in discussion forums to format readme files as well as to create rich (formatting-enabled) text using a plain text editor.

An example of a markdown script is as follows:

```
Main Heading

=======

## Sub-heading

Line break has two spaces after a line break.

Text formatting _italic text_,

**bold text**, `monospace`.

HR

---

Bullet list:

  * one

  * two

  * three

Numbered list:

  1. one

  2. two

  3. three

[Link text](http://example.com)

![Image Alt Text](ImageSource "Image Title")
```

The HTML equivalent of the preceding mark down code is as follows:

```
<h1>Main Heading</h1>
<h2>Sub-heading</h2>
<p>Line break has two spaces after a line break.</p>
<p>Text formatting <em>italic text</em>,
<strong>bold text</strong>, <code>monospace</code>.</p>
<hr />
<p>Bullet list:</p>
<ul>
<li>one</li>
<li>two</li>
<li>three</li>
</ul>
<p>Numbered list:</p>
<ol>
<li>one</li>
<li>two</li>
<li>three</li>
</ol>
<p>An<a href="http://example.com">Link text</a>.</p>
<p><img alt="Image Alt Text" title="Image Title" src="ImageSource" /></p>
```

By comparing the markdown code with its HTML markup equivalent, it is quite clear which one is quicker to edit; although an understanding of its tags is needed, as markdown is not as explanatory as HTML tags.

Markdown Editor

The Markdown Editor is a full-featured markdown editor that includes live preview, syntax highlighting and supports GitHub flavored Markdown. The Markdown editor includes these features: syntax highlighting, live preview window with scroll sync, high-DPI support, pastingimage from the clipboard directly to the document, outlining of code blocks, and keyboard shortcuts.

Working with the Markdown Editor

The following steps demonstrate how to download, install, and use the Markdown Editor extension:

1. Navigate to the Visual Studio Marketplace at **https://marketplace. visualstudio.com/items?itemName=MadsKristensen.MarkdownEditor**

2. Download the Extension.

3. Double click on the VSIX file to install the extension.

4. In the Visual Studio 2019 IDE, select **Tools | Options | Environment | Fonts and Colors**.

5. Scroll down to find the markdown formatting options, as shown in the following screenshot:

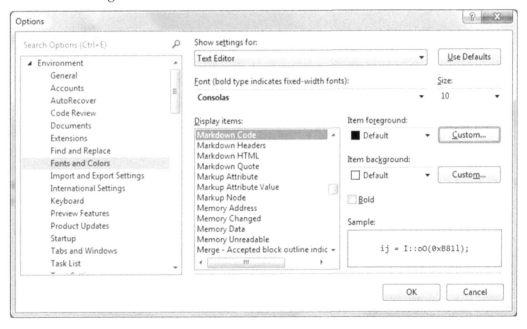

Figure 13.1: Markdown formatting options

6. Set them as desired.

7. In the same dialog box, navigate to **Text Editor**.

8. Select **Markdown | Advanced**, as shown in the following screenshot:

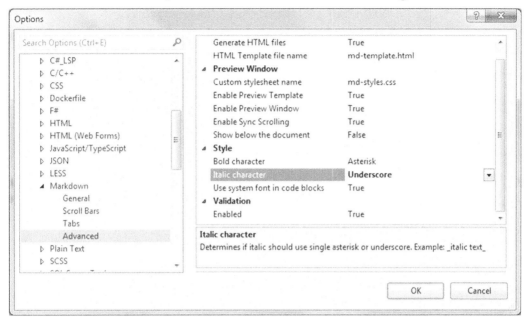

Figure 13.2: Markdown settings

9. Set the **Properties** as desired.

Web Compiler

The Web Compiler Visual Studio extension compiles Less, Scss, Stylus, and JSX files within the Visual Studio IDE or using the MS Build compiling tool.

Now, what are these files?

Let us examine them one by one:

- Less
- Scss
- Stylus
- JSX

Less

Leaner Style Sheets(Less) is a backwards-compatible language extension for **Cascading Style Sheets (CSS).** It is a dynamic pre-processor style sheet language that can be compiled into CSS and run on the client side or server side.

Less adds a few new features to CSS such as variables, mixins, and nesting. Let us take a look at each of them with examples.

Less variables

In the following example, Less variables are created, which produce the CSS output:

```
@width: 20px;

@height: @width + 20px;

#header {

width: @width;

height: @height;

}
```

The output in CSS for the preceding code is as follows:

```
#header {

width: 20px;

height: 40px;

}
```

Less mixins

Less mixins enables us to include or mix in properties from one ruleset into another ruleset. Here is an example to create the rule set:

```
.outline {

border-top: solid 2px black;

border-bottom: solid 2px black;

}
```

The following code shows you how to use the desired copied rule set in other rule sets:

```
#topmenu a {

color: #111;

  .outline();

}
```

```
#bottommenu {

color: red;

  .outline();

}
```

Less nesting

Less nesting gives us the ability to use nest rules instead of having to cascade rules. Here is an example. In CSS, we need to frequently write code similar to the following code:

```
#footer {

color: black;

}
#footer .navigation {

font-size: 15px;

}
#footer .logo {

width: 400px;

}
```

In Less, we can write it as shown in the following code:

```
#footer {
color: black;

  .navigation {

font-size: 15px;

  }
  .logo {

width: 400px;

  }
}
```

Scss (Sass)

Sass is a stylesheet language that is compiled into CSS. Sass allows us to use variables, nested rules, mixins, and functions. Sass keeps stylesheets organized and makes it easy to share designs across projects.

An example of a Scss script is as follows:

```
@mixin button-base() {

  @include typography(button);

  @include ripple-surface;

  @include ripple-radius-bounded;

display: inline-flex;

position: relative;

height: $button-height;

width: $button-width;

horizontal-align: center;

&:hover { cursor: pointer; }

&:disabled {

color: $mdc-button-disabled-ink-color;

cursor: default;

pointer-events: auto;

  }

}
```

Stylus

Stylus (influenced by Sass and Less) is a dynamic stylesheet pre-processor language that is compiled into CSS. One great feature of Stylus is that the CSS selector braces and colons are optional. The following code segments show the difference between CSS and Stylus:

CSS implementation

```
body {

font: 14px Helvetica, Arial, sans-serif;

}

a.button {

  -webkit-border-radius: 10px;

  -moz-border-radius: 10px;
```

```
border-radius: 10px;

}
```

Stylus implementation

```
border-radius()

  -webkit-border-radius: arguments

  -moz-border-radius: arguments

border-radius: arguments

body

font: 14px Helvetica, Arial, sans-serif

a.button

  border-radius(10px)
```

JSX (React)

Unlike Angular, React is not a framework. It is an extremely popular JavaScript library. React is open-source and is used to build **user interfaces (UI)** on the front end.

In the following code, we declare a variable called name and then use it.

```
const name = 'BpB Publishers';

const element = <h1>Hello, {name}</h1>;

ReactDOM.render(

element,

document.getElementById('root')

);
```

Using the Web Compiler extension

Follow the given steps to install and use the Web Compiler extension:

1. Navigate to the Visual Studio Marketplace at **https://marketplace. visualstudio.com/items?itemName=MadsKristensen.WebCompiler**
2. Click on the **Download** button.
3. After the Extension has finished downloading, double click on the VSIX file.
4. Create a new **ASP.NET Webforms** application.

5. Rightclick on a `.less`, `.scss`, `.styl`, or `.jsx` file in **Solution Explorer**. The **Web Compiler** menu item appears, as shown in the following screenshot:

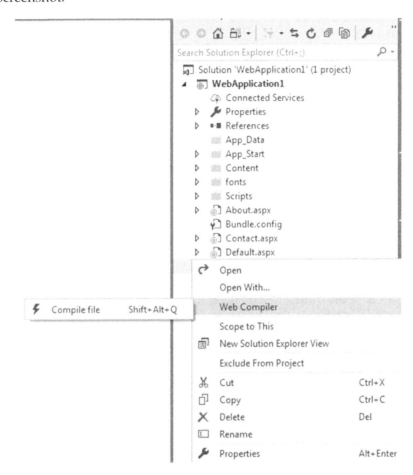

Figure 13.3: *Web Compiler menu*

6. Click on **Compile file.** A few files get created in the **Solution Explorer** window, as shown in the following screenshot:

Figure 13.4: *New files created*

7. The files include the CSS equivalent of the script that was supplied plus the `compiler config.json` files, which include the defaults for the various acceptable compliable scripts.

Web Accessibility Checker

Before we learn about the Web Accessibility Checker extension, let us quickly talk about Web accessibility.

Web accessibility

Web accessibility is the practice of ensuring interaction with, or access to, websites on the web by people with disabilities. When websites are properly designed, all users have equal access to information and functionality. For example, links that are underlined or differentiated, and colored ensure that colour blind users will be able to notice them. Videos that are closed captioned or have a sign language version available ensure that deaf and hard-of-hearing users can understand the video. When flashing effects are made optional or avoided entirely, users prone to seizures (caused by flashing effects) are not put at risk.

Web accessibility addresses the following needs:

- **Visual:** Blindness, common types of low vision, poor eyesight, color blindness
- **Motor/mobility:** Inability or difficulty to use the hands
- **Auditory:** Deafness, hearing impairments and hard of hearing
- **Seizures:** Photo epileptic seizures
- **Cognitive and intellectual:** Developmental disabilities, learning difficulties such as dyslexia and dyscalculia, and cognitive disabilities

Working with the Web Accessibility Checker Visual Studio extension

The Web Accessibility Checker extension helps perform accessibility checks on ASP. NET web applications. It supports all the major international accessibility standards. Some features include the following:

- Integrates easily with the Visual Studio error list
- Compatible with MVC, WebForms, Web Pages, and ASP.NET Core projects
- Uses Browser Link to test the running websites
- Tests the actual **Document Object Model (DOM)**

The following steps demonstrate how to download, install, and make use of the Web Accessibility Checker extension:

1. Navigate to the Visual Studio Marketplace at **https://marketplace.visualstudio.com/items?itemName=MadsKristensen. WebAccessibilityChecker**
2. Click on **Download** to download the extension.
3. After the download is complete, doubleclick on the VSIX file to install it.
4. Create a new **ASP.NET Webforms** application.

5. Click on the small drop-down arrow next to the **Browser Link** button on the toolbar, as shown in the following screenshot:

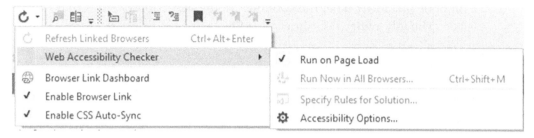

Figure 13.5: Web Accessibility Checker menu

6. Expand the **Web Accessibility Checker** menu, as shown in the preceding screenshot (*Figure 13.5*).

7. Select the **Accessibility Options**… tab.This produces a screen similar to the following screenshot:

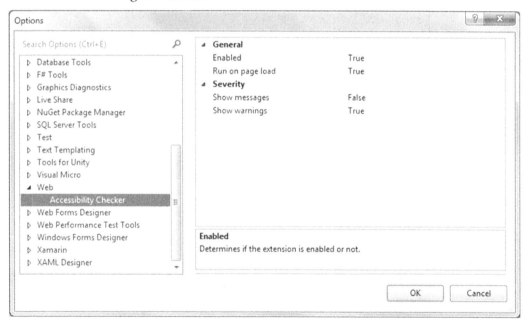

Figure 13.6: Accessibility Checker options

8. Set the **Run on page load** property to **True**, if necessary. This ensures that when a website is being run, the extension will also start running immediately.

9. Expand the **Web Accessibility Checker** menu again, as shown in *Figure 13.5*.

10. Click on the **Specify rules for Solution...** tab. A configuration file named `.a11yrc` will be created in the solution and will be visible in the **Solution Explorer** window. This file contains all the accessibility rules that can be tested. The following code shows this file:

```
{
    // See all rules at https://github.com/dequelabs/axe-core/blob/
master/doc/rule-descriptions.md
    "noscroll":  true,
    "runOnly": {
      "type": "rule",

      "values": [
        "accesskeys",
        "area-alt",
        "aria-allowed-attr",
        "aria-required-attr",
        "aria-required-children",
        "aria-required-parent",
        "aria-roles",
        "aria-valid-attr-value",
        "aria-valid-attr",
        "audio-caption",
        "blink",
        "button-name",
        "bypass",
        "checkboxgroup",
        "color-contrast",
        "definition-list",
        "dlitem",
        "document-title",
        "duplicate-id",
```

```
    "empty-heading",

    "frame-title",

    "heading-order",

    "html-has-lang",

    "html-lang-valid",

    "image-alt",

    "image-redundant-alt",

    "input-image-alt",

    "label-title-only",

    "label",

    "layout-table",

    "link-in-text-block",

    "link-name",

    "list",

    "listitem",

    "marquee",

    "meta-refresh",

    "meta-viewport-large",

    "meta-viewport",

    "object-alt",

    "radiogroup",

    //"region",

    "scope-attr-valid",

    "server-side-image-map",

    //"skip-link",

    "tabindex",

    "table-duplicate-name",

    "table-fake-caption",

    "td-has-header",
```

```
        "td-headers-attr",

        "th-has-data-cells",

        "valid-lang",

        "video-caption",

        "video-description"

    ]

  }

}
```

ASP.NET core vs Code Extension Pack

ASP.NET core VS Code Extension Pack contains a collection of extensions for developing ASP.NET core applications in Visual Studio Code.

VSCODE must first be installed on the computer.

The following steps will guide you to install the extension:

1. Navigate to
   https://marketplace.visualstudio.com/items?itemName=temilaj.asp-net-core-vs-code-extension-pack

2. Click on **Install**. VS Code will be launched.

3. Click on **Install** at the bottom-right hand corner of the screen, as shown in the following screenshot:

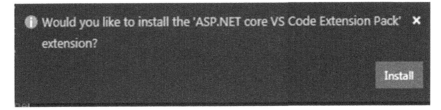

Figure 13.7: Install extension

Open VS Code

Click on the **Extensions** button to ensure the extensions were installed. The **EXTENSIONS** screen is shown in the following screenshot:

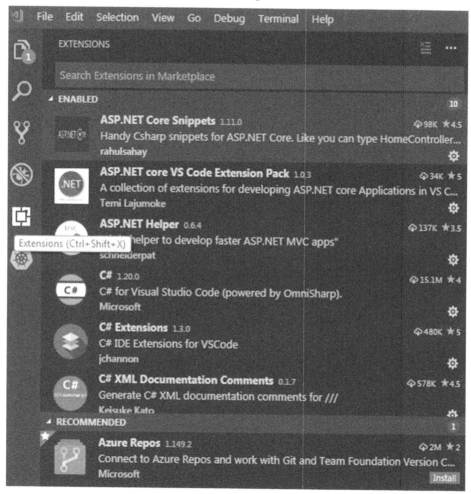

Figure 13.8: VS Code Extensions

Conclusion

In this chapter, we looked at some of the advanced ASP.NET Extensions in Visual Studio 2019. We learned about the markdown editor extension as well the markdown language in general. We learned about a few other web languages and frameworks and had a look at the Web Compiler extension.

We learned about the importance of web accessibility to provide a better web experience for everyone. For this, we used the Web Accessibility Checker extension. Finally, we installed a few extensions in Visual Code so that we can author ASP.NET websites in it.

In the next chapter, we will explore advanced mobile extensions, including SQLite, NuGet, and JSON Viewer.

Questions

Q. 1. What is the difference between markdown and markup languages?

Q. 2. What does Less stand for?

Q. 3. Explain the term JSX.

Q. 4. Name the five accessibility needs that need to be checked.

Q. 5. Can ASP.NET applications be authored in VS Code?

CHAPTER 14

Mobile Extensions

A SP.NET. Extensions provide new and improved Visual Studio features for web applications. These features enable us to do things we normally couldn't do, or it enhances an already pre-existing feature.

Structure

- SQLite
- NuGet Package Manager
- JSON Viewer

Objective

In this chapter, we will focus on IDE Extensions, especially for mobile app development purposes. We will create and install the SQLite database on an Android device and create a small project to use it. We will also learn how to create a new NuGet package from scratch and publish it on the NuGet platform.

SQLite

SQLite is an embedded SQL database engine; it does not have a separate server process like most other SQL databases. SQLite reads and writes directly to ordinary disk files. Contained in a single file is a complete SQL database that can have multiple tables, indices, triggers, and views. Furthermore, this database file format is cross-platform, which means that we can freely copy a database between 32-bit and 64-bit systems or between big-endian and little-endian architectures (endianness is the sequential order in which bytes are arranged into larger numerical values when stored in memory or when transmitted digitally).

SQLite is a compact library with a library size less than 600KB. The 64-bit version is usually larger. SQLite runs faster the more memory you give it, but in general, its performance is quite good even in low-memory environments.

SQL features not implemented in SQLite

SQLite implements most of the features of SQL. Instead of trying to list all the SQL features that SQLite supports, it is easier to list the features that SQLite does not support. The following table lists the same:

Feature	Description
right and full outer join	Right and full outer join are not implemented, but left outer join is.
complete alter table support	Only rename table, add column, and rename column are supported.
complete trigger support	For each statement triggers are not supported.
writing to views	Views in SQLite are read-only.
grant and revoke	The only access permissions needed are the normal file access permissions of the operating system.
no boolean datatype	SQLite does not have a boolean data type. True and false are generally represented as integers 1 and 0.
no datetime datatype	SQLite has no datetime datatype. Dates and times are stored in any of the following ways: • A text string • An integer (which represents the number of seconds since 1970) • A real value which is the fractional Julian day number

Table 14.1: SQL features not supported by SQLite

Installing and using SQLite for Visual Studio 2019

The following steps will demonstrate how to install and use SQLite with an Android App (with Xamarin) in Visual Studio 2019:

1. Start Visual Studio 2019.

2. Click on **Create a new project**.

3. If Xamarin is installed, create a **Mobile App (Xamarin.Forms)** project, as shown in the following screenshot:

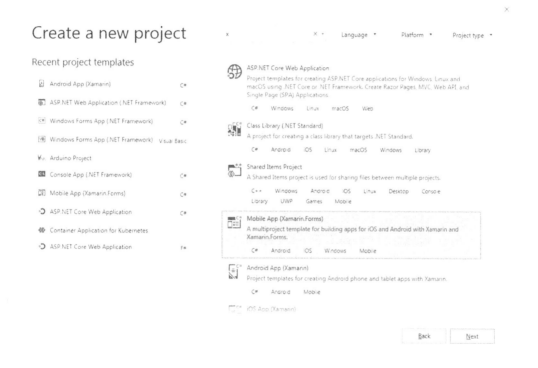

Figure 14.1: Mobile App (Xamarin.Forms) template

4. Click on **Next**.

5. Specify the project name and location.

6. Click on **Create** button.

7. In the template box that pops up, select **Blank**, as shown in the following screenshot:

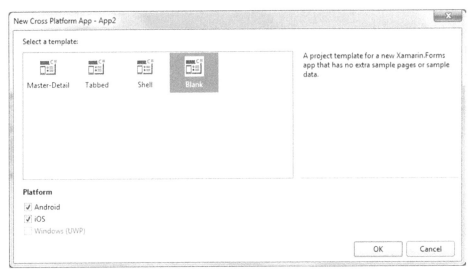

Figure 14.2: Blank Xamarin.Forms template

8. Ensure that the app uses .NET Standard as the shared code mechanism.

9. Select a project in the **Solution Explorer** window.

10. Select **Project | Manage NuGet Packages… | Browse**.

11. Type in SQLite in the **Search** bar. It will start searching.

12. Select **sqlite-net-pcl** from the list.

13. On the right-hand side of the screen, click on **Install**, as shown in the following screenshot:

Figure 14.3: sqlite-net-pcl NuGet package

Coding the logic for the database operations

The following steps will guide you to create a Student class and save the student information in the SQLite database:

1. Ensure that the project is still selected, by clicking on it in the **Solution Explorer**.

2. Right click on the selected project.

3. Select **Add | Class**, give it a name **Student.cs**, as shown in the following screenshot:

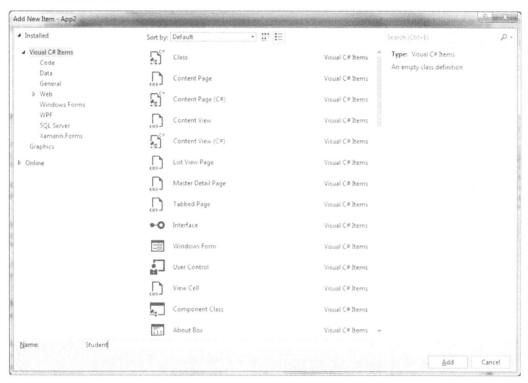

Figure 14.4: Student Class

4. Click on **Add**.

5. Edit the **Studentclass** to look similar to the following code:

```
using SQLite;

public class Student
{
    [PrimaryKey, AutoIncrement]
```

```
        public int StudentID { get; set; }
        public string StudentNames { get; set; }
        public int StudentAge { get; set; }
    }
```

6. Now, create a **Class** for the database operations, using the previous steps. Name the class `Database.cs`.

7. Edit the `Database` class to look like the following code:

```
using System.Collections.Generic;
using System.Threading.Tasks;
using SQLite;

public class Database
{
    readonly SQLiteAsyncConnection _db;

    public Database(string dbPath)
    {
        _db = new SQLiteAsyncConnection(dbPath);
        _db.CreateTableAsync<Student>().Wait();

    }

    public Task<List<Student>> GetStudentAsync()
    {
        return _db.Table<Student>().ToListAsync();
    }

    public Task<int> SaveStudentAsync(Student student)
    {
        return _db.InsertAsync(student);
    }
}
```

The preceding code creates a connection to the database. It then creates a new table named Student. The Database class has two methods: one for getting a list of all students, and one for saving the student details in the Student table.

8. Expand App.xaml in the selected project. Double click on it to open it.

9. Edit the code in App.xaml.cs to resemble the following code:

```
using System;

using System.IO;

using Xamarin.Forms;

using Xamarin.Forms.Xaml;

public partial class App : Application

{

  static Database db;

  public static Database StudentDB

  {

    get

    {

      if (db == null)

      {

        db = new Database(Path.Combine(Environment.GetFolderPath
        (Environment.SpecialFolder.LocalApplicationData),
        "students.db3"));

      }

      return db;

    }

  }

  public App()

  {

    InitializeComponent();

    MainPage = new MainPage();
```

```
   }

   protected override void OnStart()
   {
     // Handle when your app starts
   }

   protected override void OnSleep()
   {
     // Handle when your app sleeps
   }

   protected override void OnResume()
   {
     // Handle when your app resumes
   }
}
```

The preceding code defines a `Database` property that creates a new `Database` instance. A local file path and filename are passed as the arguments to the `Database` class constructor so that the database can be created in the `passed` folder and with the passed name.

10. Double click on the `MainPage.xaml` file to open it.

11. Edit the `StackLayout` section to resemble the following code:

```
<StackLayout Margin="20,35,20,20">

<Entry x:Name="studentnameEntry"

Placeholder="Enter Student Names" />

<Entry x:Name="studentageEntry"

Placeholder="Enter Student Age" />

<Button Text="Add to Students Database"

Clicked="OnButtonClicked" />

<ListView x:Name="listView">
```

```
<ListView.ItemTemplate>

<DataTemplate>

<TextCell Text="{Binding StudentNames}"

Detail="{Binding StudentAge}" />

</DataTemplate>

</ListView.ItemTemplate>

</ListView>

</StackLayout>
```

Notice that there is no entry specified for the `StudentID` field. This is because we created the `StudentID` field as the `PrimaryKey` and `AutoIncrement` in the `Students` class. This means that an ID will automatically be assigned.

The code in the `StackLayout` section creates two entries: one for the student names, and one for the student age. This information is bound to the database through the `Binding` property. A button is used to store the entered information in the `Students` table.

12. Expand the `MainPage.xaml` file to expose the `MainPage.xaml.cs` file.

13. Double click on the `MainPage.xaml.cs` file to open it.

14. Add the `OnAppearing` and `OnButtonClicked` events, as shown in the following code:

```
protected override async void OnAppearing()

{

  base.OnAppearing();

  listView.ItemsSource = await App.StudentDB.GetStudentAsync();

}


async void OnButtonClicked(object sender, EventArgs e)

{

  if (!string.IsNullOrWhiteSpace(studentnameEntry.Text) && !string.
IsNullOrWhiteSpace(studentageEntry.Text))

  {

    await App.StudentDB.SaveStudentAsync(new Student

    {
```

```
        StudentNames = studentnameEntry.Text,

      StudentAge = int.Parse(studentageEntry.Text)

    });


    studentnameEntry.Text = studentageEntry.Text = string.Empty;

    listView.ItemsSource = await App.StudentDB.GetStudentAsync();

  }

}
```

The preceding code brings everything together. When the screen appears, the `GetStudentAsync` method is called to list all the students in the `ListView`. When you click on the button and the `studentnameEntry` field is not empty, the `SaveStudentAsync` method is called to store the details in the database.

NuGet Package Manager

Throughout this book, we have continuously worked with NuGet in several chapters. Although we have worked with it, we have not actually delved into NuGet. Let us quickly do that now.

NuGet, formerly known as **NuPack**, is an opensource package manager designed specifically for the Microsoft development platform. NuGet is distributed as a Visual Studio extension and comes pre-installed by default. It is also integrated with **SharpDevelop** and can also be used from the command line or automated with scripts.

In this book, we have added quite a few NuGet packages. For a complete list of available NuGet packages, navigate to **https://www.nuget.org/packages.**

Creating and publishing a NuGet package using Visual Studio 2019

In order to create a NuGet package, the .NET Core SDK is needed so that we are able to create .NET Standard projects that use the SDK-style format. We need to perform the following steps to download and install the .NET Core SDK:

1. Navigate to **https://dotnet.microsoft.com/download.**

2. Download and install the .NET Core SDK.

Now, create an account on nuget.org, if necessary. Create a free account on **https://www.nuget.org/** by following the given steps:

1. Navigate to **https://www.nuget.org/users/account/LogOn.**
2. Click on the `Sign in with Microsoft` button.
3. Sign in with a Microsoft account.
4. Click on **Yes** to accept the permissions to be given to the `NuGet.org` application, as shown in the following screenshot:

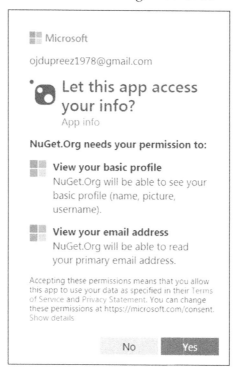

Figure 14.5: NuGet App permissions

1. After clicking on **Yes**, it will redirect to the NuGet login page.
2. Specify a username when prompted. This username is case sensitive and cannot be changed later.
3. Click on **Register**. The account is now created.

Creating the Class Library to be used as a NuGet package

We have everything we need now (the .NET Core SDK and a NuGet account). Now, we need to create a .Net Standard Class Library to host the logic we would like to distribute. We need to perform the following steps to create the .NET Standard Class Library:

1. Start Visual Studio 2019.

2. Select **Class Library (.NET Standard)** from the templates, as shown in the following screenshot:

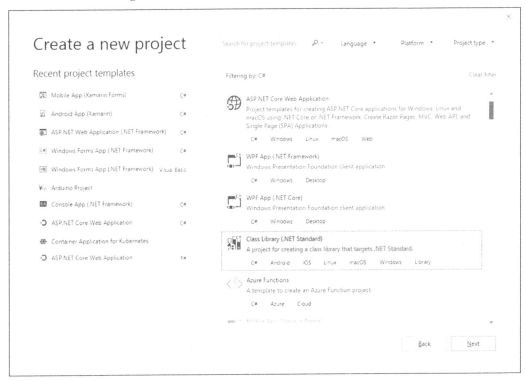

Figure 14.6: Class Library (.NET Standard) template

3. Click on **Next**.

4. Provide a decent name such as BpBSample, and then click on **Create**.

5. Rename Class1 in the **Solution Explorer** window to **BpBSample**.

6. Edit the code to resemble the following code:

```
namespace BpBSample

{

  public class BpBSample

  {

    public void Greet(string strSalutation, string strFullName)

    {
```

```
        Console.WriteLine("Hello {0}. {1}!", strSalutation, strFullName);
    }


    }
}
```

7. This code is quite simple! It outputs a message greeting the user with his or her title (such as Mr., Ms., Mrs., Dr.) and the supplied name.

8. Ensure that the BpBSample project is selected in the **Solution Explorer** window.

9. Select the **Project** menu.

10. Select **BpBSample Properties**.

11. Select the **Package** tab. If everything is done correctly, the **Package** screen should resemble the following screenshot:

Figure 14.7: Package tab

12. Fill in the desired details. These properties aresaved in a .nuspec Manifest file.

13. Then, set the configuration to **Release**.

14. Right click on the project in **Solution Explorer** and select **Pack**, as shown in the following screenshot:

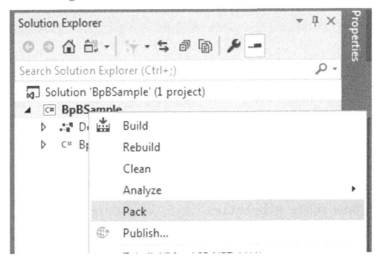

Figure 14.8: Pack command

15. Visual Studio 2019 builds the project and creates the `.nupkg` file, as shown in the following screenshot:

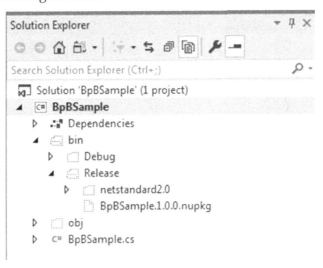

Figure 14.9: nupkg file

To see the nupkg file in the Solution Explorer window, ensure that the Show All Files button is selected in Solution Explorer.

Publishing the NuGet package

All that is left to do now is to publish this package on the NuGet platform. Follow the given steps to publish the package:

1. Sign into the **https://www.nuget.org/account**.
2. Select the user name (top-right), and then select **API Keys**.
3. Select **Create**.
4. Provide a name for the key.
5. Select **Push** under the **Select Scopes** heading.
6. Under the **Select Packages** heading, enter * in the **Glob pattern** field.
7. Select **Create**. The following screenshot shows the screen where everything has been filled in:

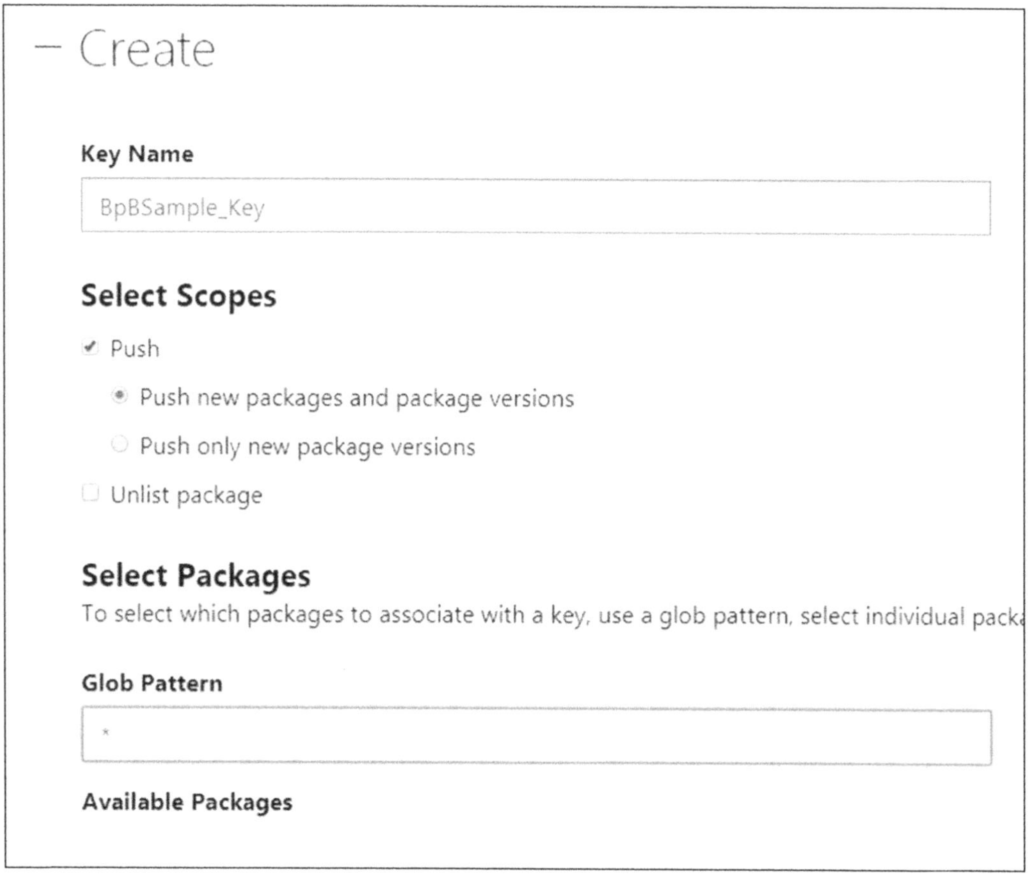

— Create

Key Name

BpBSample_Key

Select Scopes

☑ Push

    ● Push new packages and package versions

    ○ Push only new package versions

☐ Unlist package

Select Packages

To select which packages to associate with a key, use a glob pattern, select individual packa

Glob Pattern

*

Available Packages

Figure 14.10: Key details filled in

8. The key is created.

9. After the key is created, select **Copy** to retrieve the access key in the CLI.

Figure 14.11: BpBSample_Key

7. Open the Developer Command Prompt, which is usually under the Visual Studio 2019 items.

8. Navigate to the location where the `.nupkg` was created.

9. Enter the following command:

```
nuget push BpBSample.1.0.0.nupkg
oy2jveah4tpt6awvr35aqgqp5zf623pufdw7tjtsa4bcia -Source https://
api.nuget.org/v3/index.json
```

10. The following information must be provided: name of the NuGet package file, the key, and where it must be published. The following screenshot demonstrates the information with responses:

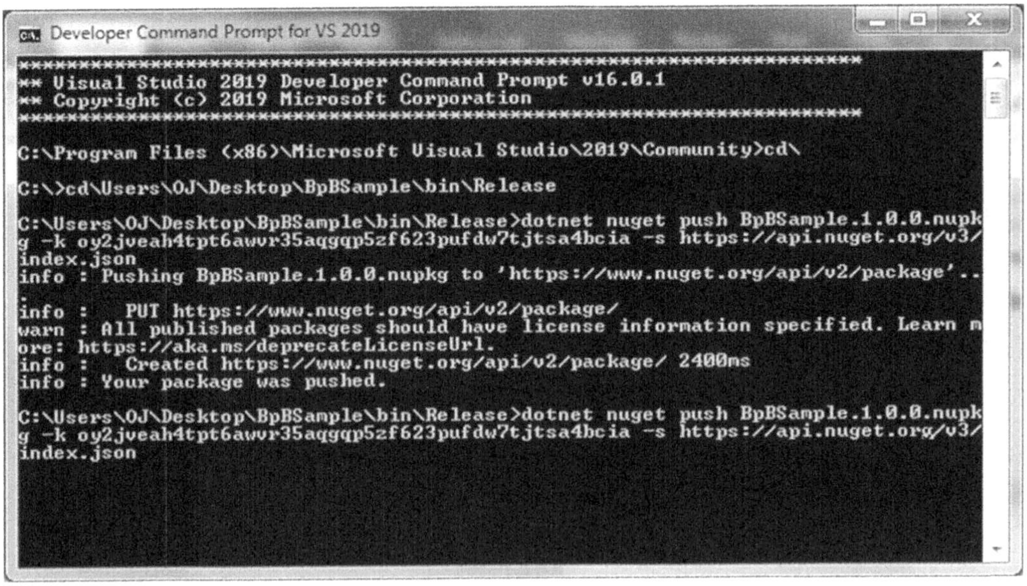

Figure 14.12: Publishing to NuGet.org

The indexing of the package may take a while, so it may not show up immediately in searches.

JSON Viewer

The JSON Viewer extension formats JSON to a friendly view, compares, and prints the formatted results as well as evaluates JSONPath expressions.

Installing and using JSON Viewer

The following steps will guide you to download, install, and demonstrate JSON Viewer:

1. Navigate to the Visual Studio Marketplace at
    https://marketplace.visualstudio.com/items?itemName=MykolaTarasyuk.
    JSONViewer&ssr=false#overview

2. Click on **Download**.

3. Install the extension by double clicking on the downloaded VSIX file. After the extension has been installed, it will be available under the **Tools** menu of Visual Studio.

4. Select it from the **Tools** menu to open it. The following screenshot shows this tool in action:

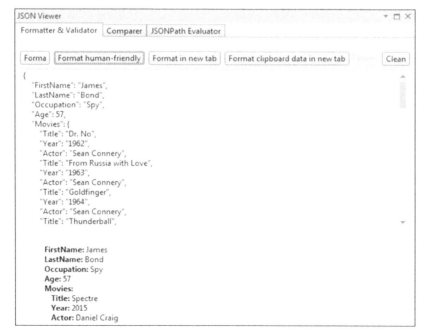

Figure 14.13: JSON Viewer in action

Conclusion

In this chapter, we explored the world of advanced Mobile Extensions in Visual Studio 2019. We learned about SQLite databases and their benefits. We installed the database on an Android device and learned how to store information in one of its tables. We then learned about NuGet and created a package for NuGet to be used by other developers. Lastly, we quickly had a look into the JSON Viewer extension.

In the next chapter, we will explore Azure DevOps Extensions, including Azure Artifacts, Code Search, and IIS Web App Deployment using WinRM.

Questions

Q. 1.   Name five SQL features that SQLite does not support.

Q. 2.   What is a `.nuspec` Manifest file?

Q. 3.   How is a table created in SQLite and C#?

Q. 4.   What is NuGet?

Q. 5.   What does the JSON Viewer extension do?

## CHAPTER 15

Azure DevOps Extensions

In the world of cloud computing, Visual Studio 2019 provides the best tools for working with Microsoft Azure. In this chapter, we will explore Azure DevOps tools and more.

Structure

- Azure DevOps
- Azure Artifacts
- AWS Tools for Microsoft Visual Studio Team Services
- Code Search
- Other noteworthy Azure DevOps extensions
  - o Test Case Explorer
  - o IIS Web App Deployment Using WinRM

Objective

In this chapter, we will focus on Azure DevOps extensions and tools. We will learn about Azure Artifacts and how to use them. We will also learn about Amazon's powerful AWS Tools for Microsoft Visual Studio Team Services. Lastly, we will take a quick look at other noteworthy Azure DevOps extensions.

Azure DevOps

We discussed Azure and Azure DevOps in *Chapter 11: Azure Tools*, but now let us does a quick recap. Azure DevOps is a practice that unifies people, processes, technology, development, and IT in five practices:

- Planning and tracking
- Developing
- Building and testing
- Delivery
- Monitoring and operations

While practicing DevOps, different teams from different disciplines such as development, IT operations, quality engineering, and security all work together.

Practicing a DevOps model

Teams across different disciplines follow the following phases through their delivery pipeline:

- **Plan and track:** Identify and track work visually using practices such as Kanban Boards and Agile.
- **Developing:** Write code with the help of version control systems such as Git to integrate continuously to the master branch.
- **Building and testing:** With an automated build process, the code is tested and validated immediately. This ensures that bugs are caught early in development.
- **Deploying:** Using continuous delivery practices, the final deployment to production is ultimately a manually controlled business decision.
- **Monitor and operate:** Once the app is live in production, monitoring delivers vital information about the app's performance and usage patterns.

Azure Artifacts

Using Azure Artifacts, we can create host and share packages with our teams. We can publicly or privately share code across teams as well as manage package types like NuGet, Maven, Python, npm, and many more. We can add a fully-integrated package management to our continuous integration/continuous delivery (CI/CD) pipelines. Azure Artifacts come pre-installed in Azure DevOps Services.

Getting started with Azure Artifacts

Follow the given steps to get started with Azure DevOps Artifacts:

1. Navigate to
   https://azure.microsoft.com/en-gb/free/?WT.mc_id=A261C142F.

2. Click on the **Start for free** button, as shown in the following screenshot:

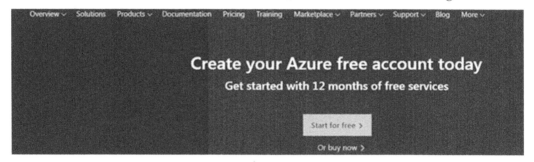

Figure 15.1: Start for free

3. Follow the prompts and fill in the desired information.

4. Select the organization.

5. Select Artifacts from the menu, as shown in the following screenshot:

Figure 15.2: Artifacts

6. Click on **Invite**. Enter the user's or group's details.

7. Fill in the team information.

8. Click on **Add**, as shown in the following screenshot:

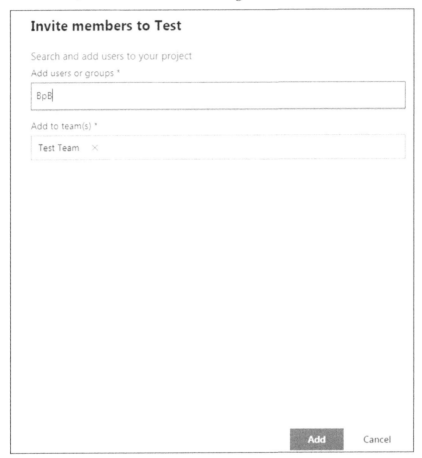

Figure 15.3: Invite members

9. Click on an assigned user. This will open up a new screen.

10. Select either **New Feed** or **Connect to Feed**. New feed enables us to create a new feed, whereas connect to feed enables us to connect to an existing feed. The following screenshot shows this option in action:

Figure 15.4: Connect to feed

11. Copy the NuGet package source URL.

12. Open Visual Studio 2019.

13. Create a new project, or open an existing project where this needs to be consumed.

14. Select **Tools | Options**.

15. Expand the **NuGet Package Manager**.

16. Select **Package** **Manager**. The screen should resemble the following screenshot:

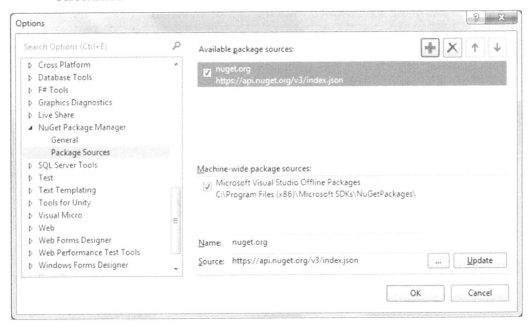

Figure 15.5: Package Manager

17. Click on **OK**.

18. Right click on **References** in the **Solution Explorer** window.

19. Select **Manage NuGet Packages**.

20. In the **Package Sources** drop-down menu, select the feed.

AWS Tools for Microsoft Visual Studio Team Services

AWS Tools for Microsoft **Visual Studio Team Services (VSTS)** adds tasks to quickly enable build and release pipelines in Microsoft Visual Studio Team Services and on-premises **Team Foundation Server (TFS)** to work with AWS services such as Amazon Simple Queue Service, Amazon S3, AWS CodeDeploy, AWS Lambda, AWS CloudFormation, AWS Elastic Beanstalk, and Amazon Simple Notification Service.

These tools also enable us to deploy serverless .NET Core applications and .NET Core C# functions to AWS Lambda and to deploy AWS CloudFormation templates to easily manage, provide, and update a collection of AWS resources straight within VSTS.

The available AWS tasks in a VSTS project or Team Foundation Server include the following:

AWS Task	Task description
AWS Code Deploy Application Deployment	Deploys applications to Amazon EC2 instances.
AWS Cloud Formation Create/Update Stack	Creates new AWS Cloud Formation stacks or updates stack if they exist.
AWS Cloud Formation Delete Stack	Deletes AWS Cloud Formation stacks.
AWS Cloud Formation Execute Change Set	Executes AWS Cloud Formation change sets to create or update stacks.
AWS Elastic Beanstalk Create Version	Creates new versions of applications.
AWS Elastic Beanstalk Deploy Application	Deploys new versions of applications to Elastic Beanstalk environments.
Amazon ECR Push	Pushes Docker images to the Amazon Elastic Container Registry.
AWS Lambda Deploy Function	AWS Lambda function deployment for supported Lambda language runtimes.
AWS Lambda .NET Core	Builds, packages, and deploys. NET Core AWS Lambda functions.
AWS Lambda Invoke Function	Invokes AWS Lambda functions with JSON payloads.
AWS CLI	Runs commands via the AWS CLI.
AWS Tools for Windows PowerShell Script	Runs PowerShell scripts that make use of cmdlets from the AWS Tools for Windows PowerShell AWS module.
AWS Shell Script	Runs shell scripts via Bash with AWS credentials.
Amazon S3 Download	Downloads file and folder content from Amazon Simple Storage Service buckets.
Amazon S3 Upload	Uploads file and folder content to Amazon Simple Storage Service buckets.
AWS Send SNS or SQS Message	Sends messages to the Amazon Simple Notification Service topics or to Amazon Simple Queue Service queues.
AWS Secrets Manager Create/Update Secret	Updates secrets, or create secrets if they do not exist.
AWS Secrets Manager Get Secret	Stores values of secrets in AWS Secrets Manager in secret build variables.

AWS SSM Get Parameter	Reads values from Systems Manager Parameter Store into build variables.
AWS SSM Set Parameter	Creates or updates parameters in Systems Manager Parameter Store.
AWS SSM Run Command	Runs Systems Managers or user-provided Commands on fleets of EC2 instances.

Table 15.1: AWS tasks available in a VSTS project

Getting and installing AWS Tools for Microsoft Visual Studio Team Services

Perform the following steps to get and install the AWS Tools:

1. Navigate to the Visual Studio market place at **https://marketplace. visualstudio.com/items?itemName=AmazonWebServices.aws-vsts-tools.**

2. Click on the **Get it free** button.

3. The next screen will open up, as shown in the following screenshot:

Figure 15.6: AWS Tools

4. Select the desired Azure DevOps organization.

5. This will check the necessary permissions for the organization.

6. Click on **Install**.

7. After it has installed, click on the **Proceed to organization** button.

Code Search

When a codebase expands or the codebase is divided across multiple repositories and projects, finding items becomes quite difficult.

The Code Search extension maximizes cross-team collaboration and code sharing. It helps to discover API implementation examples and error texts to name a few.

Installing and using the Code Search extension

The following steps demonstrate how to get the extension and how to use it:

1. Navigate to the Visual Studio market place at **https://marketplace. visualstudio.com/items?itemName=ms.vss-code-search**.

2. Click on the `Get it free` button, as shown in the following screenshot:

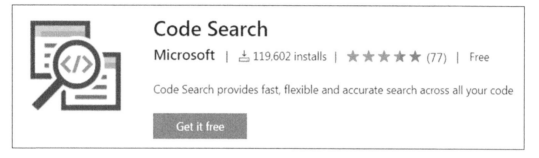

Figure 15.7: Code Search Azure DevOps extension

3. Select the desired Azure DevOps organization.

4. Click on **Install**.

5. Click on the `Proceed to organization` button.

6. The Code Search extension is now installed.

7. Open or import arepo such as **https://github.com/OJ1978/BpBRepo.git**.

8. Click in the **Search** bar on the top of the screen. It should look like the following screenshot:

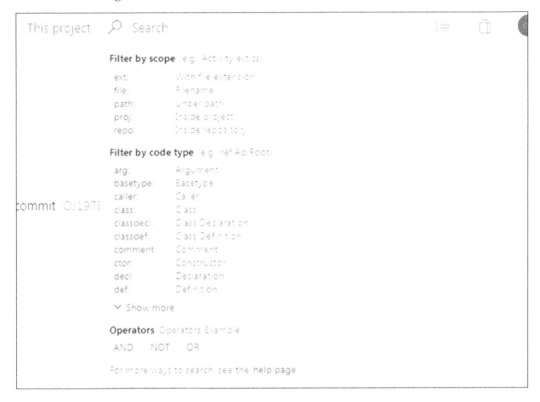

Figure 15.8: Code Search

Other noteworthy Azure DevOps extensions

There is a lot more Azure DevOps extensions. Here, I will highlight two more.

Test Case Explorer

The Test Case Explorer extension helps manage test cases better. It can be found at **https://marketplace.visualstudio.com/items?itemName=ms-devlabs. TestCaseExplorer**.

IIS Web App Deployment Using WinRM

The IIS Web App Deployment using WinRM extension can connect to the host machine when either IIS or SQL Server is installed, then manage the Web application or deploy the SQL server database. This extension can be found at **https://marketplace. visualstudio.com/items?itemName=ms-vscs-rm.iiswebapp**.

Conclusion

In this chapter, we focused on Azure DevOps extensions and tools. We learned about Azure Artifacts and how to use them. We also learned about Amazon's powerful AWS Tools for Microsoft Visual Studio Team Services. Lastly, we looked at other noteworthy Azure DevOps extensions.

Questions

Q. 1. Explain the term Azure Artifacts.

Q. 2. Name five AWS tasks.

Q. 3. Explain the purpose of the Code Search extension.

Q. 4. What is the function of the Test Case Explorer extension?

Q. 5. What is the function of the IIS Web App Deployment using WinRM extension?

Index

Symbols

.NET Core 3 189

.NET Core 3.0
  about 104
  installing 104, 105
  Windows applications, building 110

.NET Core IDE 48

.NET Core local tool 108, 109
  Windows applications, building
      with .NET Core 3.0 110

.NET platform dependent intrinsic
  about 107
  guidelines 107

A

accessibility modifiers
  adding 140
  sorting 141

Akamai CloudTest
  about 174

reference link 174

Amazon Cognito
  setting up 197

Amazon Cognito, components
  identity pool 197
  user pool 196

Analytical AI 231

Andriod emulator
  in Visual Studio 2019 223
  new device, setting up 224

Apache JMeter 171

APIs (Application Programming
      Interfaces) 107

Appium
  about 169, 170
  reference link 169

Application Programming
      Interface (API) 198

application timeline 126

Arduino IDE

for Visual Studio 260
installing, for Visual Studio 260-262
arrays
about 83
example 83
Artificial intelligence (AI)
about 66, 231
Analytical AI 231
Azure AI 232
Human-inspired AI 231
Humanized AI 231
Microsoft AI platform 231
ASP.NET
about 47
AJAX extensions 48
data section 47
HTML 48
login section 47
navigation section 47
standard section 47
validation section 47
webparts 47
ASP.NET application, types
empty 54
MVC 54
single page application 55
web API 55
web forms 54
ASP.NET core
versus Code Extension Pack 280, 281
ASP.NET Core Identity
Amazon Cognito 196
for Amazon 196
ASP.NET MVC framework
about 180, 181
controller (or input control) 180
model (or business layer) 180
view (or display layer) 180
assignment 80
asynchronous streams 99

Azure AI
about 232
agents 233
API apps 233
knowledge mining 232
machine learning 232
Azure App Service 8
Azure Artifacts
about 303-306
AWS tools, for Microsoft Visual Studio
Team Services 306, 307
AWS tools, installing for Microsoft
Visual Studio Team Services 308
AWS tools, obtaining for Microsoft
Visual Studio Team Services 308
using 302
Azure Blockchain Service 242, 243
Azure Cloud Services 8
Azure Databricks 232
Azure Data Lake Analytics 8
Azure DevOps
about 241, 302
extension 310
IIS Web App Deployment,
using WinRM 310
model, practicing 242, 302
Test Case Explorer 310
Azure Digital Twins 229
Azure, for IoT
Azure Digital Twins 229
Azure IoT Central 228
Azure IoT Edge 228
Azure IoT Hub 228
Azure IoT solution accelerator 228
Azure Maps 229
Azure Sphere 228
Azure Time Series Insights 229
Azure IoT Central 228
Azure IoT Edge 228
Azure IoT Hub 228

Azure IoT solution accelerator 228
Azure Kubernetes Service (AKS) 201
Azure Machine Learning 232
Azure Maps 229
Azure Search 232
Azure Sphere 228
Azure Storage 8
Azure Time Series Insights 229
Azure Windows Virtual Machines 9

B

BlazeMeter
  about 172, 173
  reference link 172
Blazor
  about 189
  in Visual Studio 2019 189, 190
  setting up 190-194
block body preferences
  applying 141
Bot Service 233
braces for single-line control statements
  adding 140
  removing 140

C

C++
  IntelliSense, template in 66
C# 8.0
  asynchronous streams 99
  declaration, using 95
  disposable ref structs 97
  features 93
  indices 99, 100
  nullable contexts 98
  nullable reference types 98
  pattern matching 93
  property pattern 94
  ranges 99, 100

static local functions 96
  switch expressions 94
  tuple pattern 95
Cascading Style Sheets (CSS) 269
casts
  removing 141
casts, types
  explicit casting 141
  implicit casting 141
C# language 80
class library
  creating, NuGet package used 293-296
CLI (Command Line Infrastructure) 108
Cloud Explorer 40
CLR (Common Language Runtime) 106
Code Cleanup
  about 136
  accessibility modifiers, adding 140
  accessibility modifiers, sorting 141
  block body preferences, applying 141
  braces for single-line control
      statements, adding 140
  braces for single-line control
      statements, removing 140
  casts, removing 141
  collection initialization preferences,
      applying 142
  configuring 137
  explicit type preferences, applying 138
  expression body
      preferences, applying 141
  framework type
      preferences, applying 139
  implicit type
      preferences, applying 138
  language type
      preferences, applying 139
  object initialization
      preferences, applying 142
  out variable preferences, applying 142

private fields, creating read-only 141
this. keyword, applying 139
unused variable, removing 142
Coded UI tests
  Selenium Grid 169
  Selenium WebDriver 169
Coded UI tests (CUITs)
  about 162
  creating 162, 163
  Selenium 164
Code Extension Pack
  versus ASP.NET core 280, 281
code formatting options 137
code generation tools
  about 150
  code snippets 151, 152
  Design time T4 templates 152
  quick actions 151
  runtime T4 text templates 153
Code Search
  about 309
  extension, installing 309
  extension, using 309
code snippets 151
code window 43
Cognitive Services 233
collections
  about 83, 84
  hashtable 86
  namespace 84
  queue 85
  stack 85
constant
  about 80
  data type 81
  example 80
Control Library 32
COOL (C-like Object Oriented
    Language) 80

CPU usage 121, 122
cryptographic key
  exporting 113
  importing 113

D

dataset 34
data sources 32-38
Data Sources Configuration
    Wizard window 4-7
data type 81
debugging application
  about 144
  breakpoint 144
  code, navigating at
      debug mode 145, 146
  multiple processes, debugging 147
debugging window
  about 44
  Locals window 45
  Output window 44
  QuickWatch window 44
debugging windows
  highlighting 143
  search bar 142
  search depth 144
  search navigation 143
declaration
  using 95
default argument 66
Design time T4 templates 152
design window 32
  design view 55
  source view 55
  split view 55
desktop IDE
  about 48-50
  comparing, with mobile IDE 46
  comparing, with web IDE 46

DevExtreme
  about 222
  installing 222
disposable ref structs
  about 97
  limitations 97
DotNetNuke (DNN platform)
  about 182
  using 182
do while loop
  about 92
  example 92
DSA (Digital Signature Algorithm) 113

E

ECDsa (Elliptic Curve Digital
        Signature Algorithm) 113
EditorConfig file
  about 68-73
  adding, to solution or project 73
emulator 223
enterprise resource planning (ERP) 229
entry field 9
enumeration
  about 87, 88
  example 87
explicit casting 141
explicit type preferences
  applying 138
expression body preferences
  applying 141

F

First in, first out list (FIFO list) 85
foreach loop 92
for loop
  about 91, 92
  example 91

Form Recognizer 232
framework type preferences
  applying 139

G

GitHub
  about 253
  for desktop 257
  repository, creating 253
  repository, forking 254, 255, 256
GPU profiler tool
  using 126
GPU usage 125
Graphical User Interface (GUI) 46
grouping structures 83

H

hashtable 86
HTML (Hypertext Markup Language)
        55
HTML UI responsiveness 128
Human-inspired AI 231
Humanized AI 231
HWND (Windows Handle) 111

I

identity pool 197
IDE Productivity Power Tools 62
if statement 88, 89
implicit casting 141
implicit type preferences
  applying 138
indices 99, 100
instance 210
Integrated Development Environment
        (IDE) 31
IntelliCode
  EditorConfig file 68-73

reference link 67
IntelliCode, advantages
  assisted IntelliSense 67
  code reviews 74
  code style, inferring 68
  code types, recommendations 67
  conventions, formatting 68
  IntelliCode extension, installing 74-78
  issues, finding 74
  using 67
IntelliCode extension
  using, for Visual Studio 2019 67
IntelliSense
  about 63
  default argument 66
  live edits 66
  nested template 66
  Peek window UI 66
  template, in C++ 66
IntelliSense, features
  complete word 65
  list members 64
  parameter info 64, 65
  quick info 65
IntelliTrace 128
Internet of Things (IoTs) 228
ISA (Instruction Set Architectures) 107
iteration statement 91
  do while loop 92
  foreach loop 92
  for loop 91, 92
  while loop 93

J

JavaScript memory 128
JavaScript Object Notation (JSON)
  about 41, 109, 208
  complex schema 213
  multiple subschemas, combining 211
JSON, data types

array 208
Boolean 208
null 208
number 208
object 208
string 208
JSON outline window 41
JSON schema
  about 210, 211
  keywords 212
JSON structure 208, 209
JSON Viewer
  about 299
  installing 299
  using 299
JSX (React) 273

K

Kubernetes
  installing 202-204
Kubernetes platform
  namespace 202
  pod 202
  service 202
  volumes 202

L

language type preferences
  applying 139
Leaner Style Sheets (Less)
  about 269
  mixins 270
  nesting 271
  variables 270
LIFO (Last in, First out) 85
live edits 66
Locals window 45

M

Machine Intelligence 66
markdown
  about 267
  example 266
markdown editor
  about 267
  working with 268
markup language 266
memory usage 123, 124
menus 32
Microsoft AI platform 231
Microsoft Visual Studio Live Share
  about 259
  using 259
mobile IDE
  about 50-53
  comparing, with desktop IDE 46
  comparing, with web IDE 46
model view controller (MVC)
        architecture 183
model view controller (MVC)
        pattern 22, 180
MonoRail
  about 183
  reference link 183
MSIX
  deployment, for desktop apps 114
  prerequisites 114

N

namespaces
  System.Runtime.Intrinsics 107
  System.Runtime.Intrinsics.X86 107
naming conventions
  about 83
  CamelCase 83
  PascalCase 83
nested template 66

network usage 128
Node.js
  reference link 184
notifications 40
NuGet package
  about 111, 168
  class library, creating 293-296
  creating, Visual Studio 2019 used 292
  manager 292
  publishing 297, 298
  publishing, Visual
        Studio 2019 used 292
  reference link 292
nullable contexts 98
nullable element
  disable 98
  enable 98
  safeonly 98
  safeonlywarnings 98
  warnings 98
nullable reference types 98
NUnit 168
NuPack 292

O

object initialization preferences
  applying 142
ONNX 232
Open-source WPF 115
Output window 44
out variable preferences
  applying 142

P

PaaS (Platform-as-a-Service) 204
pattern matching 93
Peek window UI 66
PerfTips 127
Platform as a Service (PaaS) 8

pre-processed text templates
  types 152
private fields
  creating, read-only 141
profiling tool
  about 121
  application timeline 126
  CPU usage 121, 122
  GPU usage 125
  HTML UI responsiveness 128
  IntelliTrace 128
  JavaScript memory 128
  memory usage 123, 124
  network usage 128
  PerfTips 127
Project Properties window 42
Properties window 4-6
Property Bag 183
property patterns 94
Pull Requests
  Azure Repo, connecting to 258
  for Visual Studio 257
  using, for Visual Studio extension 258

Q

queue
  about 85
  example 85
quick actions 151
QuickWatch window 44

R

ranges 99, 100
React.js
  using 187
Redgate SQL Change Automation Core
  about 263
  installing, in Visual Studio 2019 263
  reference link 263

reference window 42
Resource view window 41
RSA (Rivest Shamir Adleman) 113
runtime T4 text templates 153

S

SaaS (Software-as-a-Service) 204
SAP Business One 230
SAP BW/4HANA 230
SAP Cloud Platform 231
SAP Hybris 231
SAP NetWeaver 230
SAP, on Azure solutions
  about 229
  SAP Business One 230
  SAP BW/4HANA 230
  SAP Cloud Platform 231
  SAP HANA 229
  SAP Hybris 231
  SAP NetWeaver 230
  SAP S/4HANA 230
SAP S/4HANA 230
schema 210
Scss (Sass) 271
search bar
  on debugging windows 142
search depth 144
search navigation 143
selection statement
  about 88
  if statement 88, 89
  switch statement 90
Selenium 164
Selenium, components
  about 164
  Selenium IDE 164-167
  Selenium RC 168
Selenium Grid 169
Selenium IDE 164-167

Selenium RC
  about 168
  client libraries, working 168
  server, executing 168
  server, installing 168
Selenium Recorder 164
Selenium WebDriver
  about 169
  installing 169
  reference link 169
Server Explorer window
  about 4, 7
  Azure 8
  cloud services 7
  data connections 9
  servers 9
  SharePoint connections 9
  SQLDatabases 7
  Virtual Machines 7
SharpDevelop 292
SIMD (single instruction,
    multiple data) 107
simulator 223
simulator or emulators
  differences between, test apps 223
Solution Explorer 128
Solution Explorer, feature
  about 129
  solution filter file 132, 133
  solution filtering 129-131
  unloaded projects, displaying 131
  unloaded projects, hiding 131
Solution Explorer window 4, 46
solution filter
  windows search keywords,
    debugging 12
solution filter file 132, 133
solution filtering 131
  about 129, 130

benefits 129
SQL Databases 8
SQLite
  about 283, 284
  installing, for Visual
    Studio 2019 285, 286
  logic, coding for database
    operations 287-292
  SQL features, non implemented 284
  using, for Visual Studio 2019 285
stack 85
  about 86
  example 86
standard IDE Windows
  about 31, 32
  Cloud Explorer window 40
  code window 43
  Data Sources window 32-38
  debugging window 44
  design window 32
  JSON outline window 41
  menus 32
  Notifications window 40
  Project Properties window 42
  reference window 42
  Resource view window 41
  Task List window 46
  Team Explorer window 39
  toolbars 32
  toolbox 38
static local functions 96
Streaming SIMD Extensions (SSE) 107
Stylus 272
switch expressions
  about 94
  example 94
switch statement 90

T

Task List window 46
Team Explorer window 4, 39
Team Foundation Server (TFS) 306
this. keyword
  applying 139
toolbars 32
toolbox
  about 9, 38, 46
  ASP.NET 47
  Desktop IDE 48-50
  .NET Core IDE 48
  Visual Studio Code IDE 48
  Windows Forms 46
  Xamarin 48
tuple pattern 95

U

unit testing, in Visual Studio 2019
  about 158
  small test, writing 160
  Test Explorer 161
  test methods, creating 158
  unit test project, creating 158, 159
  unit test stubs, creating 158, 159
Universal Windows
      Platform (UWP) 23, 106
unloaded projects
  displaying 131
  hiding 131
unnecessary casts
  removing 141
unused variables
  removing 142
User Interface (UI) 162
user pool
  about 196
  benefits 196

V

variable
  about 80
  creating 82
  data type 81
  declaring 82
  naming conventions 83
Visual Studio
  extension, Pull Requests using 258
  pull requisites 257
Visual Studio 2019
  about 4
  additional requisites 13, 14
  Android emulator in 223
  community 19
  Data Sources Configuration
      Wizard window 6, 7
  editions 14
  enterprise 19
  hardware 13
  installation, selecting 23-28
  installing 184
  Integrated Development Environment
      (IDE) comparison 20
  IntelliCode Extension, using 67
  launching 28-30
  operating systems 13
  prerequisites 13
  preview 15-18
  professional 19
  Properties window 5, 6
  Redgate SQL Change Automation
      Core, installing 263
  requisites 13
  Server Explorer window 7
  Solution Explorer window 4
  supported languages 14
  toolbox 9
  unit testing in 158

updates 12
used, for creating NuGet package 292
used, for publishing NuGet
    package 292
using 184
Visual Studio 2019 community edition
  reference link 23
Visual Studio 2019 extensions
  about 57, 248
  creating 59-61, 249, 250
  finding 57
  image optimizer 58
  installing 57
  preview label 248
  preview label, adding to 252
  reference link 57
Visual Studio 2019, features
  about 10
  document health indicator 11
  project dialog box 10
  solution filter 12
Visual Studio 2019, installation options
  about 21
  for mobile and gaming 23
  for web and cloud 22
  on Windows 21
  other toolset 23
Visual Studio 2019 remote
        debugging tools
  about 147
  downloading 148
  reference link 148
  remote configuration wizard,
        executing 148, 149
  remote configuration wizard,
        installing 148, 149
Visual Studio Code IDE 48
Visual Studio Kubernetes Tools 201
Visual Studio Live Share
  about 120

brown bag meetings 120
  code reviews 121
  competitions, coding 120
  developer streaming 120
  hack-a-thons 120
  pair programming 120
  peer mentoring 120
  quick assistance 120
  technical interviews 121
Visual Studio Marketplace
  reference link 276
Visual Studio Team Services (VSTS) 306
Vue.js 183
  installing 184
  using 184

W

WCF (Windows Communication
      Foundation) 106
web accessibility
  about 275
  need for 276
web accessibility checker
  about 275
  working with, in Visual Studio
        extension 276, 277
Web API
  about 198
  application, creating 199
  features 198
WebAssembly 189
Web Compiler
  about 269
  extension, using 273-275
  JSX (React) 273
  Less 269
  Scss (Sass) 271
  Stylus 272
web framework
  about 180

ASP.NET MVC framework 180

DotNetNuke (DNN platform) 182

MonoRail 183

Vue.js 183

web IDE

about 54-56

comparing, with desktop IDE 46

comparing, with mobile IDE 46

while loop

about 93

example 93

Windows applications

building, with .NET Core 3.0 110

Windows community toolkit

about 111

reference link 111

Windows desktop app

creating, XAML Islands used 112

Windows Forms

about 46, 115

all Windows Forms 47

common controls 47

components 47

containers 47

data controls 47

dialogs 47

menus and toolbars 47

printing 47

Windows Presentation

Foundation (WPF) 21

Windows Workloads 25

WinUI 115

X

Xamarin

about 48, 216

cells 48

controls 48

installing 216

layouts 48

Xamarin.Forms 217

Xamarin.Forms

about 217

application, creating 217

XAML (Extensible Application
    Markup Language) 52, 110

XAML Islands

about 110, 111

NuGet packages 111

used, for creating Windows
    desktop app 112

Windows community toolkit 111